A Suitable Enemy

A Suitable Enemy

Racism, Migration and Islamophobia in Europe

LIZ FEKETE

Foreword by
A. Sivanandan

PLUTO PRESS
www.plutobooks.com

First published 2009 by Pluto Press
345 Archway Road, London N6 5AA and
175 Fifth Avenue, New York, NY 10010

www.plutobooks.com

Distributed in the United States of America exclusively by
Palgrave Macmillan, a division of St. Martin's Press LLC,
175 Fifth Avenue, New York, NY 10010

British Library Cataloguing in Publication Data
A catalogue record for this book is available from the British Library

ISBN   978 0 7453 2793 8   Hardback
ISBN   978 0 7453 2792 1   Paperback

Library of Congress Cataloging in Publication Data applied for

This book is printed on paper suitable for recycling and made from fully
managed and sustained forest sources. Logging, pulping and manufacturing
processes are expected to conform to the environmental standards of the
country of origin. The paper may contain up to 70% post consumer waste.

10   9   8   7   6   5   4   3   2   1

Designed and produced for Pluto Press by
Chase Publishing Services Ltd, Sidmouth, EX10 9QG, England
Typeset from disk by Stanford DTP Services, Northampton
Printed and bound in the European Union by
CPI Antony Rowe, Chippenham and Eastbourne

CONTENTS

ACKNOWLEDGEMENTS

As this book has been a long time in gestation – 16 years in fact – there are a considerable number of people to thank. It was in 1992 that the Institute of Race Relations (IRR) first launched the European Race Audit (ERA), of which I am head. Not only have IRR staff Harmit Athwal, Arun Kundnani and Rosie Wild provided support and inspiration, but a quite amazing bunch of volunteers from across the Continent have given of their time, translating articles and providing a network for discussion and ideas. And, as they have never received any reward for so doing, if I didn't register my thanks here, I would be a very ungrateful person indeed.

Over the last 16 years, the work of the ERA has grown in importance, and if I have grown with it, then IRR Director A. Sivanandan, is the principal reason why. When I first walked into the Institute as a hopelessly disorganised student and anti-fascist activist in 1982, I would never have predicted that one day I would come to write a book. But Siva helped me to hone my commitment and find my voice. If the reader finds clarity in this book, then the clarity is Siva's, not mine. *Race & Class* editor Hazel Waters was also a fine teacher. She has spent hours unravelling the knots in my writing, and for this she cannot be thanked enough.

But if Siva and Hazel have been the finest teachers during the last 16 years, over the last year, my best best-friend has been Jenny Bourne, whose support on this project – which I little deserved – has been unbelievable. (Different versions, of different chapters, landed on her kitchen table literally every weekend.) Writing on refugee, integration and migration policies in so many different countries is no easy task, when your natural inclination on taking up official documents (particularly EU ones) is to glaze over. Mercifully, Frances Webber was on hand for me to test out ideas, to check the text and iron out any wrong interpretations of the law. Thanks also to Naima Bouteldja, Victoria Brittain, Avery Gordon, Penny Green and Robin Virgin for spurring me on as well as my editor at Pluto Press, David Castle.

Sixteen years is a long time to labour over a book, but it has taught me a lot about myself. Most of all, it has taught me gratitude – for it was not till the making of this book that I came to recognise the tremendous hardships faced by my father, Andrew Fekete and my mother, Elizabeth Fekete – forced migrants from a different era. To them, I express not only my thanks but my remorse for taking half a century to show my appreciation.

FOREWORD

A. Sivanandan

Facts do not speak for themselves – not in an age of disinformation, spin and deceit. To derive truth from facts, therefore, is the mark of a rare political intelligence; to envisage trends and tendencies even before the fact is the mark of a rare political instinct. It is this combination of virtues that gives Liz Fekete's investigation into Islamophobia, xeno-racism and the rise of the security state in *A Suitable Enemy* its authenticity and authority. Underscoring all of which, of course, is the sociological imagination that allows her to become the oppressed and the hatred of injustice that calls her to their cause.

The ground, though, has to be cleansed of yesterday's notions of today's racism. Racism changes with changes in the economic and political system, and the nationalist racisms of industrial capitalism have yielded to the common, market racism of global capital.

Hence, for instance, the treatment meted out to (white) East European immigrants cannot be said to stem from a 'natural' fear of strangers, xenophobia, but from a compelling economics of discrimination, akin to racial discrimination, effectively racism under a different colour, xeno-racism. The treatment of the Roma, however, bears the mark of Cain, the outcast, the sub-homines – a more savage aspect of racism. And that despite the fact that they too are citizens of Europe. Asylum seekers, of course, are outsiders by definition and mostly non-white, and therefore kept from earning a legitimate livelihood, denied basic social and civil rights, and liable to end up in prison or detention centre, if not already set upon by the passing fascist.

Since 9/11, however, racism has taken a qualitative leap and spawned other racisms in the process. The immigrant is no longer just a classic outsider but also the terrorist within. Since the latter is most likely to be a Muslim, it is 'natural' to hold all Muslims suspect until proved innocent. It is like the 'Sus' law which once criminalised British black youths on suspicion of their being about to commit a crime – except that in this case the victims are marked out not so much by their colour as by their beards and headscarves. And, like the black youth, they must walk on tiptoe through the land, looking over their shoulders, inviting of more suspicion – or else give up being who they are. These are the choices: you either integrate or disintegrate.

Integration today, in any European language, has, by a political sleight of hand, been equated with assimilation, the aim of which is a homogenous society and not the pluralist multicultural society that integration envisages. Hence the attack on multicultural-ism, which, despite its success in Britain, has been interpreted by politicians and pundits in search of homogeneity to mean culturalism, ethnicism, communities closed in on themselves – the very antithesis of *multi*-culturalism. And the focus of that attack now becomes the Muslim communities who are perceived as 'self-separated' not just by culture but by religion too, a political religion at that, with its own system of laws and rules of social conduct and sanctified oppressions – a fundamentalist religion of the Book – stuck in the Middle Ages, untouched by time or place – forever waging *jihad* against the unbelievers.

That, at any rate, is the populist and rightwing rationale for the crusade against the Muslims. The Left '*liberati*', however, are far more sophisticated, ideological even, in their approach. Their opposition to Islam stems from their defence of the Enlightenment and of western values – liberty, equality, fraternity – all under threat from Islam. But when did the Enlightenment ever reach out to the 'darker races'? As for western values, they have only been observed in the breach. What Islam knows of the West is imperial exploitation, racial oppression and religious bigotry. And then it is argued that, among other things, Islam's oppression of women and of homosexuals signifies fascist and medieval characteristics – is, in fact, Islamofascism. But this is to tar the whole of Islam with its fundamentalist brush (and if Islam, why not Christianity too?). The argument, besides, is not historically specific – comparing civilisations and cultures across time and social formations. Islam, in any case, is not a monolith. It varies and develops across cultures and countries, and what we are witnessing is the emergence of a European Islam. To wantonly overlook these trends and tendencies, as the *liberati* do, is both intellectually dishonest and analytically inept.

Worse, it stokes the politics of fear on which European governments have based their catchall anti-immigrant and anti-terrorist legislation, which, as Liz Fekete eloquently shows, not only erodes civil liberties and points the way to arbitrary government but also undermines the very values that Europe vaunts. Nowhere is this clearer than in her chapter, 'They Are Children Too', which is both a passionate indictment of an immigration and asylum system that incarcerates children in detention centres for long periods prior to deportation, and a cry against the dimming of the Enlightenment: to dispossess a child of its childhood is to dispossess it of its first liberty.

But all is not lost. For, ironically enough, it is the grandchildren of immigrants, born and socialised in Europe, who are now taking up the cause of Liberty – in challenging discriminatory and repressive laws in several countries of Europe, in swelling demonstrations everywhere against the war in Iraq and the systematic destruction of Palestine and, in France, fighting against their relegation to an underclass locked up in the *banlieues* and brutalised by the police.

Contrary to the official view, however, these young people, mostly Muslim and/or black, are not into self-segregation. Nor do they want to be assimilated into a society that denies them their basic rights. How Liz Fekete characterises them, instead, is as an anti-body within the body politic, challenging the system to live up to the Enlightenment values that it has itself dissipated.

Like any good investigation, *A Suitable Enemy* contains within it the seeds of action.

INTRODUCTION

When, in 1992, the Institute of Race Relations (IRR) first set up its European Race Audit,[1] on which I have worked since its inception, neo-Nazis in Germany were on the rampage and refugee hostels at Hoyerswerda and Rostock had been firebombed.[2] In Austria, the leader of the far-Right Freedom Party (FPÖ) had just launched a twelve-point 'Austria First' petition against foreigners; in France, Jean-Marie Le Pen's Front National (FN) was putting the finishing touches to its '300 measures for the renaissance of France'; and, in Belgium, the Vlaams Blok (VB) had published a 70-point programme against immigration. The response of Chancellor Kohl to the unprecedented racist violence against asylum seekers and migrant workers in Germany, gave succour to the neo-Nazi cause by abandoning Article 16 of the German Constitution that guaranteed the right to seek asylum. Kohl was not alone in capitulating to the extreme-Right agenda. The EU harmonisation of asylum and immigration laws was leading to a new pan-European racism directed against asylum seekers and migrant workers.[3]

Yet, despite the closing of Europe against migrants and asylum seekers displaced by globalisation and the break-up of the former Communist bloc, the IRR could not have predicted, back in 1992, that the extreme-Right's call for an exclusive national preference and cultural identity would come to fruition some 16 years later. For a variant of the extreme-Right's call for national preference is today written into government social programmes that demand compulsory integration (i.e. assimilation) of minority ethnic communities into superior British, German, French (etc.) 'values'. How the nativism of extreme-Right and anti-immigration movements came to be written into European immigration, asylum and national security laws is the topic of this book. For the sake of clarity, I have divided what follows into four sections:

1

the emergence of a new form of non-colour-coded institutional-ised racism, and the links between this racism and the security state; the popular discourses that justify the introduction of racist immigration controls and nativist citizenship policies; the human cost of EU detention and deportation policies; the new resistance movements and the centrality of civil rights. But as *A Suitable Enemy* is concerned, for the most part, with developments in racism – both popular and institutionalised – and anti-racism, post-2001, the purpose of this introduction is to provide some historical context and backdrop.[4] For the processes whereby certain groups in European societies have been identified as 'enemy aliens' and 'enemy citizens' were set into motion well before the September 11 2001 al Qaida attacks on the World Trade Center and the Pentagon in the US.

Europe has, of course, had a long history of treating its ethnic minorities, most notably the Jews and the Roma, as 'enemy aliens'. But since the late 1990s, a whole host of other groups have come to be identified as 'suspect' communities as new strains of racism have erupted like sores on society's surface. Some of the responsibility for this lies, as already indicated, with the army of extreme-Right and anti-immigrant (nativist) electoral parties, which, from the 1990s onwards, were making significant electoral breakthroughs in one European country after another. The post-war consensus whereby European countries were ruled either by the forces of the centre-Right (Conservatives, Christian Democrats, Liberals) or the centre-Left (Social Democrats, sometimes with Greens, Liberals and other small Left parties as coalition partners) was beginning to break down.[5] As the frantic pace of European harmonisation transformed the nation state, exacerbated existing regional disparities and broke up working-class communities and culture, two breeds of populist extreme-Right movements emerged. The first type, epitomised by the FN in France, sought to exploit the insecurities of glo-balisation's (white) losers; the second, represented most clearly by Italy's Northern League, espoused the greed and selfishness of its (business and nouveau riche) winners. Both played on the fears and anxieties of an electorate fragmented by the social upheaval and economic adjustments that had left them, in the absence of other political moorings, susceptible to xenophobic conspiracy theories. National identity and culture, the extreme-Right and anti-immigrant parties were warning, were under threat not only from EU bureaucrats but from the cosmopolitanism of liberal elites.[6] The only solution, as they saw it, to the cultural dissolution (i.e. multiculturalism) favoured by liberal elites was cultural purity (i.e. monoculturalism), which would be fought for via campaigns for 'national preference' (i.e. natives first, hence the extreme-Right slogans 'Austria First', 'France First', etc.).

These were campaigning slogans based on an electoral politics that made a deliberate pitch for the vote of working-class constituencies, as well as vulnerable groups like pensioners, who had traditionally voted Left.[7] The new nativists presented themselves as the natural defenders of the welfare state as well as the (white) working class. Thus, the FN, whose share of the national vote in the late 1990s outstripped that of the Greens and the Communists combined, and who, at one point, controlled the naval port of Toulon, the Marseilles suburb of Marignane, the southern Rhône valley town of Orange as well as Vitrolles (the fourth largest town in the Provence-Alpes Côte d'Azur region),[8] depicted itself as the protector of the working class from the ravages of the global market. (The sociologist Pascal Perrineau coined the term 'gaucho-lepénisme' to describe the rise in urban areas of a disenchanted working-class electorate won over to the FN.[9]) Jörg Haider, leader of the FPÖ, also described himself as the protector of the Austrian poor, the elderly and the working class.[10] On doubling its share of the vote in the September 1997 general election, the Norwegian Progress Party declared that 'We are the caretakers of the working class... Labour has deserted the welfare state.'[11] It was a tune repeated by Pia Kjærsgaard, the leader of the Danish People's Party (DPP), which was formed in 1995, as a breakaway from the more avowedly far-Right Progress Party. Kjærsgaard became adept at packaging herself for media consumption as an ordinary housewife and mother, in tune with the everyday problems of Danish folk.

How did such extremist, racist parties become embedded in mainstream society? While there was much discussion, in the first half of the 1990s, of placing a political *cordon sanitaire* around parties that espoused racism, this was dissipated when the nativists gained ground in a media that popularised its message and themes. For instance, 'the boat is full' was originally the slogan of the far-Right Republikaner Party in Germany, but it soon became used by most of the German mainstream political parties. In September 1991, just eight days before the pogrom at Hoyerswerda, the right-wing popular magazine, *Der Spiegel*, blazoned the slogan on its front cover, complete with an illustration depicting Germany as a massively overcrowded boat, surrounded by a sea of struggling humanity, with a sub-title 'The onslaught of the poor'.[12]

Similarly, the extreme-Right's alarmist warnings about the threat posed by 'foreign criminality' was greatly aided by media reporting from the 1990s onwards. And today, the issue of foreign criminality is peddled freely by nearly all the political parties, particularly at election time.[13] The mainstreaming of the foreigner/criminal equation was greatly aided, throughout the 1990s, by the way in which police, interior ministries and right-wing political think-tanks issued dubious, unscientific and racialised crime statistics that purported to show that European societies were under threat from immigrant crime waves as well as duplicitous asylum seekers. Crime statistics, in their turn, were sensationalised in the media, which came to constantly link the themes of immigration, crime and security.[14] For in this, the digital age of 24-hour news coverage, where hundreds of television channels compete for viewers, the media has a vested interest in perpetuating the notion that crime and immigration are out of control. Throughout the late 1990s, much of the media, particularly the tabloids, also portrayed asylum systems as out of control, with immigration departments depicted as incapable of dealing with 'bogus' claimants whose real intention in seeking asylum was to gain access to the social benefits that accrued from a generous welfare state.[15] Not only was the media's constant focus on the numbers of asylum seekers arriving grist to the extreme-Right's mill, but anti-immigrant electoral candidates were regularly presented in the media as the authentic voice of the people battling against liberal elites who lived detached from the problems of ordinary working-class folk.[16]

This interplay between anti-immigration movements and the media was very clearly demonstrated in the November 1997 Danish local municipal and regional elections when the DPP made its first significant electoral breakthrough, scoring 6.8 per cent of the national vote. One national tabloid newspaper, the *Ekstra Bladet*, launched a campaign against refugee welfare cheats while another, the *Jyllands-Posten* (notorious in 2005 for its decision to print twelve cartoons of the Prophet Mohammed, one of which depicted the Prophet as a terrorist) claimed that elderly immigrants, who did not qualify for a state pension on the grounds of the 40-year residence requirement, were milking the system. Such was the climate of hate, that in October 1997, just one month before the elections, Danish Refugee Aid warned that 'the tone of the debate' was 'so negative' that refugees living in small towns were migrating back to city areas with larger migrant populations in order to guarantee their safety.[17]

One of the main targets of the press invective were Roma asylum seekers and migrants from eastern Europe and the Balkans who had been displaced from their 'homelands' following the break-up of the former Soviet Union and subsequent horrendous levels of racial violence. More an 'outcast' community than ever before,[18] the Roma were the archetypal 'suitable enemy'. Not only were they Gypsies and beggars, but asylum seekers to boot. A similar pattern of events to those that had occurred in Denmark unravelled in Ireland. The Immigration Control Platform was launched in May 1998 on the back of a campaign of negative press reporting during which negligible immigration was described as a 'wave crashing into Ireland'. As racist attacks escalated, the Irish Council for Civil Liberties accused the newspaper editor of the *Wexford People*[19] as well as some backbench MPs of fuelling 'racist poison' against refugees and asylum seekers, particularly the Roma.[20] In the same year as the Irish anti-asylum campaign, Roma from eastern Europe were singled out for attack in the UK. A *Dover Express* editorial also had the Roma in mind when it stated, 'We want to wash dross down the drain'. 'Illegal immigrants, asylum-seekers, bootleggers ... and scum of the earth drug smugglers have targeted our beloved coastline ... we are left with the backdraft of a nation's human sewage and no cash to wash it down the drain.' Meanwhile, in the Netherlands, sections of the Dutch media were also instrumental in popularising the themes of locally based anti-asylum groups, which in 1999 united for a brief spell under the umbrella of the Party for a Safe and Caring Society 2000. The biased, misleading and hysterical television and newspaper coverage of incidents in the Friesland village of Kollum in November 1999 played a large part in the deteriorating situation. (Asylum seekers at the Kollum reception centre were held collectively responsible for the rape and murder of a local teenage girl.[21])

This combination of anti-immigration movements and media invective proved too much for mainstream political parties. Politicians knew full well that, because of Europe's declining birth rates, an ageing population and shortage of skilled workers, in some areas, and semi- and unskilled workers, in others, Europe was in desperate need of migrant workers. But they also knew that to openly acknowledge this would be to antagonise the electorate. At the same time, governments feared that the globalisation-inspired irregular movements of people, resulting in migratory flows of labour surplus to Europe's economic needs, would derail a political strategy based on micro-managing the migration process quietly and behind the scenes. In this climate, political mileage could be gained by incorporating the extreme-Right's anti-asylum, anti-immigration agenda. A Third Way philosophy, epitomised by the British prime minister Tony Blair[22] and his Spanish counterpart José Maria Aznar, grew up to justify this accommodation with grassroots nativist movements. In vain did anti-fascists point out that the extreme-Right parties were often the winners when mainstream parties prioritised immigration, asylum and security as election ploys. It was also becoming clear that those parties that fought elections on anti-immigration, anti-refugee themes would have to seek further accommodation with the extreme-Right. Many centre-Right parties found themselves in a position where they either shared power with the anti-immigration parties (as junior partners in coalition governments) or had to bow to their demands, because these smaller parties held the balance of power in weak parliaments.[23]

There were, of course, variations to this trend from one country to another, depending on its particular history and political culture. In Germany, where the federal electoral challenge from the more openly far-Right and neo-Nazi parties was weak, the Christian Social Union became particularly adept at playing the 'foreigner card' as a way of winning votes, and, by linking immigration to crime, managed to steal the far-Right vote and become the standard-bearer for the entire German centre-Right.[24] The fear promoted by the growth of the VB in Belgium ensured that a 1996 immigration and asylum law (known as the 'Vande Lanotte' law after the Social Democratic interior minister who initiated it) actually implemented many of the proposals first advanced by the VB in its 70-point programme to end immigration (more deportations, the creation of detention centres, no social assistance, the removal of the right to work, no access to welfare benefits, etc.). In the UK, asylum was the dominant issue in the run-up to the 2001 general election with the Conservative leader William Hague, in a speech at Conservative party conference in Harrogate, warning that Labour would turn Britain into a 'foreign land'. Hague used the phrase 'We will give you back your country' eight times and devoted a whole page of text to a shrill attack on Labour's record on asylum.[25] Jean-Marie Le Pen's stock-in-trade for more than 30 years was alarmist scare-mongering about urban crime fed by unchecked immigration, a theme that was taken up by President Chirac in the run-up to the 2002 French presidential elections when facing Le Pen in the second round.[26] The TV watchdog l'Observatoire du Débat Public reported that the 'accumulation of [violent] facts on TV had given the impression that all protection has collapsed, leaving a field of ruins'. The commercial station TF1 and the state network FR2 were both blamed for serving Le Pen's theories by exaggerating accounts of the dangers of urban and rural crime waves.[27]

But why did politicians acquiesce in the process whereby immigration, asylum, crime and security came to be a dominant (if not the major) issue in elections in all EU countries in the 1990s? Part of the answer lies in the substantial reduction in the power of the state to protect its labour force from the impact of the market in a globalised economy. Impotent to deal with many rising inequalities, the mainstream political parties slugged it out at election time, each hoping to deal the knock-out blow, proving that they and only they could best manage immigration and asylum in the interests of the native people. From now on, the *cordon sanitaire* would be against refugees and asylum seekers. Thus, from the 1990s onwards, both centre-Right and centre-Left parties began to implement laws that criminalised asylum seekers (through compulsory fingerprinting of all claimants, for instance) and isolated them from the rest of society, by removing them from the welfare state altogether and/or placing them in detention centres, prior to removal. The German model of replacing cash payments to asylum seekers with food, coupons and clothes and forcibly dispersing asylum seekers across the country began to be favoured by other countries.[28]

But with the dispersal of asylum seekers went the dispersal of xenophobia. Kosovan asylum seekers in Switzerland were among the first to be dispersed to mountain huts administered by the army. Here, and in Scandinavia, the Netherlands, Ireland and the UK, anti-asylum movements (sometimes fomented by the extreme-Right, sometimes emerging spontaneously from below) sprang up in local constituencies as residents' committees formed blockades to keep the asylum seekers out.[29] Racist violence and neo-Nazi petrol bomb attacks on asylum hostels, as well as Roma camps[30] and the dilapidated encampments of migrant agricultural workers in southern Europe[31] became an everyday occurrence. The violence was constantly shifting from one region to the next. One day Oberwart, Austria (four Roma killed in a bomb attack),[32] the next day Lübeck, Germany (arson claimed the lives of ten asylum seekers, mostly African and including six children).[33] One day the Brandenburg town of Rathenow (116 asylum seekers issued a desperate plea to be transferred to a safe region),[34] the next day Glasgow (four families, fleeing racial violence, were told that unless they returned to the housing estate they fled from, all welfare support would be withdrawn).[35] By the beginning of the new millennium, a whole architecture of exclusion had been built up around asylum seekers who found themselves without civil and social rights and vulnerable also to the most basic denial of their fundamental human rights, including the right to dignity and life itself. It was this that heralded a new form of non-colour-coded institutionalised racism, xeno-racism, the parameters of which are laid out more fully in chapter 1.

ɔʒ   ʃɔ

Once structures of exclusion are erected for one group in society, they can easily be adapted for others. Thus, following the September 2001 attacks on the World Trade Center and the Pentagon, public discourse began to identify, to a much greater extent than before, minority ethnic communities who happened to be Muslim, as 'suspect' communities whose loyalty and patriotism were constantly questioned. Of course, the extreme-Right's identification of Muslim communities as constituting a 'threat' had co-existed with its demonisation of asylum seekers, throughout the 1990s. But, at this point, the Islamophobia of the nativists was neither mainstream nor linked exclusively to the supposed threat that Muslims posed to national security. Rather, extreme-Right populists saw in the lives of Muslims the same 'alien' lifestyle that once characterised the Jew – unassimilable on account of a foreign religion, inimical to monocultural, multifaith Europe on account of an obvious cultural difference. The ruling liberal elite, furthermore, was accused of nurturing Muslim immigrants' perceived difference through its support for globalisation, which they linked to cosmopolitanism and the dilution of national identity. Crude anti-Muslim racism lay behind some of the DPP's success in Denmark, as well as the rapid rise of the List Pim Fortuyn (LPF) in the Netherlands (its populist leader, Pim Fortuyn, achieved notoriety after the publication of *Against the Islamification of our Culture*). But the message was not mainstream. At this stage, governments were preoccupied not with Muslims, but with the economic integration of specific groups – Moroccans, Turks, Algerians, Pakistanis, for example – which were experiencing high levels of unemployment and poverty. And the intelligence services were less concerned with Islamicism *per se* than with the political activities of different national groups – Algerians, Kurds, Palestinians, Lebanese – as well as non-Muslims, such as Sri Lankan Tamils or Punjabi Sikhs.

However, a shift in the views of governments and security services was on its way. And once fully realised, it was quick to enclose Muslims within a parallel security state that had been surreptitiously created over previous decades. It was in 1991 that Tony Bunyan, editor of Statewatch, first warned that behind the formal institutions of (then) European Community (EC) lay a shadowy parallel state, largely undemocratic and unaccountable. Its purpose, warned Bunyan, was twofold: to create a hard outer barrier to prevent asylum seekers and immigrants from entering fortress Europe; and to develop mechanisms of internal control that would effectively police long-term residents who, although settled in Europe, lacked citizenship rights.[36] This gradual growth of a parallel European Security State provided the basis upon which more and more categories of people, mainly Muslims, and including citizens as well as long-term residents, came to be caught up within the ever-expanding loop of xeno-racism. Even prior to the events of September 11, administrative systems had been established by heads of states and civil servants that were leading to the collection of wide-ranging data on Europe's minority ethnic communities. First, the collection of extensive personal data for general surveillance purposes, which started in the 1970s, was applied to asylum seekers. Information on all asylum seekers was stored on the Schengen Information System (SIS), which is the EU's largest computer database and at the head of the EU's internal security system. In time, data registered on SIS was extended to include Third Country Nationals who, although long-term resident in Europe, for a variety of reasons, did not have citizenship. After September 11 2001, security services took the view that Islam *per se* constituted a 'threat'. The data collection systems expanded still further. The EU and member states set about building up 'risk profiles' of Muslim residents, while the European Council's Anti-terrorism Roadmap introduced a new system of 'alerts' on SIS and the creation of a European central register on Third Country Nationals present within the territory of the EU. The latest proposal is to establish a comprehensive electronic pact with the US, whereby vast volumes of information on European citizens and travellers would be passed on to the US security services.[37]

The crucial impetus for the institutionalisation of anti-Muslim racism then was not so much the populist anti-Muslim rhetoric of the nativists, as the fears and preoccupations of intelligence services, which were the principal movers behind the emergent European Security State. The German and French intelligence services, in particular, with their close ties to intelligence services in Turkey and Algeria respectively, played a key role in introducing processes that criminalised Muslim communities in Europe. For they had regarded their minority communities – Turkish, Kurdish, Algerian, Moroccan – as constituting a security threat for some years. In Germany, the Kurdish Workers Party (PKK) was banned in 1993[38] at the request of the Turkish prime minister, Tansu Çiller, who had vowed to crush the Kurdish rebels within a year. The Christian Democrats declared 1998 'the year of security' with interior minister Manfred Kanther pressing the EU to follow its lead in prioritising the triple themes of crime, immigration and security, arguing that 'in view of this threatening situation, western Europe must view itself as a security community... All our countries are potential destinations if the beginnings are not stamped out.'[39]

But it was France that had the most draconian approach to its minority ethnic communities. For its strategic interests, including its decision to assist Algeria's military-backed regime when it annulled the results of the first round of the January 1992 general election (the first round was won convincingly by the Islamic Salvation Front, FIS), demanded internal repression of France's North African communities. Thus, in August 1994, after three French gendarmes and two consular officials were killed by gunmen in Algeria, interior minister Charles Pasqua mobilised the entire police force of Paris to carry out mass identity checks on 'immigrant' areas, drafting in police reinforcements from the provinces to guard railway stations and public buildings, and interning 25 Arabs in a disused army barracks at Folembray, northern France. (They were subsequently deported, amid much controversy, to Burkina Faso.) By March 1999, the International Federation of Human Rights Leagues (FIDH) warned that France's anti-terrorist laws and special procedures (particularly the catch-all charge of 'association with wrongdoers', which is discussed at greater length in chapters 2 and 4) were a major violation of democratic values, stripping of all substance major human rights guaranteed by the French Constitution.[40] The trial of 138 men and women (known as the 'Chalabi trial' after the alleged ringleader of the 'terrorists'), accused of providing support for Islamic insurgents in Algeria, drew particular criticism. Of those accused, 27 had been held in preventative detention for nearly four years during which time no evidence for their detention was made public. At least $1 million was spent converting a gymnasium adjoining a prison at Fleury-Mérogis, Essonne, 20 miles south of Paris, into a temporary court protected by 300 gendarmes for what FIDH described as an assembly-line political show trial worthy of China or the Soviet Union.[41]

ଓ ଋ

A Suitable Enemy charts the path from nativism to xeno-racism and the institutionalised anti-Muslim racism of today. But these trends have been bolstered by the impetus coming from nation states to artificially cohere a sense of nationhood in the face of globalisation, the dismantling of the welfare state and the traditional industrial compact between capital and labour. Increasingly, European governments are openly calling for conformity in mores and values from their citizens. And the first indicators of modern-style social authoritarianism is found in the erosion of minority cultural and religious rights – a process legitimised by the popular racism and demonisation of minority ethnic communities as the unassimilable *Other* with questionable loyalties.

Today, the European quest to scapegoat specific groups as 'suspect' is ever inventive. Not only that, but one enemy morphs easily into the next, with some enemies achieving multiple identity status! Hence young Muslims are British, French, etc., and Islamic when it comes to the threat posed to national security. But they are unIslamic and foreign (i.e. Turkish, Pakistani, Somali) when they are arrested for crime – only to re-emerge as Muslim once criminalised and imprisoned. Amid political fears about radicalisation of Muslims in jail, the young prisoner resurfaces in public discourse as Islamist and a security threat.

And, then, there is the resurrection of old enemies as outcast communities re-emerge as archetypal scapegoats. As Italians, spurred on by the Neapolitan mafia, burn the 'nomad' camps where Roma and migrant workers subsist,[42] once again the supposed threat posed by the alien values, nomadic lifestyle and criminal subculture of the Roma are used to justify racist measures such as the national census on the Roma population (this entails the compulsory fingerprinting of all those living in nomad camps, including children). The Italian government's argument for such authoritarianism, warns the European Center for Antiziganism Research, recalls similar arguments deployed in Nazi Germany where the registration of Roma and Sinti were justified as a measure necessary for crime prevention.[43]

The defining feature of such hatred and violence is nativism. And the purpose of this nativism is to entrench the majority culture as the bulwark against 'acculturation', or cultural diversity. What the nativist movements demand today is no less than the cultural cleansing of Europe of all foreign influences, particularly the 'alien' religion of Islam.[44] Once again, such indecent demands are becoming official policy. New citizenship tests and integration policies are being introduced on the back of a debate that argues that newcomers need to be taught the rudiments of acceptable behaviour in western European societies, which are based (depending on your take) on superior Enlightenment (secular) values or Christian ones. And government policies as a whole are being formulated around two basic nativist principles of 'assimilation' and 'exclusion'. By advocating an assimilationist minority policy, governments legitimise the extreme-Right's attack on multiculturalism and pluralism in favour of new definitions of equality based on cultural similarity, as opposed to difference. (The idea is that we can only be equal if we are the same.) And by advocating exclusion of those who fail to assimilate (either through deportation or refusal of citizenship), governments not only legitimise the extreme-Right nativist agenda but undermine the very values that underline the European Convention on Human Rights.

But what to do with the enemy alien, surplus to economic requirement and potentially a threat to security, especially if s/he refuses to leave or cannot be deported? The answer is incarceration. The prison industrial complex (first delineated in the US to describe a 'black hole into which the detritus of contemporary capitalism is deposited'[45]) has been extended into an asylum prison complex and national security complex within Europe. The rise of the asylum prison complex and the national security prison complex as a fundamental extension of the prison industrial complex is discussed in these pages. The growth in prison regimes that favour internment and deportation of 'enemy aliens' parallels trends in asylum policy wherein the detention and deportation of asylum seekers has become an essential element of the penal state. Both 'enemy citizens' and 'enemy aliens' are subject to the new prison regimes introduced through the logic of what criminologists call actuarial penology.[46] Whole categories of people are treated as constituting risk. No longer treated as individuals, they are seen as part of a wider class of people to be collectively neutralised, incapacitated and warehoused. 'Failed' asylum seekers and *sans papiers*, including children, are locked up in private prisons run for profit, not because they have committed any crime but solely for the administrative convenience of government. And 'enemy aliens' interned on national security grounds (most of whom are also refugees and asylum seekers) are also detained without charge for the administrative convenience of governments, which includes the convenience of appeasing the demands of authoritarian governments around the world. The purpose of both forms of detention is never the rehabilitation of the offender (how can you be rehabilitated when you have committed no crime or have not been informed about the nature of the crime you are purported to have committed?). The purpose of detention is to break down the will of detainees, so as to make them compliant in their own removal. Thus, national security detainees in the UK who challenge their proposed deportation may be asked to choose between lengthy detention in the host country or return to torture in their country of origin. Only a public discourse based on xeno-racism could justify this psychological torture and fundamental attacks on human rights.

ひ   &

Despite the grandstanding of politicians, another Europe is being built from below, by new movements in support of asylum seekers and undocumented workers and by young people engaged in student initiatives, civil rights campaigns and pioneering new publishing ventures. It is such committed young people who are preserving the fabric of Europe's multicultural society and breathing fresh life into its extra-parliamentary movements and humanitarian traditions. Though these new initiatives – highlighted in the book's concluding two chapters – are positive pointers, such gains have to be balanced against the high human cost. Here, and in the pages that follow, I draw attention to those who have died or suffered permanent injury because of the racism unleashed by the nativists in the late 1990s and the first eight years of the twenty-first century. Too many people have died during deportation, or suffered lasting emotional and psychological damage owing to their indefinite detention under asylum and national security regimes. Even less-well documented have been the deaths of so many young second- and third- generation 'immigrants' and Roma of central and eastern Europe in the custody of European police forces. While the new resistances, particularly among young people living a life in poor and marginalised communities, needs to be acknowledged and celebrated, the failure of large sections of the intelligentsia to come to the aid of vulnerable and demonised communities also needs comment. In particular, the humanitarian instinct of the liberal intelligentsia – which in many cases has spoken up for refugees and *sans papiers* – has been blunted when it comes to the Muslim community. Anti-racism today needs to forge the connections between the fight for the rights of refugees, migrants and asylum seekers and the fight for the civil rights of Muslims. The groundwork for change is being laid by those groups who link anti-racism to the fight for civil rights. The opening is there, if only we have eyes to see it and vision enough to meet the challenges ahead.

Xeno-racism and the Security State

1

THE EMERGENCE OF XENO-RACISM

Once, the West saw its 'superior' civilisation and economic system as under threat from the communist world. That was the ideological enemy as seen from the US; that was the hostile, intransigent neighbour as seen from western Europe. Today, the threat posed by 37.4 million displaced people, living either temporarily or permanently outside their countries of origin[1] has replaced that posed by communism. For, in this brave new post-Cold War world, the enemy is not so much marked out by ideology as by poverty. As western security agencies, supranational global bodies, intergovernmental organisations and national governments mobilise against migratory movements from 'over-populated' and 'socially insecure countries with weaker economies',[2] a whole new anti-refugee discourse has emerged in popular culture. Those seeking asylum are demonised as bogus, as illegal immigrants and economic migrants scrounging at capital's gate and threatening capital's culture. And it is this demonisation of the people that the capitalist western world seeks to exclude – in the name of the preservation of economic prosperity and national identity – that signals the emergence of a new racism. As Sivanandan has argued:

> It is a racism that is not just directed at those with darker skins, from the former colonial territories, but at the newer categories of the displaced, the dispossessed and the uprooted, who are beating at western Europe's doors, the Europe that helped to displace them in the first place. It is a racism, that is, that cannot be colour-coded, directed as it is at poor whites as well, and is therefore passed off as xenophobia, a 'natural' fear of strangers. But in the way it denigrates and reifies people before segregating and/or expelling them, it is a xenophobia that bears all the marks of the old racism. It is

racism in substance, but 'xeno' in form. It is a racism that is meted out to impoverished strangers even if they are white. It is xeno-racism.[3]

In the UK, it was after the election of the New Labour government in 1998, that xeno-racism became fully incorporated into domestic asylum policy. By making 'deterrence' (of 'economic migrants'), not human rights (the protection of refugees), the guiding principle of its asylum policy, a government committed to dismantling institutionalised racism[4] has erected new structures of discrimination and, in the process, provided the ideological space in which racism towards asylum seekers became culturally acceptable.

'Managed Migration': the New Socio-economic Darwinism

Over the last two decades, the EU, while encouraging member states to harmonise asylum policies, has slowly been introducing measures to control 'migratory movements'. But more recently the EU's approach coalesced into an overall philosophy of 'global migration management'. Since the UN warned of the growing demographic crisis in Europe, brought on by an ageing workforce and declining birth rates,[5] there has been a growing recognition within western Europe that immigration is necessary and that refugees might even provide an important source of skilled labour. Indeed, since the European Commission indicated in November 2000 that the EU should open up legal routes for migration,[6] and national governments within Europe followed its lead by adopting skills-based recruitment programmes for foreign workers, European governments have been openly supporting 'managed migration'.

But while 'managed migration' may well be a means of opening up avenues for skilled immigrants (including refugees) to enter Europe as guestworkers, it is simultaneously leading throughout Europe to moves to abolish the right to claim asylum, as guaranteed by the 1951 UN Convention on the Status of Refugees. For global migration management is not just a philosophy within which skills shortages are addressed; it has emerged as part of

the strategic response of the powerful nations of the First World
to the economic and social dislocation engendered, first, by the
break-up of the former communist zone of influence and, second,
by the impact of 'globalism's insatiable demand' on the Second
and Third Worlds 'for free markets and unfettered conditions of
trade'.[7] It is a strategy that arises, ironically enough, from the
recognition that the global market-induced displacement of people
cannot be left to market forces but must be managed for the First
World's benefit. If global capitalists are concerned with 'building a
stable and regional environment for global accumulation' and 'a
new legal and economic superstructure for the world economy',[8]
they are equally concerned with building a new global structure
of immigration controls to decide which people can move freely
around the world, and which people will have their movement
restricted. One result of this is that the Fortress Europe 'zero
immigration' approach, which characterised the end of the
twentieth century, is not so much abandoned as refined.

But to understand how such a strategy of global migration
management leads to xeno-racism, it is necessary first to outline
the scale of international cooperation on migration issues and to
detail specific, internationally agreed measures through which
seeking asylum came to be regarded as an illegal, criminal act.[9]
Although the targets of global migration management may differ
in terms of North American, Australian and European concerns,
these power blocs share a common interest, as demonstrated by
their cooperation in supranational bodies and intergovernmental agencies in pooling information on migratory movement.
Such cooperation then informs regional policy, at the EU level,
for instance.

The industrialised nations liaise through bodies like the
International Centre for Migration Policy and Development
(ICMPD), founded in 1993, which developed out of the Inter-
Governmental Consultations on Asylum, Refugee and Migration
Policies in Europe, North America and Australia. It was originally
set up to coordinate refugee and migration policies following the
break-up of the former Soviet Union and saw its role as 'advising
governments on the prevention of migratory movements from East

to West and South to North'. Other mechanisms include regular meetings of the secretariat of the Budapest Process, a conference of ministers from some 34 states and representatives from inter-governmental organisations, which deals with the prevention of illegal migration and recommends action on issues like trafficking, smuggling and pre-entry and entry controls. By the late 1990s, there were at least 30 other networks and fora of activity set up by European states and intergovernmental organisations to predict migratory flows and to advise on border controls. On many of these, international and national security agencies were represented, as well as the governments of the US, Australia and Canada, either as fully fledged members or as observers. More recently, the focus of these fora has shifted from predicting migratory flows to combating smuggling and trafficking. The year 2000 was designated by the EU, the Group of Eight industrialised nations (G8) and the Organisation for Security and Cooperation in Europe (which includes Canada and the US) as the year of the 'anti-trafficking plan'.

Criminalising Irregular Migration

The overwhelming focus of supranational bodies and intergovern-mental fora on trafficking networks (termed by the G8 as the 'dark side of globalisation'), coupled with a complete absence of concern for refugee protection, has led Migrant Rights International to warn that 'in national and international fora, the dominant con-siderations regarding displacement of people have deteriorated from assistance and hospitality to rejection and hostility'.[10] In effect, that aspect of international law that once upheld the right of all migrants to claim asylum in another country, regardless of their means of entry, and placed on all governments the obligation not to return refugees, either directly or indirectly, to a country where they faced a real risk of persecution (*non-refoulement*), has been progressively negated.

While no one can deny the exploitative nature of the smuggling networks that control so many of the routes through which asylum seekers reach Europe, Australia and the US, what these international fora have blatantly failed to address is that it is the regimes that governments have instigated (carriers' liability, visa requirements, readmission treaties and electronically fortified borders) that have blocked legal routes for those seeking asylum and thrown them into the arms of smugglers and traffickers. Western governments refuse to countenance this. Instead, asylum seekers trafficked into Europe are described, for example by the UK Home Office, as people who seek illegal entry 'after receiving daily images of the potential economic and ... social benefits available in richer countries across the globe'. Informed by such blinkered views, international bodies, hardening themselves against the plight of millions of displaced people across the world, adopt anti-trafficking measures that elide the difference between the traffickers and the trafficked so as to treat both as points on the same shadowy continuum. Indeed, the Smuggling Protocol of the 2000 UN Convention on Transnational Organised Crime states unequivocally that the 'migrant' should not be viewed as a blameless victim but, rather, as partly complicit in the act of 'illegal migration'. It is now an offence all over Europe to assist any person in an illegal border crossing, regardless of whether she or he is a refugee in need of protection or not.[11] And, at an EU level, the November 2002 Directive and Framework Decision on 'Strengthening the Penal Framework to Prevent the Facilitation of Unauthorised Entry, Transit and Residence' is being interpreted in such a way that those providing humanitarian-grounded assistance are being penalised.[12]

Governments admit, when it suits them, that traffickers trade in human misery. The women and children thrown overboard in the Atlantic by traffickers desperate to avoid detection and the 58 Chinese who suffocated in a refrigerated lorry on its way to Dover were cited by UK prime minister Blair as vulnerable victims of the trafficking trade when he launched the joint Anglo-Italian initiative to clamp down on trafficking via the so-called Sarajevo route.[13] But when former home secretary Jack Straw implied that trafficking was carried out on such a large international scale that it threatens national sovereignty over immigration issues, then he linked trafficked and traffickers in a criminal conspiracy.

The 'war against trafficking' serves, in effect, both as the means of and justification for states to recast asylum seekers in the public mind as 'illegal immigrants'. To break domestic immigration laws (through, for instance, entering a country as a stowaway) is now treated as a criminal act, even though the 1951 UN Convention on the Status of Refugees upholds the right of refugees to break domestic immigration laws in order to seek asylum. Thus the EU succeeded in shifting the terms of the refugee debate so as to treat asylum seekers not as people from many different countries, with many different experiences and each with an individual story to tell, but as a homogenous and undifferentiated mass. Hence the fascination among its politicians and press with flat statistical projections of asylum flows; hence the offensive language in which migratory movements of displaced people are described in terms of environmental catastrophe; hence the dehumanisation of asylum seekers as a 'mass', 'horde', 'influx', 'swarm'. In this, xeno-racism against asylum seekers resonates with the past. Jews under Nazism, blacks under slavery, 'natives' under colonialism, were similarly dehumanised, held to possess mass characteristics that justified exploitation, victimisation and, at the last, genocide.

Imposing Western Immigration Controls

But there is another aspect to the 'war against trafficking' and the criminalisation of asylum seekers. For, if asylum seekers who break domestic immigration laws are treated as having carried out an illegal act that links them to an international criminal conspiracy, then the EU is justified in imposing its own immigration policies on states that tolerate illegal migratory movements or fail to control the movements of internally displaced people.

How does this work in practice? It was at the Tampere European Council summit in October 1999 that the processes were formalised under which the EU instituted policies that turned Third World governments into immigration police for western Europe. (Such structures already existed for the so-called 'buffer states' of central and eastern Europe.[14]) Prior to this, in late 1997, the EU (borrowing from the Canadian practice of posting immigration officers at airports across the globe) substantially increased the number of airline liaison officers posted at airports and other ports to stop suspected illegal immigrants from travelling. Such officers, who had no training in refugee protection, also acted as immigration staff at embassies and consulates throughout the world. The EU High Level Working Group on Asylum and Immigration,[15] which had already drawn up draft action plans to stop refugee movements from Afghanistan, Albania (and Kosovo), Morocco, Somalia, Sri Lanka and Iraq, also started to seek ways in which trade and development arrangements could be used as levers with which to achieve the EU aim of refugee reduction. The new policies instituted at Tampere, in essence, formalised arrangements that had been ad hoc and piecemeal. It ensured that the policy of 'refugee reduction' would be achieved not at the point of arrival but at the point of departure, via pre-embarkation checks. Responsibility for the prevention of refugee movements would be passed to the asylum seeker's country of origin or the countries through which asylum seekers passed on their way to Europe. This was to be encouraged by measures tying trade and humanitarian aid to the prevention of 'refugee flows' and the return of rejected asylum seekers. The Lomé convention, for instance, was redrawn in February 2000 in order to tie £8.5 billion in aid and trade agreements between the EU, Africa, the Caribbean and Pacific region (ACP) to specific rules guaranteeing the repatriation and expulsion of people deemed to be 'illegal' within the EU. But concerns within the donor community internationally regarding the linkage between migration policy and development aid forced the EU to take a more nuanced approach. Hence, in December 2007 at the EU-Africa Summit in Lisbon, a Strategic Partnership to 'foster the linkages between migration and development', through returns and readmission programmes aimed at 'jointly combating irregular immigration', was adopted.[16]

In this way, the discourse around global migration management – of opening avenues to skilled migrants – camouflages the First World's true approach to immigration controls. Effectively, it takes control of migration strategy and policy, a basic state function, from those nations that have no sway on the supranational bodies that set out the stall of global migration policy. And the EU's North African neighbour countries, anxious to enjoy good trade relations with Europe, are, likewise, co-opted through the 'Euro-Mediterranean Partnership' (otherwise known as the Barcelona Process). Just as a Third World country has to accept World Bank and IMF austerity measures imposed through Poverty Reduction Strategy Papers (PRSP) to survive in the era of globalism, it also has to accept the imposition of migration controls. And, just as poverty reduction programmes mean pauperisation and the erosion of education, social and welfare provision, western-imposed immigration controls lessen the life chances of globalism's victims still further, by denying them freedom of movement, confining them to camps in their own countries and removing the hope of obtaining sanctuary from the persecution of authoritarian regimes.

To put it another way, whereas European nation states are prepared to pool sovereignty on immigration and asylum issues in order to stop asylum seekers from getting into the EU, the poorer nations of the world lose their sovereignty over immigration controls in order to stop their citizens getting out. Unless, that is, these citizens are part of the chosen few: highly skilled computer wizards, doctors and nurses trained at Third World expense and sought after by the West. Global migration management strategy saps the countries of the Third World and the former Soviet bloc of their economic lifeblood, by creaming off their most skilled and educated workforces. Since the Tampere summit, the thrust of EU refugee policy has shifted to include integratory measures for officially recognised refugees (henceforth 'genuine refugees'), while moving towards the total exclusion of asylum seekers (henceforth 'bogus claimants' and 'economic migrants'), preferably through pre-embarkation controls. The ultimate aim is to create an entirely different model of 'refugee protection' based, not on individual rights, but on a system of warehousing the displaced in large camps in their region of origin until a conflict has been resolved to the satisfaction of the western powers.[17] From such camps, a chosen few will be selected for resettlement in Europe under an Australian-style quota system.

But what would be the criteria for such selection? Given the EU's eager support for a policy of managed migration, are we now to see a situation develop in which the displaced people of the world are screened and selected, sectioned off into categories of skilled and unskilled, through a sort of economic natural selection process ensuring the survival of the economically fittest? Global migration management heralds a new Darwinism. Not the old Social Darwinism that believed that the advance of civilisation was dependent on the advancement of the superior race, but a socio-economic Social Darwinism that allows the rich First World to maintain its economic dominance by emptying the poorer worlds of their skilled workforces. In the era of globalisation, the skills pool, not the gene pool, is key.

The New State Racism and the Philosophy of Deterrence

These international and EU-wide shifts have led, at a domestic level, to a new form of state racism. While the details may vary from country to country, the broad canvas remains the same. Take the UK, for instance. For many decades, campaigners in the UK have fought against the racism of the British state as epitomised in discriminatory immigration laws. The Commonwealth Immigrants Act of 1962 had, for the first time, limited the entry of (black) British subjects, imposing on them the requirement of work vouchers and, by 1971, primary immigration was all but abolished for black people. The state racism of today, however, differs from that of the earlier period in that the national state is not its primary originator; rather, state racism is derived from a globalised racism that is designed by supranational bodies, incorporated into EU programmes and transmitted to the member states for inclusion in their domestic asylum and immigration laws. With the EU intent on institutionalising policies that undermine Article 31 of the 1951 Geneva Convention by criminalising illegal entry, it was only a matter of time before the UK government followed in the footsteps of its counterparts across Europe. But it was not until the 1999 Immigration and Asylum Act (the passage of which coincided with the EU's harmonisation of asylum and immigration policy at Tampere) that the UK government put in place internal mechanisms reflecting the EU view of asylum seekers as the outriders of a criminal fraternity in need of constant surveillance. The creation of a separate system of welfare provision for asylum seekers, linked not to social care but to immigration control, and the introduction of a special asylum detention regime, ensured that from this time on asylum seekers living in the UK would be treated as a suspect community, a rightless group, within a framework designed to contain them specifically.

But, of course, none of this was acknowledged by the New Labour government, which introduced the 1999 Immigration and Asylum Act as a progressive reform designed to bring about centralised control of an asylum system that had spun out of control under the previous Conservative administration. Whereas the Conservatives had an unplanned and piecemeal approach to asylum, New Labour would base its 'fairer, faster and firmer' approach on a system that was 'comprehensive and cohesive'.[18] It was certainly true that the Conservatives had sought to divest the state of its responsibilities, off-loading the costs of asylum seekers' welfare on to local authorities (an attractive option as most asylum seekers were accommodated, at that time, in Labour-controlled London boroughs) while presiding over an asylum claims system that was on the point of breakdown. And it was also true that it was the Conservatives who first began to divest asylum seekers of their welfare rights. At the beginning of the 1990s, a person's immigration status had very little direct bearing on his or her entitlements to welfare and housing services. This gradually changed between 1993 and 1996, under the impact of successive pieces of Conservative legislation. Prior to the 1996 Immigration and Asylum Act, asylum seekers were entitled to the same welfare benefits as UK citizens, but at 90 per cent of the normal rate; they could also claim housing benefit to cover rent. But the 1996 Act removed all rights to housing and financial support from asylum seekers who failed to claim asylum at a UK port of entry or who received a negative decision on their asylum claim. What this meant was that these asylum seekers had to be provided for by local authorities which, under the National

Assistance Act 1945 and the Children Act 1989, were compelled to provide accommodation and food for the destitute. London local authorities – where 90 per cent of all asylum seekers were living – came to resent the burden that asylum claimants placed on budgets. So, at a time when London property prices were booming and temporary accommodation was both costly and in short supply, London local authorities decided to get round their responsibilities by unofficially 'dispersing' asylum seekers into cheaper temporary accommodation outside London, in 'bed and breakfasts' in seaside 'resorts' on the south coast that had fallen on bad times, and even further afield.

New Labour, anxious to sell its asylum package as a progressive reform, held out that asylum seekers were the responsibility of central and not local government. Yet, at the same time as re-establishing a national asylum system, New Labour was quite clear that its overall approach to asylum issues in future would be governed by the philosophy of 'deterrence'. For, according to the Home Office, traffickers from 'overpopulated' and socially and politically unstable 'countries with a weaker economy' were 'facilitating the migration of people who are not entitled to enter the UK'.[19] And this, in turn, was leading to the mushrooming of manifestly unfounded claims, based on a 'tissue of lies', and the subsequent breakdown of the asylum system. Hence, in its 1998 White Paper on immigration and asylum ('Fairer, faster, firmer'), the Home Office argued that it was essential to introduce new legislation to 'minimise the attraction of the UK to economic migrants' by removing access to social benefits and making cash payments as small as possible. Home Secretary Jack Straw later made it clear that he viewed the introduction of vouchers as essential, as 'cash benefits in the social security system are a major pull factor that encourage fraudulent claims'.[20] The only obligation that the state had towards asylum seekers, who could not be wholly supported by friends or relatives, implied the White Paper, was to protect them from absolute destitution.

What signal does it send out when a home secretary broadcasts that the purpose of social legislation is largely punitive, to deter the unfounded claims of bogus asylum seekers? The overall message

– that asylum seekers, in future, will be treated as a suspect group – is one that justifies popular resentment and fuels prejudice. Held under suspicion of being illegal entrants and economic migrants, and guilty – until proved innocent – of lodging false claims, asylum seekers were, henceforth, to be subjected to policies designed not to protect their human rights but to protect the public from them. They were to be enclosed within a separate system of administrative controls designed to act as a *cordon sanitaire* around mainstream society, as though seeking asylum was an infectious disease that needed to be quarantined.

The philosophy outlined in the White Paper was soon followed by changes in the government's administrative apparatus, in line with the White Paper's proposal that 'all funding for support of asylum seekers should be brought into a single budget managed by the Home Office'. Since the 1999 Immigration and Asylum Act, responsibility for the housing and welfare of destitute asylum seekers has passed from the Department of Social Security (welfare benefits) and the Department of Environment, Transport and the Regions (housing benefits) to the Home Office. In other words, the housing and social care of asylum seekers is no longer considered an issue of social welfare but one of immigration control, to be administered by Home Office officials trained to detect false claimants. Furthermore, an entirely new administrative body, the National Asylum Support Service (NASS) was established in the Home Office's Immigration and Nationality Department to oversee the new control mechanisms.

Compulsion, Exclusion and the Denial of Dignity

What characterises a 'deterrent asylum system'? In exchange for basic subsistence and shelter, asylum seekers must accept a regime that denies them access to the welfare state. In exchange for protection from homelessness and starvation, asylum seekers are, quite literally, stripped of human dignity and divested of even the most basic civil and social rights. In this, the state's approach to asylum seekers' 'welfare' is without parallel in modern times. Indeed, the only parallel lies within the pre-welfare state administration of poor relief, most specifically the Poor Law of 1834, which institutionalised the dreaded workhouse system, forcing paupers who passed the 'workhouse test' for indoor relief to submit to a regime so awful as to deter them from seeking refuge in the workhouse in the first place.

Just as that reforming Whig government of the early nineteenth century instituted the workhouse regime as a utilitarian response to increasing pauperisation, so New Labour created NASS as an administrative response to the housing shortage in London and the burden asylum seekers were placing on services both in London and the south-east generally. And like their nineteenth-century counterparts, who saw it as essential to make the workhouse so grim as to deter all but the most needy, New Labour established a regime for asylum seekers so stringent as to deter, or turn away, all but the most desperate. Though destitute asylum seekers did not have to face the workhouse, they did have to face an inhumane 'relief' system, applying to NASS for support, either for living costs, accommodation or a package comprising both. Those who opted for both housing and welfare support, and passed the NASS destitution test, then received the accommodation part of the package – transportation to accommodation in a part of the country selected by NASS. The fact that no consent was needed and no choice given, the fact that those absent from accommodation for more than seven days lost all right to financial support, were the first major components of New Labour's 'deterrent regime'. It was modelled on the 'designated accommodation system' already practised in Germany, the Netherlands, Switzerland and Scandinavia, where asylum seekers were accommodated in reception centres and refugee hostels while their claims were considered.[21]

Removal of Housing Rights

Compelling asylum seekers to live in designated accommodation may seem bad enough, but the system was made worse by changes in housing legislation. Previously, homeless asylum seekers could apply to a local authority for assistance and gain access to the local council housing register. But the 1999 Act was complemented by amendments to housing law that, under the Housing Accommodation (Persons Subject to Immigration Control) (Amendment) (England) Order 1999, stripped asylum seekers of their former eligibility for council housing. In addition, the 1999 Immigration and Asylum Act stipulated that anyone housed through the NASS scheme would be excluded from the security of tenure provisions of current housing legislation, ensuring that he or she could be legally evicted from accommodation with just seven days' notice, and had no legal redress from landlord harassment. Thus, the cumulative effect of the 1999 Act and these new housing regulations was to strip asylum seekers of housing rights afforded to the rest of society, including the homeless. Rendering asylum seekers en masse a group without legal redress, with no security of tenure and no protection from eviction, is a fundamental underpinning of the NASS scheme.

In the initial stages of the new regime, NASS did not itself provide housing for dispersed asylum seekers but contracted out the delivery of support services, including housing (and until 2002, vouchers), to 'accommodation providers' in both the public and private sectors. Initially, NASS had hoped to work with twelve regional consortia in the dispersal areas, made up of local authorities and social or private landlords. But, for a variety of reasons, only 40 per cent of the beds needed for 2000/01 were provided by the consortia, while a staggering 60 per cent were provided via direct private contracts. To make matters more complicated, the majority of private providers were accommodation agencies that subcontract accommodation from private landlords. This led the housing charity, Shelter, to conclude that 'complicated subcontracting arrangements, involving several tiers of subcontractors are developing, with small landlords becoming subcontractors without any checks being made about their past record or suitability'.[22]

The state's policy of denying basic civil rights to asylum seekers was well understood in the twilight zones of the unregulated private housing sector where, huddled in bedsits, shared houses, overcrowded hostels and bed and breakfasts, they faced private landlords who saw in them a lucrative business opportunity. According to Shelter, new landlords were entering the market to take advantage of profitable contracts providing accommodation for asylum seekers, who were actually preferred to other groups precisely because of their rightlessness and their inability to complain effectively. Asylum seekers became the 'new exploited homeless'.[23]

From 1999 onwards, as the new system was put into place, reports of abuse were commonplace. Some of the worst examples came from the large hostels where hundreds of asylum seekers were herded into dormitory conditions. Under New Labour's 'deterrent' regime, food was often inedible, sanitation and hygiene deplorable, heating insufficient and fire and safety regulations ignored. Scarcely any shred of dignity was left to the asylum seeker. Nor was there any privacy in the meagre living space, which could be searched at a moment's notice by police and immigration officials to ensure that only the person designated to live at the accommodation was actually there. And private landlords, too, assumed similar rights. From Liverpool came reports that residents of two tower blocks (the Landmark and the Inn on the Park), deemed unfit for council tenants, were not allowed visitors without the prior consent of the landlord. Individual rooms had no locks and staff had access to all flats. Inmates who complained were threatened with violence or eviction.

Similar stories began to pour in from other parts of the country. As a result, protests erupted as the 'politics of deterrence' provoked the politics of defiance. In September 2000, following a series of hunger-strikes at an asylum hostel in Langley Green, West Midlands, inmates held a rooftop protest and occupied the main road to protest at cramped living conditions, poor food and inadequate health care. There were also at least two mass protests at the Angel Heights Hostel in Newcastle, punished by the arrest of those Iraqi Kurds who were deemed ringleaders. And in January 2001, asylum seekers at the International Hotel in Leicester, a run-down former hotel, who for months had complained about severe problems of hygiene, inadequate heating and poor food, took their beds out on to the streets in protest. These were the same conditions that were among the factors that led a young Iranian resident to commit suicide. 'We came to England to seek safety but have been treated worse than animals', commented one asylum seeker.[24] By introducing measures that strip people of basic rights, the state had issued private landlords with a charter for abuse and victimisation as well as, incidentally, landlord fraud.[25] By 2001, the government was promising to phase out the use of run-down council estates and private accommodation to house asylum seekers and replace them with accommodation centres – 'asylum camps designed to house 750 people in the middle of nowhere, detention centers in all but name, where asylum seekers would be housed, fed and, most controversially of all, their children educated, segregated from mainstream provision'.[26] The White Paper 'Secure Borders, Safe Haven' outlined how these centres would operate alongside induction, reporting and removal centres to form part of an 'end-to-end' asylum process, housing asylum seekers from arrival through refusal of their claim and appeal to departure, keeping asylum seeking families segregated from mainstream society and therefore easier to remove. But by June 2005, the plans had been abandoned,[27] owing to a combination of spiralling costs, shrinking numbers of asylum seekers, fierce local resistance, opposition from refugee groups and the development of alternatives (see below).

Such was the first component of New Labour's 'deterrence regime'.

Removal of Benefits and Access to Health Care

The second component of the 'deterrence regime' was the replacement of cash benefits from 3 April 2000 by NASS vouchers, issued only to a named recipient at a post office. Church bodies, trades unions, professional medical organisations and the voluntary sector immediately mobilised against the degrading and stigmatising voucher system. But while an overarching voucher system for all asylum claimants was abolished in 2002 (on the grounds that the system was unworkable and unfair), the Nationality, Immigration and Asylum Act (2002) introduced new benefits-related legislation, with some categories of asylum seekers removed from even the meagre support offered by NASS, while others (as well as failed asylum-seekers who could not be removed) still remain within the voucher system to this day.

The voucher scheme, in operation from 1991 to 2001, was modelled on existing schemes in Switzerland and Germany.[28] The then home secretary Jack Straw justified the introduction of vouchers as necessary to prevent fraud[29] and to stop what he described as the phenomenon of 'asylum shopping' in which asylum seekers are said to shop around for the European country with the best and most easily obtainable social security benefits. Vouchers are worth only 70 per cent of income support (a benefit of last resort to prevent destitution), amounting to just £36.54 per week for a single person aged over 25 (£10 of which is in cash), and must be spent at designated supermarkets. Any change for unused portions of the vouchers was pocketed by the retailer.

Just as NASS contracted out the provision of accommodation, the voucher system was contracted out to the French multinational, Sodexho Pass International, which already operated a similar scheme in Germany where vouchers were introduced in the 1990s as an essential component of the 'politics of dissuasion'. The UK government chose to ignore the sustained critique provided by the German voluntary sector, which had argued that vouchers were evidence of regression from inclusive post-war social security provisions that reflected the constitutional protection of human dignity, towards a system based on the type of compulsion, exclusion and denial of dignity last seen under National Socialism. For, just as the pink triangle and the yellow star of David marked out gays and Jews as 'deviant', vouchers brand asylum seekers as fraudsters, they argued. Given that no other social group in the UK was given welfare benefits in voucher form, commentators in the UK were quick to point out that the vouchers were in essence discriminatory and regressive.

In that the politics of deterrence leads to the degrading voucher system, the government demeans the authority of the state by making it the instrument of the systematic humiliation and stigmatisation of asylum seekers. Soon after its introduction a number of influential organisations were drawing attention to the misery and degradation of the voucher scheme: children unable to go to school because parents didn't have the bus fare; old people left without warm clothing for the winter because they lived on half of what a UK pensioner had; disabled people who did not enjoy the same benefits as disabled citizens and could not afford the specialist items they needed; mothers of newborn children who had no cash to purchase the essential baby equipment that other parents take for granted.[30] And even bereaved asylum seekers were subjected to the same privations. NASS refused to pay even the most basic funeral expenses on the grounds that, once an asylum seeker had died, he or she was no longer NASS's responsibility 'because they are no longer seeking asylum'.[31]

Health organisations also rallied against the voucher scheme. Research by the King's Fund concluded that there was a marked deterioration in asylum seekers' mental health in the first six months of their stay, particularly in the form of depression and anxiety.[32] Such mental health problems were a direct result of the politics of deterrence, as those who must shop with vouchers and who are ferried around the country, not knowing where they will end up, experience disorientation, uncertainty, loneliness and isolation.

Thus, in the light of such united opposition, vouchers were phased out for most asylum seekers in 2002. But the overall system was merely refined, with the principle of using benefits removal as part of a politics of deterrence remaining firmly in place. The Nationality, Immigration and Asylum Act (2002) deprived late[33] and failed asylum seekers of any form of support whatsoever, leading to an army of destitute asylum seekers on the streets until in November 2005 the House of Lords ruled that leaving asylum seekers with no shelter or food breached the government's obligations under the Human Rights Convention.[34] And Section 9 of the Asylum and Immigration (Treatment of Claimants) Act 2004 extended this exclusion to failed asylum-seeking families, who were henceforth denied the support of NASS as well as other forms of social services, resulting in the threat of eviction from local authority housing for those families who failed to take 'reasonable steps' to leave the country. (Mindful, though, of its obligations under international legislation regarding the rights of the child, the Home Office kindly included a provision to save children from possible starvation by taking them away from their parents faced with eviction, and placing them in the care of social services.) In addition, free NHS treatment was removed from failed asylum seekers (except in emergency cases) under NHS regulations introduced in 2004, leaving cancer sufferers unable to afford radiotherapy and newly diagnosed HIV/AIDS patients unable to access hospital out-patient treatment or anti-retrovirals,[35] and pregnant women refused antenatal care and forced to give birth at home. Then, in December 2007, the Home Office and the Department of Health announced proposals to ban failed asylum seekers from primary care from GPs. The proposals, which prompted an immediate rebellion from hundreds of GPs furious at this denial of their Hippocratic Oath,[36] were overturned following legal challenge in April 2008.[37] The only concession the government made to the absolute destitution faced by a growing desperate army of failed asylum seekers was to introduce workhouse-style 'hard cases' support under Section 4 of the Asylum and Immigration Act 2004. While this comprises accommodation on a no-choice basis, and food or vouchers, it is only available to certain groups such as those who agree to return to their home country 'voluntarily'.

The UK and other European governments are using access to the welfare state as a lever to compel asylum seekers to give up their fight for asylum and leave the country 'voluntarily'. But how voluntary is a return, if a failed asylum seeker is effectively starved out of the country? Grinding down the victims of torture, AIDS sufferers, children, pregnant mothers and the elderly has today become the harsh medicine that unctuous politicians prescribe for the protection of the deserving majority from the undeserving – foreign – poor. Such is the second component of the deterrence regime.

Internment and Xenophobia

At the same time as producing the 1998 White Paper, the government initiated a major review of existing facilities within the immigration and prison services, with the express aim of identifying new sites in which to detain asylum seekers arriving at UK ports and airports. It was vital to do so. For another key aspect of the government's 'deterrent' response to asylum seekers was to speed up the asylum determination process and to keep more and more asylum seekers in detention throughout that process. Having created a new asylum detention centre at a former military barracks in Oakington in which to hold 400 asylum seekers (including, for the first time, women and children) whose applications for asylum would be fast-tracked;[38] having transformed Aldington prison, near Ashford, into a special detention centre for asylum seekers; having commandeered a wing of South Yorkshire's Lindholme prison for the same purpose, the Home Office was, by January 2001, ready to set specific targets for detention and removal.[39] For it was in these new detention centres that failed asylum seekers and *sans papiers* could be held, pending removal by a deportation machine armour-plated against corrosion from any sense of compassion or responsibility (see chapter 5).

What lies behind this extraordinary attempt to create a separate prison regime for asylum seekers detained at the point of arrival in the UK or held for administrative purposes, pending removal? How, indeed, can democratic European states justify imprisoning individuals who have not been brought before a court for a criminal offence but are targeted by the state and committed to prison owing to their outsider status? In fact, the imprisonment of asylum seekers in this way is not new. Part of New Labour's justification for the creation of a factory-style system for the detention and removal of asylum seekers was the mess left by the previous Conservative administration. Despite the Conservatives' repeated calls on New Labour to mandatorily detain all those who apply for asylum in the UK, the Tories, in power, presided over chaotic detention arrangements that developed ad hoc and piecemeal. While there were small detention centres near airports and, by 1993, a new purpose-built high-security immigration and detention centre at Campsfield House, Oxford, the vast majority of a growing population of immigration detainees were held in existing prisons, often for extremely long periods of time. Both within Campsfield House and ordinary prisons, asylum seekers were denied meaningful activity or employment and treated, in many respects, far worse than those convicted of a crime – as was at that time acknowledged by a former chief inspector of prisons.[40]

New Labour, however, in attempting to cohere the elements of these ad hoc arrangements into a special asylum prison regime linked to the politics of deterrence was attempting to establish something qualitatively different. And, once again, it was a system that bore the stamp of the EU, designed as it was to harmonise UK practices with those already existing on the European mainland where asylum seekers were imprisoned at different stages of the asylum process. It is a system that today is characterised by centres to fast-track the applications of new arrivals; special holding centres for interning problem applicants; discrete detention centres close to airports, where asylum seekers are held pending deportation. What has resulted, in all EU member states, is a separate prison complex for asylum seekers, underpinned by specific legal powers and instruments in a Europe-wide system of control and surveillance. The use of measures more germane to serious criminal investigation, such as the compulsory finger-printing of all asylum seekers, including children of five, has become routine, as has the complete disregard for civil liberties in the storage of personal data on asylum seekers on the Schengen Information System. This, the EU's largest computer database, can be accessed from 50,000 terminals across Europe. As around 90 per cent of the information stored on it concerns immigration rather than criminal cases,[41] and as this database is considered to be at the heart of the EU's internal security system, it follows that the EU considers the movement of the world's 32.9 million displaced people the most important security issue it faces.

By detaining vast numbers of asylum seekers,[42] the UK government replicates on the domestic plane the EU's linkage of asylum with internal security. From 1999, little by little and step by step, New Labour implemented measures that targeted asylum seekers, enclosing them in a separate system of surveillance and control. But even as it created what is, in effect, a separate police state for asylum seekers, New Labour denied that it was doing so. To this day, it continues as a signatory to the UN Geneva Convention, despite the fact that it has brought in laws violating Article 31, which expressly states that asylum seekers should not be criminalised for entering a country illegally. And while, on paper, it remains bound to the European Convention on Human Rights, it blatantly ignores its stipulation that immigrants (including asylum seekers) should only be detained for short periods at the border (to prevent unauthorised entry) or for a limited period in pre-deportation detention (to aid removal). And with characteristic spin and subterfuge, it attempts to argue that those detained in 'privately run reception facilities' are held not in prisons but hotels, depicting inmates at Oakington (who are not allowed to leave or move between buildings unless escorted by security guards) not as prisoners but as guests.[43]

In fact, New Labour is right. These so-called guests are not prisoners under domestic UK law, for then a court would have had to detain them for a specific criminal offence. The unpalatable truth that must be camouflaged is that detained asylum seekers are internees – and internment is a wartime measure usually invoked against 'enemy aliens' (yet more proof that New Labour has gone to war with the displaced people of the world). Internees are separate from other prisoners in that, historically, they have usually been committed to detention by 'emergency powers' such as those that obtained during the First and Second World Wars, under the Prevention of Terrorism Act (Northern Ireland), or during the 1991 Gulf War, when male Iraqi students were interned in British jails. In fact, in December 2004, the House of Lords held that the internment of foreign terrorist suspects was discriminatory and breached the government's human rights obligations. Nevertheless, today, asylum seekers can still be detained indefinitely under the Immigration Acts, so long as they are being detained 'with a view to removal'.

In Italy, with its experience of fascism, progressives within the criminal justice system have argued that the imprisonment of asylum seekers constitutes internment: the Italian Association of Democratic Magistrates, for instance, denounced the creation of a 'special legal regime for foreigners' as a 'threat to democracy'.[44] But in the UK, a New Labour government that purported to be progressive seems to have little regard for democratic traditions, as well as scant historical awareness, remaining apparently oblivious to the direct link between the onslaught against asylum seekers and the internment of Jewish refugees during the Second World War.[45] But then, this lack of historical and political recall is hardly surprising, given the doublethink that characterises the government's approach to asylum. By its actions and policies, New Labour treats asylum seekers as though they are enemy aliens and a threat to national security; yet government ministers repeat the mantra that they welcome 'genuine refugees' (without expressly detailing just how). By its language, New Labour declares itself a government opposed to institutional racism, yet by its actions it embraces and mobilises xeno-racism. The internment of asylum seekers, the third component of the politics of deterrence, legitimised the increasingly hysterical press climate against new arrivals.

But what finally set the seal on xeno-racism, legitimising even further its populist and inflammatory expression in the press, was the passing of the Terrorism Act 2000. This, the first permanent anti-terrorism law in 25 years, directly targeted exile organisations. Even as Sir William Macpherson in his report into the death of the black teenager Stephen Lawrence warned of the danger of stereotyping black communities as criminal, the government gave legitimacy to a new set of stereotypes: asylum seekers are phonies and fraudsters; refugees are terrorists and the 'enemy within'.

What is happening today in the field of immigration and asylum policy, we are constantly told, has nothing to do with racism. How can we be racist, asks the *Sun*, when most asylum seekers are white?

If this is not racism, what is?

Xeno-racism, the new racism against asylum seekers, marries up the worst racist practices throughout the western world: the segregation of asylum seekers mirrors the anti-black racism of apartheid, or of segregation in the US; the debate about asylum numbers throws us back to Britain's anti-immigrant racism of the 1970s; the scapegoating, victimisation and internment of asylum seekers mirrors the treatment of Jews during the Second World War; the targeting of refugee communities under the 2000 Terrorism Act mirrors the anti-Irish racism of the earlier period of PTA emergency powers.

2

ANTI-MUSLIM RACISM AND THE SECURITY STATE

Europe is, we have been warned, facing a 'global threat', posed, post-September 11, by 'Islamic extremism'. In a speech to his Sedgefield constituency, former British prime minister Tony Blair spoke in apocalyptic tones of a threat that is 'real and existential'; it needed to be fought 'whatever the political cost'.[1] Yet the threat to our 'values', to nations that are 'free, democratic and benefiting from economic progress', comes not just from Blair's many-headed monster of 'international terrorism', but from a domestic peril of Europe's own making. And, arguably, it will have longer-lasting results and inflict greater damage on European civil society, traditional values and way of life than any external danger. It derives from the very way that that danger is conceived and, hence, countered. It is inherent in the counter-terrorism measures the EU has adopted since September 11, which extend the definition of terrorism, and in the emergency laws passed by member states so as to undermine the fundamentals of justice. It is based on a concept of national security that is shot through with xeno-racism – the precise term Sivanandan uses to describe the new racism that has emerged across Europe over the last decade and is directed at those who, displaced and dispossessed by globalisation, are being thrown up on Europe's shores.[2] It is xeno in form in that it is directed against foreigners irrespective of colour; it is racism in substance in that it bears all the hallmarks of demonisation and exclusion of the old racism – and the mechanisms that set that foreign-ness *in situ* are legal and structural and institutional.

Post-September 11 the parameters of institutionalised xeno-racism – anti-foreignness – have been expanded to include minority ethnic communities that have been settled in Europe for decades, simply because they are Muslim. Since Islam now represents 'threat' to Europe, its Muslim residents, even though they are citizens, even though they may be European-born, are caught up in the ever-expanding loop of xeno-racism. They do not merely threaten Europe as the 'enemy within' in the war on terror, their adherence to Islamic norms and values threatens the notion of Europeanness itself. Under the guise of patriotism, a wholesale anti-Islamic racism has been unleashed that itself threatens to destroy the fabric of multiculturalism.

It is in this context that we need to understand the new drive across Europe towards assimilation.[3] Assimilation is being forced through by the adoption of a number of measures, which include the recasting of citizenship laws according to security consider-ations; the introduction of compulsory language and civics tests for citizenship applicants; codes of conduct for the trustees of mosques; a cultural code of conduct for Muslim girls and women who, in some areas of Europe, are being forbidden to wear the hijab in state schools and other state institutions.

But in order to understand how an assimilationist minority ethnic policy serves as an adjunct to anti-terrorist laws in the security state, it is first necessary to consider the political rhetoric of security that European leaders deployed in the aftermath of September 11 to justify the subsequent invasions of Afghanistan and Iraq. It is impossible to divorce the current debate on the 'limits of cultural diversity' from the war on terror.

The Securitisation Agenda

After the events of September 11, no one could argue that al Qaida did not pose a threat to the US or that its tactics were not those of terror. As close allies of the US and active participants in the first Gulf War, EU governments would have considered themselves at risk from al Qaida suicide bombers and the activities of sleeper cells. The German authorities, shocked that the September 11 plot had been hatched in Hamburg, arrested four Algerians after uncovering evidence of a conspiracy to bomb the Strasbourg Christmas market in 2000. The British authorities, too, were alarmed when Richard Reid, a young British-Caribbean convert to Islam, attempted to blow up a commercial flight using explosive devices hidden in his shoes. EU states would have been irresponsible had they not taken proportionate measures to protect their citizens from al Qaida terror attacks. The problem, however, was that the response to September 11 was not proportionate. Not only did the EU pass resolutions and initiate legislation that brought a whole array of unrelated issues under the rubric of the war against terror, but the most prominent European heads of state (with the exception of the German chancellor and the French president) played a vital role in creating the myth that the West was in 'imminent' danger from Saddam Hussein's weapons of mass destruction and that Saddam had high-level contacts with al Qaida going back a decade.

Even in the immediate aftermath of September 11, when the focus on al Qaida might have been expected to be at its sharpest, the EU reacted by bringing a whole array of dissidence – not just 'foreign terrorist organisations' but anti-globalisation protests, animal rights activism, subversive youth subcultures and so on – under the remit of counter-terrorism. The EU Common Positions and Framework Decision on combating terrorism, passed in December 2001, broadened the definition of terrorism considerably. Terrorist activity was no longer confined to extreme violence committed for political ends; now any action designed to 'seriously damage a country or international organisation' or that 'unduly compel[led]' a government to act in a particular way could fall within the definition. If the notion of undue compulsion or serious damage still implies that extreme violence is integral to the concept of terrorism, this was belied by the subsequent inclusion under the definition of all those who gave terrorism 'any form of support, active or *passive*' (emphasis added).[4] In this way, new crimes of association with terrorism were created. Henceforth, for instance, individuals fighting for ethnic self-determination who do not pursue their goals by violent means, or knowingly assist

with the preparation of violent acts, could come under the scope
of European anti-terrorist laws.

Member states subsequently began incorporating the EU
Common Positions and Framework Decision into domestic
laws, leading to the introduction by some states of emergency
legislation and new anti-terrorist laws. Others amended existing
public order, criminal justice and aliens' legislation and extended
police powers. Crucially, both approaches led to the creation of
a shadow criminal justice system for foreign nationals, including
asylum seekers, who would, in future, be denied basic civil
liberties and human rights. France, Italy and Sweden moved
to deport foreign nationals suspected of posing a security risk,
thus abandoning the principle of *non-refoulement* according to
which foreign nationals cannot be extradited to a state where they
risk persecution, the death penalty, torture or other degrading
treatment.[5] The UK Anti-Terrorism Crime and Security Act 2001
(ATCSA) introduced internment without trial for foreign nationals
only, twelve of whom were incarcerated at Belmarsh and Woodhill
prisons.[6] The detainees were charged with no crime, were unable
to see the evidence against them and were confined to their cells
for 22 hours a day.

In effect, EU governments were using the opportunity that
September 11 afforded to expand the definition of terrorism and
spread the tentacles of the security state in previously unthinkable
ways – albeit Europe is no stranger to political movements that
target civilians for bombings and other attacks. The 30-year war
in Northern Ireland, the ongoing conflict between Spain and
Basque separatists, and in France over the future of Corsica, are
the most obvious examples of conflicts that have claimed the
lives of civilians, either at the hands of the state or paramilitary
movements. Yet these real material outrages never led to the
kind of blanket security measures engendered by September 11
and now justified post hoc by the terrorist attacks in Madrid
and London.

This is not to say that European states did not attempt to
manufacture consensus for draconian policies in Northern
Ireland or the Basque Country, for instance. But consent was

manufactured through the idea that separatist violence could be contained on the periphery; the general public were encouraged to maintain a Blitz-style solidarity in the face of further potential attacks. However, after the events of September 11, European publics have been encouraged to think in an entirely different way, viewing any bombing in any part of the world as a direct threat to each individual's personal security. Criminologist Janne Flyghed has argued that the expansion of anti-terrorist measures has come through the depiction of 'imminent danger of dramatic proportions without a shred of empirical support'. 'Repeated references to certain spectacular events produce a false consciousness of impending danger' and are linked to 'perceptions of non-specific and diffuse, but nonetheless serious threats. The objects of these threats are also often quite difficult to define', but include '"the national security", "the safety of the nation", or "public order and safety", concepts whose content and applicability can vary according to the political situation'.[7] In essence, there are no distant parts of the world any more, no peripheries.

Or, rather, the periphery is at the centre, its boundaries determined by xeno-racism.

The constant reference to spectacular events, like those of September 11, then, serves a wider political agenda; that of manufacturing consent to increasingly intrusive surveillance and the circumscription of personal freedoms through the evocation of fear. The British government, for instance, has been engaged in 'illiberal experiments to govern by way of the exception' involving the adoption of 'extraordinary measures against those we are encouraged to consider as the outcast'.[8] The 'outcast' is necessary, as both threat and scapegoat. Radical lawyer Gareth Peirce has described how the politics of fear emerging around 'national security' takes effect:

'National security' has a seductive ring. It frightens off political disagreement. It frightens the population and makes it more subservient to authoritarian measures. It widens a circle of fear as the ever-expanding notion of national security perceives a nation's interests as being capable of being directly affected by events all around the world. It creates an exaggerated degree of fear and an exaggerated degree of threat, and it is of immense importance to governments and governmental institutions which have an inherent desire to act in secrecy and to hide material from which vital national decisions are made from scrutiny.[9]

The Role of the Security Services

In this climate, security services across Europe are expanding rapidly. In the UK, for example, the Special Branch is now two-and-a-half times larger than it was during the Cold War and the conflict in Northern Ireland. At the same time, western interventions in Muslim countries provide yet more opportunities for the media to demonise particular groups, even nations, serving 'to weave general public opinion into a global warfare against Muslims'.[10] As lawyer John Upton has noted, public opinion is often manipulated through the grossest of stereotypes and simplifications:

> We are told that we face a complex, overwhelming threat, yet we are given the crudest means of deciphering our predicament: caricatures of Saddam, of bin Laden, of suicide bombers and evil imams. These are the cartoon ogres in whose shadows we are encouraged to unite.[11]

A System of Religious Profiling

Evidence suggests that, rather than taking targeted action against individuals with a demonstrable link to al Qaida or its associates, security services are systematically building up widespread intelligence about particular groups or communities deemed potential security risks. This bears out the criminologist Magnus Hornqvist's observation that belonging to a particular community or group is, in itself, a security threat.[12] From this, it is a short step to the deployment of coercive measures against particular groups, whether the punitive nature of detention for aliens under terrorism acts or low-level police harassment around mosques.

Profiling by the security services has developed in two stages. The first concentrates on suspected 'enemy aliens', primarily foreign students, asylum seekers and refugees, overwhelmingly (but not exclusively) from Muslim regions of the world. The EU Common Positions on combating terrorism instructs all member states to vet all asylum seekers to determine whether they have any connection to terrorism, including that notorious catch-all of 'passive' support for it. A file is created on each person/family, detailing information on their political and trades union activity in their countries of origin or any country they have stayed in. In Denmark, Germany and Norway, intelligence services have specifically targeted foreign students as a high-risk group and embarked on a process of religious profiling of non-EU students. The Danish Police Intelligence Service (PET) and the Norwegian Police Security Service (PST) place a duty upon universities to collaborate with security services' intelligence-gathering procedures on the grounds that foreign students may attempt to register at university to access information or equipment that might be used to produce weapons of mass destruction.[13] The German system of religious profiling of foreign nationals from Islamic states, which started with universities but has since been extended to private businesses, is unprecedented in scale. By April 2002, the federal state's criminal investigation department had assembled six million personal records and singled out well over 20,000 potential suspects, even though there was no concrete evidence against them. To qualify for inclusion on this list, a suspect has to be of (presumed) Islamic religious affiliation, 'from an Islamic state', aged between 18 and 24 and not previously have come to the notice of the criminal investigation department.[14] Who is more suspect than a young Muslim man with no police record?

Second, in the UK, as elsewhere in Europe, the intelligence services move on to profile Muslim communities wholesale, citizens and non-citizens alike. By 2001, British lawyers and the Campaign against Criminalising Communities (CAMPACC), had built up a detailed picture of how the intelligence services were operating.[15] Support for international causes is key to whether a Muslim will come under scrutiny. According to the former home affairs editor of the *Observer*, Martin Bright, the police and the security services, in viewing Islam *per se* as the threat, fail to recognise the diversity of the Islamic movement. In the event, they lump together genuine political dissidents and numbers of ordinary Muslims with individuals whom most would regard as terrorists, thus obfuscating rather than clarifying any possible genuine threat.[16] Furthermore, given the attacks that followed September 11, western security agencies have become more dependent on intelligence agencies in the Arab and Muslim world, leading to even more confusion. These agencies are hardly noted for their political independence or respect for human rights; rather, they most often act as the repressive arm of authoritarian regimes practising state terrorism. Such agencies could well attempt to use European intelligence services as a vehicle for targeting dissidents from domestic Islamist movements, albeit those dissidents do not share the same ideology as al Qaida and have sought refuge in the West. In Britain, Muslim individuals are apparently suspect if they fought in Afghanistan against the Russians (when the US was funding the Mujahedin) or in Bosnia (against ethnic cleansing). They may have opposed, either actively or passively, the military junta in Algeria or the Russian occupation force in Chechnya. As Palestinian refugees opposed to Israeli state terror, or opponents of the western-backed regimes in Morocco, Tunisia, Turkey and Egypt, they also come under scrutiny. From here, the intelligence services go on to 'stigmatise whole communities as terrorist networks with communal, friendship and political networks stigmatised as "associated with terrorism"'.[17]

Even the giving of small amounts of money is treated as evidence of financing terrorism. The trustees of mosques fall under suspicion if they have been involved in fundraising for international causes, as do Muslim charities and NGOs involved in humanitarian relief to Palestinians in the occupied territories, for instance, or Chechens in the refugee camps of Ingushetia. Under anti-terrorist laws, all these acts can be construed as 'passive' support for terrorism on the grounds that, even though the emergency relief was not destined for terrorist organisations, some of it may have ended up in their hands.

For governments and intelligence services that view the Muslim community through the lens of Islamophobia, support for all such international causes is proof of Islamic fanaticism. But viewed through the lens of human rights, coming to the aid of people under occupation and at risk of serious human rights violations, even genocide, could be construed as the same kind of idealism that motivated anti-fascists to join the International Brigade and risk their lives fighting Franco.

Policing a Suspect Community

The reaction of European intelligence services, caught off guard by September 11, was to expand their sources of information. The formation of the International Coalition against Terror ensured, as already stated, that additional intelligence would be derived from intelligence services abroad. Not only are these the agencies of states that have their own repressive agendas, but their already skewed information is then to be fed into the pre-existing ignorance and prejudice of western security agencies. Failure to understand the history and socio-economic conditions of the Arab and wider Muslim world that have given rise to popular Islamist movements is a poor starting point for liaison with and evaluation of foreign intelligence sources.

How this works in practice is evidenced in a study by Fouzi Slisli, published in 2000. He details how the military junta in Algiers, which prevented the Islamist FIS government from contesting the second round of the 1992 general election (after convincingly winning the first round), created a 'comprehensive circuit of misinformation, feeding directly upon western prejudice and hatred of Islam'.[18] Restored to power, the Algerian junta's security services set out to terrorise the FIS's popular base. From 1994 to 1999, an estimated 12,000 people disappeared after being arrested. Another 17,000 were sent to concentration camps in the desert and an estimated 120,000 people were killed. Yet, today, it is that same Algerian security service, together with others of its ilk (and not just in the Arab world) that feeds information to European intelligence services.

If our intelligence services are caught up in this circuit, if they cannot distinguish between ordinary Muslims and terrorists, then the security state hardly represents the people's best hope of protection from al Qaida-style terrorist attacks. It is also quite conceivable, in such a climate, that anti-terrorist police operations are premised on anti-Muslim stereotypes and a culture of suspicion.

Indeed, a pattern of punitive policing was soon to emerge across Europe, characterised, in the first instance, by large-scale police operations in Muslim communities based on misinformation from the intelligence services. For example, in January 2003, 16 North Africans were arrested in coordinated raids throughout Catalonia, accused by the Spanish authorities of being part of a cell that provided information and support to other Islamist terror groups and conspiring to manufacture the poison ricin. During the raid, one of the accused, who was asleep in bed, awoke to find his door being blown open. Thinking at first that there was a fire and the men charging into his room were firefighters, Smail Boudjelthia was forced face down on to the floor by armed police demanding, among other things, how often he went to the local mosque. Three Muslim organisations issued a joint statement expressing horror at the 'indiscriminate' nature of the raids. They complained of 'unnecessary violence', with police 'breaking into homes in which children and pregnant women were sleeping'. Police actions of this kind, they said, wiped out years of collaborative work with the local authority and voluntary organisations 'to promote mutual respect, harmony and integration'. The statement warned of the 'danger of equating Islam or religion with terrorism, or, which is the same thing, seeing an immigrant and a terrorist as the same'. The organisations condemned terrorism – anyone responsible should be punished – but 'you can't generalise and blame a whole people for terrorism, in the same way you can't say that all the Basques are terrorists because we know ETA kills too'.[19]

In January 2003, in Germany, the Central Council of Muslims in Baden-Württemberg and ten other Muslim organisations issued a statement criticising the arbitrary and irresponsible nature of police raids that had been carried out simultaneously on houses of prayer and the offices of Muslim organisations in Stuttgart, Mannheim and Freiburg. The raids on mosques (13 December 2002), during which a total of 617 worshippers were checked and detained for several hours, led Muslims to feel that they were being treated as criminals and as though they were engaged in some sort of war. It is alleged that, during a raid on a mosque in Stuttgart-Cannstatt, a 77-year-old pensioner was led away in handcuffs because he did not have his identity card on him. In Mannheim, 600 police officers, with truncheons drawn, forced their way into the mosque of the Islamic Workers' Association.

The police justified the operation on the grounds of the danger posed by Islamic terrorism and on the basis of a suspicion that false passports were being manufactured and distributed at 'particular Islamic meeting places' to aid 'a network of Islamic extremists'. All in all, the raids led to eight arrests, most of which were connected to infringements of the aliens' law.[20] For the Muslim organisations, the raids had broken down trust and all possibilities of future cooperation. At a stroke, it would seem, the police and intelligence services, by alienating potential allies in enhancing the security of all, exacerbated and made more opaque any potential genuine threat.

The effect of heavy-handed police raids on Muslim meeting places and homes was, in the aftermath of September 11, also of primary concern to the Muslim community in the UK. The Muslim Safety Forum, set up in the wake of September 11 to liaise with the Metropolitan Police, was soon reporting that British Muslims felt discriminated against and victimised and were losing faith in the police. There was particular concern about the extension of stop-and-search powers. According to *Statewatch*, more than 71,000 stop and searches were conducted in the year 2002–03 as part of anti-terrorist operations. But arrests were made in only 1.18 per cent of cases, the vast majority of which were not connected to terrorism.[21]

How can Muslim organisations, which backed strong action after September 11, be expected to acquiesce in such methods of policing? One has only to look at the history of Northern Ireland to see where military-style policing operations lead. Following the

Prevention of Terrorism Act 1974 and the Emergency Provisions Act 1978, an estimated 60,000 people, the overwhelming majority of whom were innocent, were brought into police stations for questioning.[22] Widespread alienation of the Catholic community from the policing process was the outcome. Or take France, where a series of bomb attacks on the Paris underground in the 1990s led to the launch of the *Vigipirate* anti-terrorist plan. Under this, gendarmes and riot police were deployed to guard schools, transportation hubs, government buildings and centres of tourism in French cities. In recent years, these security measures have been tightened in the 'Islamic suburbs', effectively militarising French housing estates. But this massive extension of police anti-terrorist powers has not been matched by checks and safeguards on police behaviour. Between 1992 and 1998, at least 17 young North Africans died in police custody, yet no police officer has ever been successfully charged with manslaughter, let alone murder.[23] Meanwhile, the French ideal of the 'indivisible Republic', which means that every citizen is regarded as solely and equally French and that the existence of ethnic minorities is not officially recognised, ensures that the impact of the *Vigipirate* on the Muslim communities and others is never investigated. The anger of young people at the injustices they suffer from the forces of law rages on. Sporadic uprisings are quelled by the police who are given more and more powers; Muslim youth are locked into a cycle of discrimination and criminalisation, which is not only a major injustice in itself, but serves to promote, rather than dissipate, any threat, and heightens already widespread perceptions of insecurity among the population at large.

Crimes of Association

By the end of 2004, only one person, Mounir al Motassadeq, had been convicted in relation to the September 11 attacks. Despite al Motassadeq's initial conviction in 2003, the case has dragged on for years. Al Motassadeq was convicted but acquitted on appeal, with the initial conviction reinstated on further appeal in January 2007. (Lawyers are now considering a further appeal at the European Court of Human Rights.) There is not space here to discuss this controversial case in detail. What is critical, however, is that Mounir al Motassadeq's initial conviction does not appear to rest on any substantial material evidence but on the fact that he was a friend of the Hamburg September 11 hijackers. Al Motassadeq's retrial came after the earlier collapse (in December 2003) of a second case arising out of September 11 involving the Moroccan Abdelghani Mzoudi, a friend of al Motassadeq. The judge ruled that there was not enough evidence to proceed against Mzoudi. Mzoudi's lawyers had submitted that the only evidence against him was that he had fought in Afghanistan, that he was a friend of the hijackers and that he had done them favours. But these were simply of the kind typical between Muslims and not evidence that Mzoudi was part of a terrorist conspiracy.

These two cases are indicative of a wider trend, in which arrests and prosecutions are based not on material evidence but on 'crimes of association' – that is, association with terrorists or with the associates of terrorists. (It is a moot point how far such regression could be taken.) France, in particular, is guilty of using the vaguely defined offence of *association de malfaiteurs en relation avec une enterprise terroriste*[24] (association with wrongdoers) to arrest large numbers of people on the basis of minimal evidence, some of which may be provided by foreign intelligence services abroad with poor records on torture. In fact, the vast majority of French terrorist suspects are arrested and detained (sometimes for years in pre-trial detention) under the *association de malfaiteurs* offence, a crime that is so legally imprecise, and open to creative judicial interpretation, that all sorts of 'conduct', including speech, is prosecutable. It allows the authorities to cast such a wide net that family members, neighbours, members of the same mosque, or even those who frequent the same restaurant can come under suspicion.[25] The case brought against Smail Boudjelthia (see above) also apparently stemmed from the presumption of guilt by association. The French intelligence services originally requested the Spanish to act on the grounds that a terrorist suspect linked to the plot to bomb the Strasbourg Christmas market had stayed at Boudjelthia's apartment. But, as Boudjelthia commented after his release, 'Many Algerians who come through Banyoles stay here. I could not tell you who they all are. Even the local Red Cross brings Algerians to our door if they arrive in town and ask for help.'[26] Also in Spain, a prosecution was mounted against the Al Jazeera war correspondent Tayssir Alouni,[27] who was initially charged in 2003 with membership of al Qaida, financing an al Qaida cell and acting as a courier for al Qaida. This, too, seemed to be based on guilt by association. Alouni had taken money (around US$4,000) to Afghanistan for a wedding and to the relatives of Syrian exiles who wished to help their families back home. Alouni's argument is that he transported the money and opened his home to people now under investigation out of Arab hospitality; other contacts with suspected terrorists in Afghanistan took place as a result of his journalistic enterprise in gaining access to al Qaida and the Taliban. Al Jazeera's directors immediately wrote to the Spanish prime minister describing the charges against Alouni as 'verging on the absurd'. The International Federation of Journalists also took up the case, describing the arrest as the 'continuation of a concerted campaign against the Arab media in general, and al-Jazeera in particular'.[28] Nevertheless, in September 2005 Alouni was convicted of collaboration with a terrorist organisation and sentenced to seven years' imprisonment. He was set free in October 2006, owing to a heart complaint, on condition that he serve the remainder of his sentence at home under supervision via electronic tagging.

For media workers, the case brought against Tayssir Alouni was a crucial one. It demonstrates just how difficult it has become, post-September 11, for journalists to do their job without falling foul of anti-terrorist legislation. Criticising the 'gossamer-thin' judgment of the Spanish prosecutors, US journalist Peter Bergen writes:

> Indeed, if it were a crime to deliver cash to people in Afghanistan before 9/11 many journalists, including myself, would be found guilty. At the time there were no functioning banks in the country and no way to wire money to people.

Furthermore, if it was proof of terrorist intent for a journalist to have interviewed Osama bin Laden (as Alouni had done for Al Jazeera), then every journalist who had 'interviewed bin Laden in the past such as myself, Peter Arnett, Scott MacLeod of *Time* magazine, Robert Fisk of the *Independent* newspaper in Britain, John Miller of ABC News and several other Arab and Pakistani journalists' could be prosecuted. And finally, concludes Bergen, if the logic generated by the new crimes of association is followed through, then we shall soon see prosecutions of journalists who 'meet with and report on the insurgents in Iraq'.[29]

Trial by Media

In all these cases, the bias of the intelligence services, the police and the media has combined with the current political agenda to create a culture of suspicion against Muslims. The intelligence services and the police are often the only sources of information for the media, which then feed off them to construct alarmist and distorted pictures of spectacular threats. Speeches are made in parliament demonising the accused, and police and intelligence services are praised for foiling devastating plots and preserving 'national security'. The mass media substitute for the court – the press becomes not only the arena where the suspect is tried, but judge and jury too. The prosecution's case is enunciated by anonymous 'security' sources, while the defence is denied a voice. There is, as UK human rights lawyer Gareth Peirce has noted, 'a tidal wave of contemptuous coverage, putting in jeopardy any hope of a fair trial'.[30] But then, in the current punitive climate, media furore has to stand in for due process – for so weak are some of the 'cases' initiated that many do not come to trial at all.

Take, for instance, the case of 28 impoverished Pakistani street vendors who were arrested in Naples in January 2003, while prime minister Berlusconi was in Washington to express Italy's support for a US-led war to disarm Iraq. These 28 men, many of whom were without residence papers and scraped a living on the streets of Naples, were arrested on suspicion of 'association with the aim of international terrorism, possession of illegal explosive material, falsification of documents and trafficking'. The press immediately reported that an 'al-Qaida terrorist cell' had been uncovered, citing an anonymous police source who claimed that a plot to assassinate Britain's chief of defence staff Admiral Sir Michael Boyce had been foiled, as well as plots to attack the US consulate in Naples and nearby tourist spots from Pompeii to Capri. The combination of dynamite, explosive fuses and detonators seized 'could', said the police official, 'have blown up a ten-storey building'. He added ominously that religious texts in Urdu and other documents had also been found in the men's apartment, as well as photos of 'martyrs of the Jihad'.[31]

The Pakistani community in Naples and the Pakistani embassy in Rome were shocked at the way the men were depicted as terrorists. Friends told the press that the street vendors had been living in appalling conditions in a room in a building rented from the local mafia; one of the substances seized was a kind of sugar sent from Pakistan; the fanatical texts cited by the police were nothing more than laminated prayer cards from the Qur'an. Two weeks after the men's arrest, a judge ordered the release of all 28. There was no evidence that the defendants were linked to al Qaida and they had not been aware of the explosives in the flat (probably deposited there by the building's mafia owners).

A series of arrests linked to plots to poison commuters on the London underground and on the London streets, demonstrates the hysterical nature of the interplay between the intelligence services, media and government.[32] The first 'poison plot' story emerged in the UK on 17 November 2002, when the *Sunday Times* claimed on its front page that MI5 had foiled a poison-gas attack on the underground. Six men arrested under the Terrorism Act (2000) were said to be part of an al Qaida network operating out of Europe that had been planning to release a 'gas bomb' on a crowded tube train. Home secretary David Blunkett, although distancing himself from the *Sunday Times* article, commented on the arrests and described the men as part of a 'terrorist cell'.[33] When the six appeared in court, no allegations about explosives or chemicals were made, and there were no claims that the suspects had any materials for the manufacture of bombs. During a television interview, the home secretary had to be reminded of the Contempt of Court Act and deputy prime minister John Prescott later admitted that there was no evidence of any plan for a gas or bomb attack.[34] Despite this, three of the six men were charged with possessing articles for use – in terrorism – then false passports.

This was not the end of the 'poison plots'. In January 2003, police arrested 20 Algerians in a series of raids in north London, Bournemouth and Manchester (where a police officer was stabbed to death), and said they had discovered a cache of ricin, as well as recipes for making it and other poisons. This time, the poison was allegedly to be smeared on the handles of cars. Eight people were charged with offences related to developing or producing a chemical weapon. The 'ricin plot' quickly developed a life of its own, with stories in other countries immediately linked to the UK terror horror. In Ireland, two months after the arrests, the security services told the press that anti-terrorist Gardai and military intelligence were on full-scale alert amid fears that associates of the ricin cell arrested in Britain might move to Ireland to escape the massive police pressure on them in English cities.[35] In France, the arrest in January 2004 of a Muslim family accused of providing logistical support for the Muslim fighters in Chechnya was linked to the UK ricin plot.[36] Meanwhile, the arrest in Spain of 16 North Africans in January 2003 led to a major 'ricin scare' that was immediately linked to the UK ricin plot; the defendants were said to be in possession of white powder. A police press release stated that the men had 'provided information and support to other Islamist terror groups, had explosives, used chemical products and had connections with terror cells in Britain and France'. The Spanish president José Maria Aznar held a press conference declaring that the men 'comprised an important network of terrorists connected to al Qaida' and that their arrests highlighted 'the danger of terrorist groups getting hold of [weapons] of mass destruction'.[37] President Bush congratulated the Spanish authorities on their pre-emptive action, and, in a speech to the UN Security Council on 5 February 2003, US secretary of state Colin Powell cited the arrests as an example of the links between Baghdad and bin Laden. His slide-show presentation connected the Spanish suspects to London's ricin plotters.

After months of such prejudicial coverage, the case against the 16 North Africans collapsed before it was brought to trial. The bottles and flasks containing what police claimed were explosives and chemical products held cologne, olive oil, honey, household ammonia and washing powder.[38] Back in the UK, after a seven-month trial, the first four 'ricin plot' defendants were acquitted in April 2005. It transpired that no ricin had been found at the Wood Green flat where its discovery had been trumpeted two years before, and that the 'plot' was a product of the interrogation under torture in Algeria of Mohammed Meguerba, an acquaintance of some of the defendants. Following the acquittal, the prosecutor dropped the charges against the other defendants.[39] The acquittal did not stop the government from pressing ahead with its plans to deport the ricin defendants, however, and most of them still faced deportation in mid-2008.[40]

CB BO

So far, most – though not all – of the cases discussed have involved migrants and exiles, the flotsam and jetsam of a global tide that enriches the few, impoverishes the many and criminalises the mere struggle to survive. Thrown up on Europe's shores, they are vulnerable both to the awesome power of the European state and to the repressive reach of their countries of origin; they are vulnerable because of their marginality, their lack of rights, their poverty. They are an easy target. But any self-respecting threat to national security demands not only an enemy at the gates, but also an enemy within. Fortuitously for the state, the enemy without and the enemy within are linked by their adherence to a faith that stresses community. As some of the cases discussed above indicate, this has already been turned to account by a xeno-racism that views Tayssir Alouni's hospitality as evidence of criminality, or Smail Boudjelthia's open house as evidence of conspiracy.

The enemy within presents a more thorny problem. While the 'threat' posed by foreign nationals may be dealt with by heavy-handed policing and any combination of repressive measures (who, apart from a few 'airy-fairy' civil liberties lawyers, is really going to care?), how is the state to monitor and control suspects if they are Muslim by religion, but European by birth or naturalisation? While 'enemy aliens' have few legal rights and can be dealt with via a shadow criminal justice system, 'enemy citizens' are protected by written (or unwritten) constitutions, the rule of law and the European Convention on Human Rights. And the judiciary, as the British home secretary found to his cost when he proposed extending anti-terrorist legislation to British citizens, is loth to accept this fundamental expansion of the security state.[41]

Yet, across Europe, the state presses on. For at the same time as each state exaggerates fear to legitimise its foreign adventures, it too is fearful. The intelligence services are fearful because any bombings that do take place on the European continent reflect a failure of intelligence (as seen so clearly in the aftermath of the Madrid and London bombings). Politicians are fearful that political Islam may take root in socially deprived 'immigrant' communities. Thus, Belgium threatened to proscribe the Arab European League, which rose to prominence in 2003 following the racist killing (never officially acknowledged as such) in Antwerp of an Islamic religious affairs teacher of Moroccan origin. It fears that the League, with its self-defence patrols and Black Power rhetoric, signals the emergence of a Belgian version of African-American Islam. Danish newspapers, even before the 'cartoons affair',[42] were warning of the 'time bomb' posed by Copenhagen neighbourhoods that are overwhelmingly populated by 'immigrants'.[43] France is fearful that the Islamic subcultures practised in 'cellars and garages' (the words are those of the French interior minister) bring rage, pathology and dysfunction.[44] The UK is fearful that the shoe-bomber Richard Reid, the two British-Asian suicide bombers recruited by Hamas, and the 7/7 suicide bombers, are indicative of a wider trend. Governments and security services fear the mosque where global injustices towards Muslims are discussed; they fear the influence that 'foreign imams', with their anti-western agenda, could have on disaffected youth; they fear anything and everything associated with Islam.

But they are so lost in their own political machinations that they are unable to appraise these fears rationally. To do so would mean adopting economic and political solutions that do not conflate domestic problems with the war on terror. It would be to recognise that the alienation of second- and third-generation 'immigrant' youth was widespread long before the rise of radical Islamic movements like al Qaida. A rational approach would address the socio-economic exclusion of working-class Muslim communities from mainstream society, grant basic citizenship rights so long withheld in many European states, especially from the youth. A rational approach would speak to young people's grievances over policing by commissioning inquiries into the high number of deaths in police custody of young North African people; and as in France, so in Belgium. But because governments appear to have lost all ability to appraise their fears rationally, the fear takes on the form of paranoia in which any sign of cultural difference – wearing the hijab, for instance – is interpreted as 'a sort of aggression' (the words are those of French president Chirac) and a symbol of a subversive anti-western sentiment.[45]

National Identity and the Move to Monoculturalism

It was via the debate on national identity, which soon opened up across Europe, that the state sought to steer 'race relations' policy away from multiculturalism towards monoculturalism and cultural homogenisation. In each country, the national identity debate coalesced around a pattern of events and themes specific to that country; with new policy directions grafted on to the approaches traditionally adopted towards minority communities. Each nation moves towards the assimilationist model in a way that is consonant with the myths upon which that nation has been built. In the Netherlands, the theme of the national debate has been 'standards and values'; in Sweden and Norway, cultural barriers to inclusion; in the UK, 'community cohesion'; in France, the principle of *laïcité* (state secularism); in Germany, the primacy of the '*Leitkultur*' (leading culture); in Denmark, the 'intolerant culture' among immigrants that prevents integration; in Spain, public safety and crime. But even though the terms through which the debate is entered differ, it is always linked back to immigrant communities and cultures and the threat that multicultural policies pose to core values, cultural homogeneity and social cohesion.

One consistent element of all the debates is the implicit premise that Muslims are collectively responsible for the reactionary cultural practices and customs upheld by a few. (This mirrors the pattern established in anti-terrorist prosecutions founded on defendants' guilt by association.) The views of a few rabble-rousing anti-western imams are presented as symptomatic of the whole Islamic community. 'Honour killings', genital mutilation of African girls, North African youths who carry out gang rapes are, it would seem, all part of one Islamic cultural continuum. Girls who wear the hijab are linked to patriarchal Islam. Mothers who cannot speak the host state's language bring up children who cannot be educated who grow up into criminals who refuse to be integrated. The debate is always one of 'us' and 'them'. The idiom used humiliates and stigmatises. Seldom is the 'other' given a hearing, except to confirm *our* prejudices.

The stereotyping of all aspects of Muslim culture as backward creates a climate in which politicians and the media can attack multiculturalism as the cover behind which reactionary cultural practices flourish; according to them, it is liberalism that, by treating different cultures as of equal merit, endorses religious fundamentalism. Government policy-makers have been at the forefront of this debate. In the UK, we are told that criminal practices such as forced marriage and genital mutilation have been allowed to continue because of an overemphasis on 'cultural difference' and 'moral relativism' (former home secretary Blunkett).[46] In France, that '*communautairisme*', which takes account of the cultural needs of minority communities, has led to a 'guilty mentality which has led our country to doubt its own values and its own history' (Fillon, former social affairs minister).[47] In the Netherlands, that the nation 'does not constitute an aggregation of different cultures' (Balkenende, Dutch prime minister);[48] in Spain, that 'Multiculturalism is precisely what splits society' (former president Aznar).[49]

In almost every case, the debate about 'diversity' was first opened up through one specific event, or combination of events, and taken up intensively by the media and parliament. In several countries, including France, the Netherlands, Sweden and the UK, there have been parliamentary or quasi-parliamentary investigations into the failures of past integration policies. While the urban riots in northern England in summer 2001 followed years of heavy-handed policing of Asian communities, especially youth, economic collapse of those areas and local authority collusion in de facto segregation, the later deliberations of the government into these events, and the conclusions reached, came to be underscored by the fears and stereotypes engendered by September 11. The Home Office's Community Cohesion Task Force (set up before September 11) had already been charged with opening up a national debate around the need for a new framework of core values, based on instilling a sense of civic responsibility into communities that were perceived to be culturally lacking in such qualities. September 11 sealed the fate of that debate. In Sweden, the trigger for a review of integration measures was the tragic murder, by a member of her own family, of Fadime Sahindal, a Swedish-Kurdish woman who had campaigned against extreme patriarchal values in the Kurdish community. Even though the media debate allowed alternative migrant voices to break through and provide explanations not couched solely in 'cultural' terms, the parliamentary committee set up to investigate integration focused just on culture as the barrier to it.

In the Netherlands, it was not a perceived cultural deficit that first triggered the national debate about 'standards and values' but the 2002 assassination by an animal rights activist of the anti-immigration populist leader Pim Fortuyn and the subsequent emergence of his party List Pim Fortuyn. Nevertheless, cultural deficit was where it ended up. Prime minister Balkenende kicked off the debate when he announced that it would focus on two themes: young people who abuse the tolerant mainstream culture and people from other cultural backgrounds who are not open to Dutch culture and fail to learn the language. In the process, a parliamentary commission set up to investigate 30 years of official integration policy fell victim to the debate. The impartiality of the Hilda Verwey-Jonker Institute, which in the past had advised the government on multicultural policies, was questioned and, even before the ink was dry on the commission's report, there was cross-party criticism of its findings. The commission's crime, it seems, was to suggest that integration was a two-way process. Most migrants, it reported, had in the past succeeded in integrating into the Netherlands 'in spite of' rather than 'thanks to' government policy. This was all too much for government coalition parties which condemned the report as 'wrong' and 'weak'. A cross-party parliamentary report published in January 2004 concluded that the attempt to create a multiethnic society had been a dismal failure; huge ethnic ghettos and subcultures were tearing the country apart and the risk of polarisation could only be countered by Muslims effectively 'becoming Dutch'.[50]

Given the vast amount that has been written about the French government's 'Law concerning the application of the principle of secularism in schools, junior high schools and high schools', it would seem self-evident that the trigger for debate about national identity in France was the growing number of young Muslim girls wearing the headscarf.[51] But, according to statistics from the Education Ministry and Renseignements Généraux, in 2003, there were just 1200 reported occasions on which girls wore the hijab at school.[52] Rather, the 'national identity' debate was triggered when the first football match between France and Algeria since the war of independence was stopped prematurely after huge numbers of French-born Arab youth, seeing Algeria losing, ran on to the pitch chanting 'bin Laden! bin Laden!' The incident shocked French sensibilities and was presented as evidence of Islamic fundamentalism, leading to hysterical warnings about an intifada simmering at the heart of France, an Islamic fifth column, the 'unassimilability' of certain immigrants and an American-style 'race problem'. Press and parliament began to debate whether French housing projects (cités) – already the focus of the Vigipirate (security policing) – had become nodes in a global jihadi network stretching from Algeria to Chechnya to Afghanistan.[53] Two commissions were set up, the most important of which was the Stasi Commission (a cross-party group of parliamentarians headed by the former minister Bernard Stasi). Both were charged with evaluating the state of *laïcité*. The Stasi Commission immediately cast doubt on the official statistics on those wearing the headscarf, alleging that the number was far greater. It peppered its report with claims that the girls were being manipulated by 'politico-religious activists', 'extremist politico-religious tendencies', an 'activist minority', 'organised groups testing the resistance of the Republic', 'communalist politico-religious groups', without giving any clue to the actual identity of these shadowy bodies.[54]

The End of Multiculturalism

The security state demands a cultural policy towards minorities based on cultural homogenisation and forced assimilation. It eschews pluralism and fears diversity. That the security state spells the death of multiculturalism was demonstrated by developments in race policy from 2001 to 2004.

The Integration Contract

By 2004, citizenship laws were being redrafted to provide a new code of conduct for applicants for citizenship and family reunification. Specific measures penalised those who fail to abide by it. Multilingualism, when the languages involved are non-European, was to be discouraged. Dual citizenship in itself began to be viewed as a threat to European integrity, while attempts were also made to restrict the citizenship rights of second- and third-generation youth, as well as to subsume citizenship laws to anti-terrorist legislation.

While many of these changes will be discussed in greater detail in chapters 3 and 4, it should be noted here that subsequent reforms in procedures regarding family reunification were made possible by the European Union Directive on the Right to Family Reunification (2003). This allowed member states to subject children over twelve to an integration test before authorising their entry and residence.

During this period also, many northern and western European countries began the process of revising integration policy, introducing new measures often referred to in popular parlance in terms of an 'integration contract'. The responsibility of applicants for citizenship to integrate was emphasised. Hurdles were erected over which new applicants need to clamber in order to establish that they had accepted European values and norms. Each country had its own approach, but in each the 'integration contract' was linked to the debate over national identity. Thus, in October 2003 the French social affairs minister François Fillon was reported as saying that an integration contract was necessary 'to combat the threat of dissolution into culturally distinct communities that would threaten France's national identity'.[55] The most far-reaching version of the integration contract was drawn up by the Dutch. Newly arrived immigrants, those who have lived in the Netherlands for decades, the Dutch-born children of immigrants and even those who hold Dutch passports if they are from Netherlands Antilles and Aruba all came under its scope. However, those holding a certificate testifying that they were officially 'integrated' were exempt, as were citizens of the US, Canada, Australia, New Zealand and Japan.

In other countries, to gain residence rights or citizenship, applicants were now told that they would have to pass new language and civics tests (or take instruction in 'values'); in the UK, applicants for citizenship had also to take an oath of allegiance to the Queen (although technically we are her subjects, not her citizens). The tie-up between language and integration is, of course, not in itself intrinsically racist. But the compulsory element of the tests, the negative manner in which the debate is carried out – as though migrants are not eager to learn European languages given the opportunity – all fuel hostility towards outsiders. It sends out a political signal that those with a different mother tongue and from a different cultural background pose a threat to national homogeneity. And, in a climate of fear, hostility and suspicion, homogeneity is fast becoming western Europe's security blanket. In relation to Switzerland, Stefanie Gass, an ethnologist specialising in immigration affairs, has identified an additional factor. She believes that a written language test imposed by the town of Ostermundigen for those applying for citizenship is really a form of immigration control; that communities are adding extra requirements for citizenship in a bid to reduce numbers. 'It doesn't look like a vision of integration to me,' said Gass, 'more like a criterion for selection.'[56]

There is also a punitive element to these policies. Those who fail tests will have to leave the country (Austria) or be fined (Netherlands, Austria), have social security payments cut (Netherlands) or have residence rights removed or limited (France). In Norway (not an EU country), a new crime against the state has even been created. An African-Norwegian man who refused to allow his Algerian-born wife outside the home without permission and without the veil, and who repeatedly beat her and their children, has been jailed for three years. He was convicted of 'actively preventing his wife integrating in society'. The tough jail sentence implies that Norway finds the crime of 'preventing integration' more offensive than the actual bodily harm of women and children. So much for the campaign against domestic violence.

It was not long before the notion of an 'integration contract' was being extended to those with citizenship rights or refugee status. It was at this time then that a Europe-wide assault on dual nationality began to be detected. In a security state, dual nationality can no longer be tolerated for it implies an allegiance to elsewhere. Even to speak your mother tongue, it would seem, suggests latent disloyalty and lack of patriotism. When Dutch immigration and integration minister Hilbrand Nawijn (a member of List Pim Fortuyn) told imams in Dutch mosques to preach in Dutch, he also asked them to convince Muslims to comply with the values and customs of Dutch society.[57] And the Dutch Christian Democrat MP Mirjam Sterk stressed that 'The keeping of two passports hinders the integration of immigrants.' 'You are not a real, complete Dutch person because you also have another passport.'[58]

New Rules for Mosques

European states began to erect legal and administrative structures in order to build up detailed information on Muslims not because they were terrorist, but simply because of religious affiliation. Establishing Muslims as a community apart was a further step towards xeno-racism; was it also the first step towards criminalising a whole faith? As already noted, a system of religious profiling was, by 2004, already established in Germany. But another chilling example of administrative xeno-racism was provided by the Dutch parliament, which, soon after the events of September 11, initiated a national survey on the beliefs and activities of its 800,000-strong Muslim population. This, among other things, sought to quantify how many Muslims could legitimately be classed as fundamentalists.

An unwritten code also emerged across Europe to govern the activities of mosques. The entry of foreign clerics to Europe was to be restricted. Those allowed in would have to undergo training focusing on European values. The swift deportation of foreign clerics who represented a threat to public safety, public law and order, health, public morality or other rights was to be ensured. In the UK, the trustees of mosques were to be more closely regulated, particularly through charity laws. Trustees had to submit the mosque to intrusive intelligence-gathering exercises by the security services. In August 2003, Muslim organisations in the UK complained of visits from the security services to 100 mosques and Islamic organisations in which imams were interrogated about their attitudes towards al Qaida and the Taliban.[59] Already, in June 2003 Italian interior minister Giuseppe Pisanu had told the press that mosques were henceforth to be kept under close supervision for the 'wagers of Holy War and agents of foreign interests'.[60] It was also proposed that the building and financing of any new mosque be subject to a local referendum – for the mosque is 'symbolic of a civilisation ... in antithesis to Western culture'.[61] In less overblown tones, Danish interior minister Bertel Haarder announced that Friday prayer sessions would be monitored to ensure that imams did not advocate anti-democratic values and attitudes.[62]

In vain did Muslim organisations plead with governments not to exaggerate the influence of 'political Islam' in the Muslim community or to stigmatise all Muslim religious leaders for the anti-democratic attitudes of the few. They believe that clerics who preach a message of virulent hate represent a danger to the Muslim community, in much the same way that the British National Party and neo-Nazi skinheads pose a threat to the white working class. Governments should deal with the genuine problems posed by foreign clerics who oppose the rule of law through dialogue with the Muslim community. They choose instead full-on ideological confrontation, often using the megaphone of the popular press. In the process, they blur the terms of the security debate from the need to take action against the 'evil imams' to more generalised accusations against Islamic sites of worship – a case of 'tough on mosques, tough on the causes of mosques'. Indeed, they go further, using the security debate to suggest that Islam needs to be purified of 'foreign influences'. This was expressed most clearly at this time by the interior ministers of France ('we want to rid Islam in France of foreign influences') and Italy ('We envision an "Italian Islam", that is, one that is integrated into the reality of our country, that abides by the laws and that speaks Italian').[63]

In these ways, government policies, propaganda and prejudices paved the way for the development of the new European nativism.[64] For it was the pronouncements of politicians that made respectable local populist campaigns – often spearheaded by the far-Right – against the building of new mosques (the site of terrorism, after all). Indeed, the very design of the mosque was to come into question. A number of local authorities asked that the design of mosques to be less Islamic, less 'ostentatious' and more integrated into European architectural practices. For example, in 2004, it was estimated that there were a total of 1500 Muslim meeting places and mosques in France, but only a handful had domes or minarets because planning permission was denied by local authorities on the grounds that such identifying details are unnecessarily different, even inflammatory.[65] In the Netherlands, following a campaign by Liveable Rotterdam, Rotterdam Council asked the Moroccan community to modernise its architectural plan for a new mosque in order to incorporate a 'concept of integration'. The original was considered 'too Arabic' or, as the Rotterdam mayor helpfully put it, 'the dissemination of faith is sometimes expressed more by reserved, rather than explicit dissemination'.[66]

State-imposed Dress Codes

Banning the headscarf was the final facet of anti-terrorist-inspired assimilationist measures put in place across Europe. The French law banning the wearing in all state schools of 'oversized' religious symbols, which also includes the Jewish skullcap, the Christian crucifix and the Sikh turban, came into effect in September 2004. As of April 2004, two German states had also approved bans on Muslim teachers from wearing the hijab and several other states were in the process of approving similar legislation. This followed a ruling by the German Constitutional Court in a case brought by the Baden-Württemberg education authority against Fereshta Ludin, whose wearing of the headscarf was deemed 'a sign of holding on to the traditions of her society of origin' and thus an expression of 'a lack of cultural integration'. While the Constitutional Court ruled that wearing the hijab did not violate the religious neutrality of the state, it held that individual states were free to bring in legislation expressly forbidding religious symbols in the classroom.[67]

Once again, the debate stigmatised and humiliated Muslims. And the debate, as we shall see in chapter 3, became even more virulent when it is led by western feminists, particularly parliamentary feminists, who claim to draw inspiration from the struggles of Muslim women in the Arab world against state-imposed dress codes. But the fact that some countries force women to wear the hijab can never justify other countries forcing them to take it off. A secular state should ensure the same range of choices to all its citizens, excepting only that these do not cut across the range of choices of any other citizen.[68] While European governments should certainly uphold the rights of girls or women forced to wear the hijab against their will, they should not use state power to force on any individual a dress code, whether culturally or religiously determined.[69] Human Rights Watch concludes that to recognise this in no way undermines the principle of state secularism. 'On the contrary, it demonstrates respect for religious diversity, a position fully consistent with maintaining the strict separation of public institutions from a particular religious message.'[70]

Where will it all end? After the French law was passed, the paranoia about the hijab threatened to take on the dimensions of a modern witch-hunt. The French government announced that it was considering introducing a 'secularism charter' for other public institutions, including town halls. President Chirac said that he wanted the law changed so that private businesses could also ban the hijab and other religious symbols. Other proposed measures would stop patients refusing treatment from a doctor or nurse of the opposite sex; would ban women-only sessions in municipal baths. Education minister Luc Ferry said that he was determined to ensure that the ban would not be 'circumvented' by new religious symbols. 'As soon as anything becomes a religious sign, it will fall under the law,' he told MPs. 'When a beard is transformed into a religious symbol it will fall under the law.'[71] And Fillon, the minister responsible for integration, called for the French nationality code to be revised so that the wearing of the hijab be reasonable grounds for the Conseil d'Etat to reject an application for citizenship.

Nor was the paranoia confined to France. In Belgium, Sweden and Norway, the hijab began to be hotly debated. In Baden-Württemberg, a new state law forbidding teachers from wearing it cited a paragraph in the regional education act, which said that a teacher's behaviour should not demonstrate that s/he is against human dignity, equality and human rights. The hijab does not merely stand for religion, but is also a symbol of cultural self-isolation and part of the history of the oppression of women, argued the education minister. But as this does not hold for western religious educational and cultural values, the law will not apply to the crucifix or Jewish skullcap. The Dutch parliament, for its part, considered a proposal to allow the state to deny immigrant parents the right to select a school for their child – after all, their choice might reflect pressure from the local imam. The suggestion was that a 'family coach' be appointed to assist 'problem' immigrant families whose children fall behind at school; the coach would then choose the school.

France boasts of the Enlightenment values it spread throughout Europe. But its ill-conceived ban on the hijab represents a direct threat to the European tradition of human rights. It is an assault on the European Convention on Human Rights and Fundamental Freedoms and the Universal Declaration of Human Rights, both of which protect freedom of religious expression. By opposing the creation of a shadow criminal justice system beyond the ordinary rule of law for 'enemy aliens' and by opposing a system of compulsory assimilation for 'enemy citizens', we uphold the most important principle of all: the universality of human rights as indivisible by race, nationality or religious affiliation.

Islamophobia and
Accusatory Processes

3

ENLIGHTENED FUNDAMENTALISM? IMMIGRATION, FEMINISM AND THE RIGHT

Anti-immigration, Islamophobic and extreme-Right electoral parties have long been a feature of the European political landscape. But the views and policies promoted by such parties are no longer on the political fringe. On the contrary, they mesh with the security agenda of the European Union (EU) and are braided into the policies of conservative and liberal governments throughout its member states. States' national security agendas overlap with the immigration control programmes of xenophobic movements, and integration measures imposed by governments reinforce the Islamophobia of the extreme-Right. Today, in Europe, xenophobia and Islamophobia are the warp and woof of the war on terror.

In fact, the influence of xenophobic and Islamophobic parties, either as junior partners in coalition governments or as the recipients of the popular vote, is unprecedented, and reflects the major realignment of forces that has taken place as a direct consequence of the war on terror. With its aggressive call for 'integration' (meaning assimilation), to be achieved through 'the scrubbing out of multiculturalism',[1] the realigned Right – whose elements range from post-fascists to liberals and even some social democrats – is using state power to reinforce fears about 'aliens' and put into place legal and administrative structures that discriminate against Muslims. Most alarmingly, even some feminists and gay activists are now part of an overtly rightwing consensus that calls for immigration controls specifically targeted at immigrants from the Muslim world. Central to such a process is a generalised suspicion of Muslims, who are characterised as holding on to an alien culture that, in its opposition to homosexuality and gender equality, threatens core European values. Strict monocultural policies, besides, are seen as a necessary corrective to the multicultural policies of the Left that, in the name of cultural diversity, have turned a blind eye to patriarchal customs such as polygamy, clitoridectomy, forced marriages and honour killings.

Islamophobia Moves Into Policy

Since September 11, every EU country has introduced citizenship reforms, revised integration policies and brought in immigration laws that limit the rights of existing citizens and long-term residents to family reunification.

Citizenship: From Aptitude to Attitude

Take citizenship first. An applicant's integration would, previously, have been measured by his/her basic language acquisition or knowledge of the host society and its political and social institutions. But, today, a new approach is emerging as more and more hurdles to citizenship are introduced. First, the language requirement is set so high in some countries as to exclude all but the most highly educated. Second, applicants must submit themselves to a loyalty test. In one German state this has been extended to an attitude test that seeks to measure private beliefs, particularly on issues of sexuality.

Consequently, there is a growing rapport between government policies and the demands put forward by Islamophobic parties. The background to citizenship reform in Denmark, for example, was a debate on immigration and integration (focused on Muslims) that became so offensive that it moved the Council of Europe's Commissioner for Human Rights, Alvaro Gil-Robles, to describe Danes as 'primitive nationalists'.[2] But then, Denmark's coalition government, made up of the Liberal Party of Denmark (Venstre) and the Conservative People's Party (Det Konservative Folkeparti), relied on the backing of the openly Islamophobic Danish People's Party (Dansk Folkeparti – DFP) to stay in power. (Since the 'cartoons affair' the DFP has become even more influential, emerging in the 2007 general election as the third largest parliamentary party, with 25 seats in parliament.) The citizenship test introduced by the first Liberal-Conservative coalition government (2001–06), under pressure from the DFP, is so difficult that even some parliamentarians are unable to answer all the history questions, while the level of language proficiency demanded is equivalent to that in higher education. All new citizenship applicants have to sign a declaration of loyalty stating: 'I will work actively for the integration of myself and my family into Danish society.' The ministry of integration's website for those who want to become citizens stipulates: work, pay tax, don't hit your children and show respect for equal rights between the sexes.[3] According to the UNHCR, the 'way the declaration is formulated creates anticipation that foreigners will not respect certain values that are fundamental in a democratic society, and that they will commit the type of crimes mentioned in the declaration'.[4] Dismissing such criticism and warnings from the Council of Europe that the government's reform of immigration and integration legislation contributes to a hostile environment for minorities, Rikke Hvilshoj, the then, minister for refugees, immigrants and immigration, defended the loyalty oath on the grounds that she was tired of political correctness and the softly-softly approach to immigrants.[5] DFP leader Pia Kjærsgaard suggested that immigrants should not only master Danish but should also be examined on their respect for Danish society and values.[6] In addition, the DFP sponsored a bill to make it easier for social workers to place immigrant children whose parents 'forbid them to integrate into Danish society' into foster care because the child's 'best interests are not being served by raising them to be hostile to Danish society'. The system must step in and remove these children, so that they can be raised 'according to democratic values'.[7]

As in Denmark, the political landscape of the Netherlands – a country that takes pride in its liberal values – has changed dramatically under the influence of openly Islamophobic movements. It was a liberal, Fritz Bolkestein, who, as the (then) leader of the opposition People's Party for Freedom and Democracy (Volkspartij voor Vrijheid en Democratie – VVD), first introduced the anti-Islamic theme into national politics. In a speech in 1991, Bolkestein suggested that Islam was a threat to liberal democracy and a hindrance to the 'integration' of immigrants. In the late 1990s, a cruder Islamophobia was introduced into Dutch politics by the sociologist-turned-media-personality Pim Fortuyn. Author of *Against the Islamification of our Culture*, Fortuyn, who was gay, argued that he could not possibly be a racist because he had sex with Moroccan men. Following Fortuyn's assassination by an animal rights activist, the List Pim Fortuyn made a stunning electoral breakthrough at its first parliamentary attempt, polling 17.5 per cent of the vote in the 2002 general election. Fortuyn's death, followed by the assassination of the film director Theo van Gogh by a Muslim fundamentalist in November 2004, polarised the debate on integration still further, with conservatives and liberals relying on Islamophobia unbound to stay in power.

It is hardly surprising, then, that the 'integration contract' introduced in the Netherlands is considered the harshest and most demanding in Europe. In 2006, the Netherlands became the first European country to argue that integration should begin while migrants were still in their country of origin.[8] It brought in the Integration Abroad Act, with its pre-arrival civic integration test to prove assimilability, directed principally at applicants for family reunification and would-be spouses – mostly Moroccans and Turks.[9] (Immigrants with a certificate showing they are officially integrated are exempt, as are those from EU member states, Switzerland, the US, Canada, Australia, New Zealand and Japan.)

The 'syllabus' for the test (which has to be sat at a Dutch embassy or consulate in the applicant's country of residence) includes a DVD entitled 'To the Netherlands', which illustrates Dutch life by showing gay men kissing in a meadow and topless women on the beach. Dutch officials deny that the basis of the integration test is to stop the flow of immigrants from Muslim countries, claiming that they merely want all applicants to consider whether or not they would fit into a permissive society (which would doubtless automatically disqualify orthodox Dutch Catholics).[10]

The fact that Islamophobia and xenophobia have been so woven into the law (via legislation like the Integration Abroad Act),[11] has left a poisoned chalice for subsequent administrations. Much of the blame rests on the Liberal party, the VVD, and the hardline stance of its former immigration and integration minister Rita Verdonk.[12] Though some of Verdonk's most openly offensive proposals were rejected by parliament – such as her plan to introduce integration badges, subsequently compared to the Star of David forced on Jews by the Nazis – she had pressed ahead with the introduction of a general code of conduct for the public that emphasised Dutch identity. This was based on a seven-point charter on conduct introduced by the local authority in Rotterdam, which included calls for only Dutch to be spoken on the streets and by immigrant families in the home. Verdonk's reworked integration plan also obliged residents up to the age of 65, who had had less than eight years' schooling in the Netherlands, to undergo a course on how to integrate into Dutch society. The Equality Commission pointed out that the law institutionalised discrimination by ethnic origin, as the obligation was only imposed on naturalised Dutch citizens (and not those who were citizens by birth). Likewise, Human Rights Watch has shown how the Integration Abroad Act, with its blanket exemptions for certain nationalities, was from its very inception discriminatory.[13]

No populist xenophobic party has emerged in Germany on the scale of those in Denmark and the Netherlands. But, then, Germany has never officially accepted cultural diversity as a positive feature of society. And in certain ultra-conservative and largely Catholic German states, the Christian Democrats (CDU) and the Christian Social Union (CSU) have succeeded in marginalising the extreme-Right by speaking themselves to popular fears about immigration. Bavaria's interior minister Günther Beckstein (CSU) was one of the most prominent advocates of compulsory integration, demanding sanctions (such as the loss of social benefits) for anyone who refused to take an integration course. But the state that has gone furthest in its attempt to measure and isolate the attitudes that supposedly threaten the host society is Baden-Württemberg (which was also the first German state to ban civil servants from wearing the hijab). There, applicants for citizenship from some 57 Islamic countries face a lengthy interrogation that includes questions on belief and attitudes towards religious freedom, equality of the sexes, promiscuity, freedom of expression, the concept of honour and forced marriages. 'When we came to Germany, they examined our teeth to determine our state of health. Now they're testing our feelings', said a Turk interviewed by the *Frankfurter Rundschau*.[14] Among the questions asked are: 'Do you think a woman should obey her husband and that he can beat her if she is disobedient?' It was only in 2007, after concerted pressure, that questions on homosexuality, such as, 'Imagine that your adult son comes home and says he is homosexual and plans to live with another man. How do you react?'[15] were withdrawn.

Baden-Württemberg officials justify their intrusive tests by citing research that indicates that Muslim beliefs on such issues as forced marriages and honour killing conflict with constitutional law. 'If there is a suspicion that the person who wants to become German does not share our fundamental principles and values', said a spokesman, 'the new system of interrogation can find this out.'[16] The OSCE Representative on Combating Intolerance and Discrimination Against Muslims, Ambassador Ömur Orhun, warned that posing such questions to adherents of one religion only was an affront to their dignity, a violation of human rights and discriminatory.[17] There were further protests from the Social Democratic Party (SPD) mayor of Heidelberg who declared that the city would not administer the questionnaire because to do so would cast fundamental doubt on Muslims' loyalty to the German constitution, thereby infringing the principle of equality enshrined in it. But no district is to be allowed to exempt itself: the mayor's refusal has been deemed 'inadmissible'.[18] All of which goes against the writ of the German constitution, which guarantees the basic rights: to life, to human dignity, to freedom of expression and to religion.

Family Reunification

Also being 'reformed' is the right to family reunification under immigration law. Across Europe, this is being undermined by measures that give civil servants greater discretion to deny requests for family reunification on the grounds that marriages have not been freely contracted, but are the result of cultural practices such as forced or arranged marriages. A European Council Directive on Family Reunion has created a much tougher framework for family reunification, with children as young as twelve being subject to an integration requirement.

The country with the strictest such measures in Europe is Denmark.[19] The Danish Aliens Act 2002 removed the statutory right to family reunification on the grounds of wanting to secure 'the best possible base for integration'. Henceforth, applicants were to be individually assessed to establish, among other things, whether a marriage had been voluntarily contracted. Any administrative doubt on this score was sufficient to deny a reunification request. That marrying abroad was a barrier to integration was reiterated in the 2003 'Action plan on forced, quasi-forced and arranged marriages', which states that arranged marriages militate against integration, not least because, traditionally, they have been contracted transnationally and result in increased immigration. The Danish Institute for Human Rights has pointed out that the new provisions, by removing family reunification from a rights-based framework, allow for considerable administrative discretion – enabling state officials to act unimpeded on their suspicions of Muslims.[20]

The then Danish immigration and integration minister Bertel Haarder justified the family reunification laws as necessary to protect Nordic values and human rights.[21] But Denmark is not alone. In France, limitations were placed on family reunification and marriage rights after the urban disturbances of October and November 2005. In his new year's day address to the nation, the then interior minister Nicolas Sarkozy cited his concern for the 'immigrant woman, trapped at home, who doesn't speak the language because her husband doesn't let her leave and doesn't put her in contact with literacy groups or French lessons'. Such an unequal partner, he said, 'cannot have the right to residence'.[22] Similarly, in the UK, family reunification and marriage rights were limited following urban violence in the northern cities of Oldham, Burnley and Leeds. The then home secretary David Blunkett argued that the riots were caused by young male South Asian immigrants who held 'backward' attitudes and perpetrated oppressive practices (like forced marriage) against women.[23]

The thinking behind such 'reforms' is that Muslims *per se* pose a threat to gender equality and human rights standards, which dovetails neatly with the Right's project to end all primary immigration from Muslim countries. Listen to the anxieties of former Dutch immigration and integration minister Rita Verdonk. Strict immigration controls directed at non-EU countries (principally Turkey and Morocco) were necessary, she said, to stem the tide of 'young females who are not allowed to go on the street, who do not get the same chances as Dutch women'. She added: 'We Dutch women fought for equal rights. What I will not allow, and will do my utmost to prevent' is the return 'to the time when women were inferior to men'.[24]

If such legislation inherently discriminates against Muslims and erodes their civil rights, then so be it. First, we were told post-September 11 that new anti-terrorist laws were needed, and that, if necessary, we had to give up some of our civil rights in the name of preserving security. Now we are told that many of the principles guaranteeing equality and non-discrimination enshrined in the European Convention of Human Rights (including the right to a private life) need to be given up – in the name of equality. The bizarre logic seems to be that the best way to counter possible discrimination against women (brought about, it would seem, by the Muslim birthrate and increasing Muslim influence in society) is by bringing in laws that discriminate against ethnic minorities (that is, Muslims). And when it comes to individual cases of Muslim men violating Muslim women (via forced marriages, domestic violence and the like), the solution is not for the state to offer Muslim women better protection and equal access to justice in the host country, but to deny them rights of residence or settlement via stricter immigration controls.

Cultural Fundamentalism and the Enlightenment

The parliamentary and media debates surrounding these reforms constantly stress the 'alien culture' of Muslims, that Islamic and European values are irreconcilable and that, even in Europe, Muslims cling to their culture, refusing to 'integrate'. The discrimination against Muslims, therefore, is justified.

Cultural justification has taken the place of racial justification. The specific problems that Europe's Muslim citizens face – unemployment, discrimination, poverty, marginalisation – are now viewed through a cultural lens. This tendency to treat culture as the key analytical tool for understanding developments in European society accords with the French Arabic scholar Olivier Roy's observation that cultural and religious paradigms are now being widely used in popular debate to explain societal and political issues. Besides, Muslim culture is no more a monolith than Christian culture, and, as Roy shows, there are as many Muslim cultures as there are Muslim countries. 'How', asks Roy, 'do we begin to isolate and categorise the complex and multilevel practices of more than one billion Muslims living in so many different social, cultural and geographical conditions? How are we to designate a specific attitude as "Muslim" or "Islamic"?'[25]

The anthropologist Verena Stolcke warned in the early 1990s that anti-immigrant Right parties and politicians had adopted a repertoire of ideas and a conceptual structure of 'cultural fundamentalism'.[26] And they were using a 'political rhetoric of exclusion in which Third World immigrants' were 'construed as posing a threat to the national unity of the "host" countries because they were culturally different' – so shifting the anti-immigrant discourse from protecting one's race to protecting one's 'historically rooted homogenous national culture'. More recently, the ideas of cultural fundamentalism have been strengthened by recourse to the

Enlightenment as the foundation of western European culture, which therefore needs to be defended. Non-western immigrants must cast off their 'backward culture' and assimilate into the modern, secular values of the Enlightenment. If, for Christian and Islamic fundamentalists, the Bible and the Qur'an are sacred texts, not open to interpretation or adaptation, for cultural fundamentalists, the Enlightenment is an equally sacred, finished process. But, as Sivanandan has argued, the Enlightenment has yet to extend its remit of liberty, fraternity and equality to the non-white peoples of the world.[27] 'An Enlightenment project which excludes "the darkies" of the world is clearly benighted.'[28]

Ideas predicated on Enlightenment fundamentalism would never have achieved the dominance they are afforded today if it had not been for the war on terror, the invasions of Afghanistan and Iraq and the primacy subsequently given in political and media discourse to Samuel Huntington's 'clash of civilisations' thesis.[29] Huntington's belief that civilisational conflict occurs not just between nations, but within those western nations that fail to control immigration and/ or preserve civilisational coherence and homogeneity, has become the bedrock of the current debate on citizenship. Within days of the New York and Washington attacks of September 11, key players on the Right were popularising Huntington's themes by establishing a binary between western, European, Enlightenment values (based on the Judaeo-Christian tradition) and those of the 'other' (that is, Islam). The then Italian prime minister Silvio Berlusconi, for instance, stated that we should be 'conscious of the superiority of our civilisations'; Pim Fortuyn warned that Islam was a 'backward culture'; and the Danish populist leader Pia Kjærsgaard told parliament that September 11 was not the start of the clash of civilisations as 'a clash would indicate that there are two civilisations', when there is 'only one civilisation, and that's ours'.[30] The idea that a diversity of influences creates civilisations was dismissed. Different religions came to be viewed as fixed entities that could not possibly share common, universal values. And civilisation did not emanate from a shared humanity. If radical Islam posed a threat abroad, Muslim communities within western countries also needed to be strictly monitored. 'Islam is the biggest threat to world peace since the fall of Communism', commented the DFP's Kristian Thulesen Dahl, comparing it to the cuckoo in the nest. 'It is eating us [from within and] destabilising [our societies].'[31]

It was in this intolerant climate, against a backdrop of anti-terrorist measures targeting the Muslim community, that the debate about citizenship and national belonging opened up across Europe. Its thrust was that a set of fixed cultural norms and values was needed to establish on what basis foreigners should gain access to, or be excluded from, the national community and its territory. Today, long-term residents in Europe – even those who have become naturalised citizens and have taken the loyalty tests and passed the integration exams – may find themselves under threat of expulsion. Under new immigration laws, governments have granted themselves yet more administrative discretion to deport long-term residents or revoke the citizenship of naturalised citizens who display 'unacceptable behaviour' (UK); constitute a threat to public order (Germany); or espouse anti-western and anti-Enlightenment values (France). In fact, what frames the whole citizenship debate, argues anthropologist Marianne Gullestad, is the constant reference to a 'lack of belonging' owing to some 'innate' quality such as ancestry, a shared cultural heritage, and so on. Non-western citizenship applicants are being asked to 'become European' at the same time as it is tacitly assumed that this is something they can never really achieve.[32]

Monoculturalising the Nation

Cultural fundamentalists monoculturalise the nation. Their culturalist rhetoric, argues Stolcke, 'reifies culture ... as a compact, bounded, localized, and historically rooted set of traditions and values transmitted through the generations'.[33] And, for Gullestad, the debate on values falsely assumes that there is a single homogenised set of values, with the state as the expression of the collective identity associated with them. Immigration is 'construed ... as a political threat to the national identity and integrity on account of immigrants' cultural diversity ... the nation-state is conceived as mobilizing a shared sense of belonging and loyalty predicated on a common language, cultural traditions and belief'.[34] Cultural fundamentalism, in other words, roots nationality and citizenship in a hereditary cultural heritage.

And the integration measures adopted by European governments following September 11 have allowed for culturalist notions of nationality to flourish. In the process of steering race relations policy away from multiculturalism towards monoculturalism, national cultures have been shorn of their contradictions, of their seamier side, and valorised. According to the new mantra, the shared Enlightenment tradition that shapes European national cultures ensures that Europeans are basically forward-thinking, progressive, given to democracy and social justice. We children of the Enlightenment inhabit an imagined moral community wiped clean of fascism and authoritarianism. And if racism is mentioned at all, it is only to note its absence. If there is anything amiss in this, our European homeland, it is the consequence not of evil, but of too much goodness. Over-tolerance towards people from different cultures is our Achilles' heel. We must preserve our cultures at all costs and not let them be contaminated by what is alien. But, as Sivanandan has pointed out, cultures survive and flourish through bastardisation and hybridisation. Pure cultures, like that of the Nazis, die.[35]

When extreme-Right and anti-immigration politicians attack multiculturalism, what they are really attacking is diversity, difference. Politicians like Austrian parliamentarian Peter Westenthaler are part of a cultural heritage that has nothing to do with Enlightenment values and everything to do with the far-Right. Hence, when, after the attacks in Washington and New York, he declared that 'multicultural society was buried on 11 September 2001', he was using multiculturalism as a code for attacking the culturally diverse societies that extreme-Right politicians traditionally abhor.[36] Politicians from conservative and liberal parties have likewise sought to elevate multiculturalism into some sort of monstrosity that threatens national culture. Silvio Berlusconi was applauded by the Northern League's Roberto Calderoli for declaring on state-run radio in March 2006 that 'We don't want Italy to become a multiethnic, multicultural country. We are proud of our traditions.'[37] According to Calderoli, who had been sacked as reforms minister after ripping off his shirt on live television, revealing a T-shirt printed with one of the Danish cartoons of the Prophet Mohammed, 'Our values, our identity, our history, our traditions must be defended against immigration.'[38]

Spain, like Italy, is a country with a not-so-distant fascist past. Yet, in 2002, President José Maria Aznar told a gathering of international Christian Democrats that multiculturalism posed a great threat to Europe. 'Multiculturalism is precisely what splits society. It is not living together. It is not integration.'[39] And here starkly presented is the fundamental (perhaps deliberate) error of conflating multiculturalism and culturalism, on the one hand, and assimilation and integration, on the other. It is not multiculturalism that 'splits society' but culturalism. Multiculturalism envisages a pluralist society abounding in many cultures enriching each other and seeking unity in diversity (as in India or Britain in the late 1960s and 1970s). Culturalism envisages society as a conglomeration of ethnic enclaves, separate and ostensibly equal (as in apartheid South Africa).[40] Nor does integration equal assimilation. They are not interchangeable.

Integration, in Roy Jenkins' classic formulation, is 'not a flattening process of assimilation but equal opportunity accompanied by cultural diversity in an atmosphere of mutual tolerance'.[41] To use the term integration to mean assimilation is therefore intellectually inept and morally dishonest, as it is to use the term multiculturalism to mean culturalism. But what makes such 'thinking' dangerous is the further conflation of the two misuses of language to produce the spurious thesis that cultural homogeneity is the *sine qua non* of a democratic society.[42]

Not surprisingly, along with the emphasis on multiculturalism as one of the greatest threats facing Europe has come racism. Where once the archetypal Jew was seen as inimical to Europe, now it is all too often the archetypal Muslim. Unchanging across time and continents, Muslims are the sole carriers of patriarchy, the germ of which they transmit via a fossilised culture to successive generations. Multiculturalism was unacceptable to the Spanish immigration minister Enrique Fernández-Miranda because 'With our democratic culture, we cannot accept the stoning of an adulterous woman, or the cutting off of a thief's hand, or the existence of caste as the basis of social organisation', things that, he claimed, multiculturalism approves of.[43]

For the extreme-Right, the 'barbarous' customs of Muslims have, for some time, been part of the argument of cultural fundamentalists to justify exclusion. In Denmark, Pia Kjærsgaard attacked multiculturalists for ignoring the fact that immigrants arrive in Denmark with 'male chauvinism, ritual slaughtering, female circumcision and clothes that subjugate women, all of which belong in the darkest middle ages'.[44] Once such views were mocked, now they are accorded respect. For example, in the Netherlands, where Fortuyn asserted that Muslim attitudes were incompatible with individual rights, Ayaan Hirsi Ali (until 2006 an MP for the VVD) was applauded when she derided Islam as a 'backward culture' that subordinated women and stifled art, adding, helpfully, that the Prophet was, by western standards, a 'perverse man'. The only possible answer to such moral backwardness is for immigrants to assimilate into the national *Leitkultur* or leading culture – the yardstick of integration, according to Germany's CDU.[45]

Anti-racists – like immigrants – are vilified for allowing barbarous customs to flourish because of their celebration of cultural difference. Fritz Bolkestein summed up the position of Dutch Liberals in a speech in Rotterdam in 2003 in which he attacked those who failed to criticise the 'wanton abuse' of Muslim women in Muslim culture by glossing 'over it with references to multiculturalism'. Multiculturalism, furthermore, threatened to erode the Dutch political tradition of equality since those who criticised reprehensible practices in other cultures were 'tarred with the epithet racist'.[46]

Feminism Versus Multiculturalism

This ever more strident attack on multiculturalism has been associated with the leadership (usually, but not exclusively, male) of the Right. But, surreptitiously, another group has been jumping on the bandwagon: women, often self-proclaimed feminists, with an ideological axe to grind. The late Harvard professor of ethics and political science, Susan Moller Okin, was a feminist standard-bearer and defender of the national culture. Around the same time as Samuel P. Huntington was advancing his 'clash of civilisations' thesis, Okin asked, in the pages of the *Boston Review*, 'Is multiculturalism bad for women?'[47] Okin's central thesis was that multiculturalism and concessions to difference now posed a threat to the fragile gains made by western liberal feminists over the decades. She criticised the western liberal tradition for recognising value in the very existence of cultural diversity, proposing instead an assimilationist model for the integration of immigrants.

But Okin's criticisms of multiculturalism went further than those of the mainstream Right. She explicitly attacked multiculturalism as a form of state policy widely pursued by liberals, who were accused of arguing for the protection of 'special group rights' or 'privileges'.[48] Such a framework allowed a 'special legal treatment on account of belonging to a cultural group' to emerge. To back up her argument, Okin cited the French tolerance of polygamy. But Okin's argument that tolerance of polygamy in France equals multiculturalism, equals group rights, is a clear misinterpretation to anyone with even a cursory understanding of the French tradition of an indivisible republic and its inherent hostility towards multiculturalism. A more logical conclusion would have been to equate French indifference to polygamous marriages with French indifference to immigrants *per se* – an indifference that is rooted not in multiculturalism, but in a *laissez-faire* racism that ignores the minority ethnic experience altogether.

In fact, Okin's thesis is tendentious, elevating multiculturalism as it does into a philosophical doctrine and investing it with meanings that are not there, in order to show that special privileges afforded to immigrants threaten the fragile human rights of western women. Okin further argues that minority women locked in 'a more patriarchal minority culture in the context of a less patriarchal majority culture ... may be much better off if the culture into which they were born were either to become extinct' (a sort of culturocide to help its members to become assimilated into the less sexist majority culture) 'or, preferably ... be encouraged to alter itself so as to reinforce the equality of women – at least to the degree to which this is upheld in the majority culture'.[49]

The weak foundations of Okin's thesis did not go unnoticed by respondents to her analysis, who drew attention to her poor scholarship; paternalistic approach; tendency to stereotype the 'other'; viewing of patriarchy as the special domain of immigrants; and her casting of all immigrant women as the victims of their cultures. Okin was also accused of racism and of advocating the forced assimilation of ethnic minorities into a single dominant culture. As Azizah Y. Al-Hibri, president and founder of Muslim Women Lawyers for Human Rights, put it: 'If Western women are now vying for control of the lives of immigrant women by justifying coercive state action, then these women have not learned the lessons of history, be it colonialism, imperialism, or even fascism.'[50]

Despite such criticism, Okin had succeeded in legitimating in academic discourse the pitting of women's rights against immigrant rights (as though the battle for social justice were divisible) and allowing white western feminists to make sweeping claims about the incompatibility of non-western cultures with western liberal tradition. Okin's misrepresentation of multiculturalism was, in time, incorporated into the repertoire of the mainstream Right, the members of which began to exploit for their own ends issues of domestic violence in immigrant communities.

And, as the war on terror began to reshape domestic social policy, these tendencies became accentuated. Following September 11, and the furore over the nature of Islam it produced, a western agenda highlighting crimes against women began to emerge. Honour killing came to be cast as emblematic of Islam's problematic nature and its treatment of women. According to Purna Sen, programme director of the Asia region of Amnesty International, the contemporary 'discovery of, and subsequent opposition to, crimes of honour in the West have meshed together the perception of a "foreign" concept (honour), an alien and terrorist religion (Islam) and the bogey of violence against women into a politically potent mix'.[51]

But it is in the supposedly liberal and freedom-loving Scandinavian countries, particularly Denmark and Norway, that Islamophobia and xenophobia have most successfully been woven into the campaign around 'forced marriages' (all too often conflated with arranged marriages). Denmark, as already noted, has the harshest family reunification policies in Europe, while in (non-EU) Norway, the xenophobic Progress Party has, for some time, polarised the immigrant debate by using gender issues. In addition, the Human Rights Service (HRS), an 'independent think-tank' established in 2001 to examine 'issues and problems peculiar to multiethnic societies', has been influential in pushing the discourse further to the right in Norway.

Under the guise of concern about forced marriage, the HRS has fuelled an argument for stricter immigration controls. In *Human Visas*, HRS's information director Hege Storhaug generalised about cultural traits within immigrant communities, building, it would seem, on earlier research into 90 instances of forced marriage in which she found that, in all but three cases, the bride had been raped.[52] On the untested presumption that marriage is only a pretext for more immigration from such communities, she legitimated her call for immigration controls. Storhaug's research methods have been criticised as unethical and several interviewees have come forward and stated that, under pressure from Storhaug, they had exaggerated their stories.[53]

But methodology aside, Storhaug's credentials as an independent and non-partisan observer on gender and immigration issues are, in any case, questionable.[54] In *Human Visas*, Storhaug claimed that immigrants from non-western (read Muslim) countries have imported into Norway 'patriarchal structures, values and traditions'. Unable to adapt to European values, these new immigrants live 'disconnected from civil society' in a 'kind of self-imposed isolation ... largely imposed and enforced by anti-democratic forces' that 'prevent integration by controlling marriages and pressurising families to bring relatives from abroad, to the extent that children become "human visas".' While no one should be against 'immigration to Norway from, say, Sweden or Denmark', the 'huge cultural gap between Western and non-Western countries' means that 'immigration from places like Pakistan or Somalia' should be considered far more problematic. 'The greatest challenge to integration in Norway ... is posed by population groups from non-Western countries. And the reason for the challenge is cultural difference.' For the 'modern history of immigration in Europe has involved the importation of undesirable practices that simply cannot be reconciled with democratic values'. To 'prevent the children or grandchildren of immigrants' from being 'married off to persons in their ancestral homeland' in a 'modern form of human commerce', Storhaug advocated a new test of integration: an examination of the marriage patterns of immigrants.

Storhaug marshals feminist sentiment to support giving the state additional powers to enforce assimilation, adding yet another authoritarian layer to the body of ideas exploited by cultural fundamentalists. Like them, she represents the state as free from racism. For Storhaug, Norway is in a better position to shake off a false multiculturalism because, unlike France or Britain, it does not suffer 'an acute sense of historical guilt' over colonialism.[55] The French and the British have set aside 'key democratic principles and values ... out of a misguided sense of "understanding" and respect for culture', she writes. In this, she reflects the dominant concept of Norway as an unblemished country with an 'innocent humanitarian state with no colonial account to settle',[56] which also explains its return to what Sivanandan terms a 'primitive nativism', uncontaminated and unenriched by other cultures including that of the Sami people (the aboriginals of Norway), who continue to be dispossessed.[57]

In other European countries, prominent feminists who attack cultural diversity also replicate dominant ideas about national identity. In Germany, Alice Schwarzer, the TV personality and founder of the feminist journal *Emma*, holds that multiculturalism is a threat to individual autonomy, equality and freedom. It is an inherently 'dishonest' ideology, she asserts, accusing those who disagree with her of averting their 'eyes from the Muslim oppression of women in Germany'.[58] She repeats Storhaug's claim that, given their history, Germans are full of a self-hatred which leads them to 'love everything foreign, with their eyes closed tightly'. Those who criticised Schwarzer's views were judged traitors to the feminist cause. Marieluise Beck, the federal commissioner for integration policy, who disagreed with Schwarzer's call for a ban on the hijab, was accused of 'frenetically supporting the minority of Muslim women who demonstratively wear the headscarf' by 'stabbing the majority in the back who deliberately don't cover themselves. Does the integration representative even know what kind of moral pressure a headscarf-wearing teacher can exert on a Muslim school girl and her parents? After all, the Islamists consider an unveiled woman to be a whore.'[59]

An assimilationist, monocultural society needs its feminist cheerleaders. The struggles of minority ethnic women who have long campaigned against domestic violence are ignored if they fail to regard gender as the only contradiction and campaign also against societal racism. Governments look to minority ethnic women, like the prominent German-Turkish lawyer and SPD member Seyran Ates, who do not criticise dominant narratives, but validate them. Ates argues that 'It is certainly not exclusively but largely the "wrong" implementation of the multicultural society that we have to thank for insular and hardly accessible parallel societies' where 'forced marriages, honour killings and human rights violations are endemic'.[60] Yet post-war Germany has never officially accepted that it is a country of immigration, let alone followed explicitly multiculturalist policies.

Another servant of the cultural fundamentalist cause is Hirsi Ali. A *Reader's Digest* woman of the year and recipient of countless other awards, she emerged as a cultural icon of the new Right in the late 1990s. For many Dutch Muslims, as well as feminists and anti-racists, Ali's stock-in-trade (prior to her departure from the Netherlands in 2007)[61] was 'stirring up Islamophobia on behalf of a cabal of right-wing politicians and columnists'.[62]

Hirsi Ali's twelve-minute-documentary *Submission* was made with the film director Theo van Gogh (a man who once described feminists as 'ossified vaginas' and Islamists as 'goat-fuckers').[63]

In *Submission*, episodes from the lives of four fictional Muslim women who suffer violence at the hands of men are related to verses from the Qur'an, calligraphed on to the skin of the actresses' alluring, whipped and semi-naked bodies. The implication is that, if you do away with the Qur'an and Islam, violence against women will be done away with as well! *Submission* is, in essence, little more than the age-old Orientalist sexual fantasy – a call to white men to save Muslim women from Muslim men.[64] Historian Geert Mak believes it is even more dangerous than this. The techniques used to essentialise Muslims are, he explains, similar to those used by Goebbels in his infamous Nazi propaganda film *The Eternal Jew*.[65] Certainly the film appears to condemn Muslims for their original sin – of beating their wives and daughters – until they, like Hirsi Ali, renounce their faith. For Hirsi Ali, there is only one route to personal liberation for Muslims – her way – by compulsion if necessary. It is of a piece with her advocacy of a state ban on the hijab.

Feminist Paternalism?

It is, indeed, via the debate on the hijab that feminists – to paraphrase Azizah Y. Al-Hibri – have sought to justify coercive state action and control the lives of immigrant women. The most divisive measure to compel Muslims to assimilate into the dominant culture is, despite all the rhetoric about 'women's rights', targeted against Muslim women, with the support of other women. What an irony! Hasn't feminism been built on resistance to the male control of women's bodies? Muslim women, though, such feminists argue, are too passive or enslaved to resist the power of Muslim men, who seek to control female bodies by enforcing the wearing of the hijab. So the state has to act as the liberator of Muslim women by stepping in and forcing them to unveil. In both Germany and France, state bans on the hijab are seen as necessary both for the liberation of Muslim women and the protection of women's rights generally.

There is no federal state ban against the wearing of the hijab in Germany, but at least half of Germany's 16 states have banned women wearing it in public buildings and when working for the state. Such initiatives have been loudly endorsed by prominent conservative female politicians. The ultra-conservative state of Baden-Württemberg was, as we have already seen, the first to ban female teachers from wearing the headscarf – on the grounds that a teacher's behaviour should demonstrate his or her commitment to human dignity. Baden-Württemberg's interior minister Annette Schaven argued that the hijab was a 'symbol of cultural self-isolation and a part of the history of the oppression of women'. The Bavarian education minister Monika Hohlmeier also evoked this view to justify a similar ban in Bavaria.

Although the French ban was instituted ostensibly on grounds of secularism, covering all religious symbols including the Sikh turban and Christian crucifix, the issue of women's emancipation was used to justify the ban on the hijab.[66] An open letter addressed to President Chirac, signed by dozens of prominent women, appeared in the glossy magazine *Elle*, expressing support for the ban on the grounds that the 'Islamic veil sends us all – Muslims and non-Muslims alike – back to a discrimination against women that is intolerable'.[67] Before this, the doyenne of French feminism, the philosopher Elisabeth Badinter, had argued that the *foulard* represented the 'oppression of a sex'.[68]

Choosing to wear the veil, she argued, was tantamount to renouncing one's personal autonomy. Even if Muslim girls might appear to choose this practice autonomously, that did not mean that they were autonomous. This is because the content of their cultural norms – namely, the Muslim values of female restraint, modesty and seclusion – are opposed to personal autonomy.

Badinter, then, knows the inner state and thought processes of any Muslim girl better than she does herself. Her paternalist justification of coercive state action is redolent of a colonialist, imperialist western tradition. She has essentialised Muslim culture and deemed that, as it prevents Muslim girls from realising their own individuality, anti-headscarf measures are benign and in the best interests of the child. The state has to act as the 'good father' to liberate the Muslim child from her bad, biological and cultural father. Indeed, issues of child protection are often invoked to justify state bans. Hirsi Ali, too, called for a ban on the hijab on the grounds that children are not autonomous and need to be protected from the reactionary cultural practices of their parents (as well as from Muslim men in general).

It could reasonably be argued that, where Muslim parents have acted oppressively by forcing girls to adhere to a specific dress code against their will, then the state is justified in intervening in the best interests of the child. Yet, even in such cases, French policy has done exactly the opposite in terms of freeing children. For it has led to the removal of children from state schooling altogether.[69] Souad Benani, founder of Les Nana Beurs, a French organisation of women of North African descent, had warned of precisely such dangers when she argued that if the state were to exclude 'twelve or thirteen year-old girls from school' on account of their wearing the veil, then it would deny them 'the opportunity to learn, grow and make their own choices'.[70] Saida Kada – the only veiled woman invited to give testimony to the Stasi commission and founder of the organisation Activist French Muslim Women – argued that the ban fans the flames of extremism. Indeed, it has led to a situation in which orthodox religious families in deprived communities who have removed their children from state schools then find the children removed from them. In January 2006, four girls – aged 4, 10, 13 and 14 – were placed in care after a court in southern France stripped their mother and father of parental rights. The father (whose name was not made public in order to protect the children) refused to let the girls attend school on the grounds that they would be made to remove their veils.[71]

Ironically, the call to ban the hijab in the name of individual autonomy relies on essentialist arguments about Islam that deny any personal autonomy to Muslim women and girls: the reasons for veiling have not changed since the time of the Prophet; and those who wear the hijab, whether in Kabul or Paris, do so for exactly the same reasons (with the addition, in the case of French girls, of the internalisation of oppression). A debate claiming to be about the furthering of Enlightenment values leads to the exclusion of Muslim women and girls from the culture of civil rights. Because veiled women are not, in the eyes of their 'liberators', autonomous beings (they are either representatives of, or victims of, a fundamentalist culture), they are denied political agency altogether.

Creating a New Feminism

As Islamophobia and xenophobia are woven into the war on terror, sections of feminist opinion have bought into the incorporation of discriminatory anti-terrorist measures aimed at Muslim communities into criminal and administrative law. But, the very tensions generated by the war on terror have given rise to the emergence of another feminism. Some European women are beginning to resist state measures that create enemy images and isolate Muslim women. In the words of Nextgenderation (a network of feminist academics and scholars), 'we will not allow' these 'self-proclaimed "guardians of women's rights", whom we have never encountered as participants in nor supporters of our women's movements and struggles over many years', to 'use "the emancipation of women" for anti-immigrationist, assimilationist, Islamophobic and ethnocentric policies'. 'We say to them a determined NOT IN OUR NAMES.'[72]

In Germany, around 780 women from across the political and cultural spectrum (from the Green Party to the CDU) signed a petition opposing state bans on the hijab.[73] Feminists, too, are among those who support the French movement 'One School for Everyone' (Une École pur tou(te)s), which while taking no stand on the appropriateness of headscarves worn by Muslim girls opposes all expulsions from schools. And, in a separate but related move, a European Muslim feminist voice is breaking through the cultural and religious confines of mainstream debate to demand civil rights, particularly a woman's right to choose whether or not she wears the headscarf. For European Muslim women speaking from within their communities, the challenge of combating the sexism they face in their daily lives, while also confronting mainstream Islamophobia, can be exhausting. Yet some feminists, who seem to believe a woman can only be liberated by travelling the fixed pathways of western feminism, respond to the predicament of their Muslim sisters by vilifying and demonising them. The German feminist Alice Schwarzer, one of the most offensive in this respect, explicitly links campaigns against the headscarf to the war on terror, warning that the headscarf has been 'the flag of Islamic crusaders'.[74] And, in France, Saida Kada was personally humiliated by feminists who successfully sought her exclusion from a human rights association run by the mayor of Lyon on the grounds that, by wearing the veil, she was an 'accomplice to gang rape'.

Some feminists are resisting the campaign by the Right to link the issue of forced marriage to stricter immigration controls targeted at the Muslim world. One of the canards propounded by the supporters of Hirsi Ali and Hege Storhaug is that it was only through their brave interventions that the problem of forced marriages was ever discussed in Europe.[75] But this is a self-serving myth. Minority ethnic women's organisations were combating forced marriages long before Hirsi Ali wrote *The Cage of Virgins*. However, because such organisations did not racialise forced marriages or sensationalise the issue in the media or with policy-makers in terms that accorded with the dominant Islamophobic discourse, their message was neither popular nor marketable. Indeed, such campaigns were often also simultaneously critical of discriminatory immigration controls, which were seen as part and parcel of state racism towards immigrant communities.[76] A thoroughgoing realisation that violence against women cuts across race, class and religion (and not just a token acknowledgement of this truth) entails dismissing the myth of western moral and civilisational superiority and of the Enlightenment as a completed project at its heart.

It is around precisely these arguments that a new feminism, free of racism, needs to be built – a feminism that roundly rejects the Islamophobia and xenophobia built into the war on terror, and its underlying claim that patriarchy has nothing to do with 'us' (white, Christian, European) and everything to do with them ('aliens' from an Islamic culture). Such a feminism would clearly scorn the absurd liberatory pretensions of conservative and extreme-

Right parties (the bastions of white male heterosexual privilege and the purveyors of traditional values about a 'woman's place' for decades). The new feminist voice is breaking through: these new Enlightenment crusaders for women's rights are certainly not our champions.

4

THE NEW McCARTHYISM

After eight years of draconian emergency laws, the mood in Europe is veering towards nativism. On the one hand, populist nativists, rallying around the extreme-Right's call to 'Stop the Islamisation of Europe', are openly hostile towards any visible sign of cultural difference, whether it be the headscarves that mark Muslim women out or the mosques and minarets that threaten European skylines and Christian heritage. On the other hand, EU-wide anti-radicalisation measures, introduced after the London and Madrid bombings amid debates about 'home-grown terrorism', accompanied by security-inspired citizenship reforms and integration policies, have nourished an official nativism. Today, Europe's Muslims are routinely represented in the media as untrustworthy citizens, subject to foreign allegiance and divided loyalties. And out of the turmoil provided by anti-terrorist measures, security and integration policies, a new strain of McCarthyism has emerged.

From Communist 'Subversive' to Islamic 'Radical'

As Islamism replaces communism as the new totalitarianism against which we are urged to unite, the 'Islam scare' supplants the 'red scare'. While the 'reds' were potentially allied to the evil Soviet Empire, Muslims may be secretly allying themselves to an equally evil and totalitarian fundamentalist empire: the *Umma* of global Islam. A revamped version of McCarthyism, with its highly public loyalty reviews and congressional committee hearings, is being injected into the body politic, with particular mutations developing in particular contexts. The first strain, which primarily affects young Muslims, is a direct result of the intelligence services' promotion of anti-terrorist measures to counter the 'radical ideas' that are influencing 'the youth'. For just as the 'red scare' was used to argue that traditional security methods could not adequately safeguard the US against the communist threat, the 'Islam scare' now holds that certain beliefs are so dangerous that any measure to restrict them is justified. As progressive lawyer Gareth Peirce has warned, 'radicalisation' has become 'a condemnation as conveniently imprecise as the label "subversive" used in the post-war McCarthyite witch-hunts in America'.[1]

European intelligence services have promoted the view that young Muslims are increasingly receptive to radicalisation. For the Dutch intelligence service, the AIVD, for instance, the 'principal causes' of terrorism today are 'the processes of radicalisation and recruitment among young Muslims' with radicalisation defined across a 'spectrum', at the extreme edge of which lies *jihadisation*.[2] Because the evolution of a European *jihad* comprises a 'spontaneous, interactive and largely autonomous process', subversive opinions, impulses and emotions, it would seem, have to be criminalised before they ignite into violence.

In reality, the security services' view that the 'radical ideas' of young Muslims should be brought within the purview of anti-terrorist laws because young Muslims are the most likely vectors of terrorism is not borne out by the facts. Leaving aside the fact that statistics prove that in Europe, in 2006, a greater number of civilians died in separatist-related terrorist attacks than at the hands of Islamic terrorism,[3] research into those arrested for Islamic-related terrorism reveals that there is no typical terrorist profile, either by age or social and economic background. Edwin Bakker, a senior research fellow at the Clingendael Institute in The Hague, analysed 242 convictions for terrorist offences carried out in Europe between 2001 and 2006. Using 20 variables concerning the suspects' social and economic backgrounds, he set out to discover whether there was a typical terrorist profile. He concluded that there was 'no standard jihadi terrorist in Europe' as the cases he analysed involved men (and five women) from all social and economic backgrounds and of all ages.[4]

Nevertheless, EU intelligence services are now so anxious about the mindset and emotions of all young male Muslims (and, increasingly, young females)[5] that they have within their sights both well-educated and un-educated youth. The well-informed Muslims are aware of the plight of Muslims across the world, and therefore deemed open to recruitment by sophisticated Islamic groups on university campuses. The less educated may be alienated young Muslims open to indoctrination by jihadi war veterans, extremist preachers and net surfing. Young Muslims, from all social and economic backgrounds are considered suspect, as though they all are potentially programmed for violence. Mindful of a number of high-profile arrests of young Muslims for terrorist-related offences and anxiously observing outbreaks of violence in the UK, France and Denmark, the authorities fear that European social and integration policies may have failed, leading, on the one hand, to the creation of a dangerous 'Muslim underclass', and a resentful educated class, on the other. In this way, the 'terrorism issue' comes to 'colour the interpretation of all inequalities and potential troublespots in society in much the same way as the Cold War made it possible to suspect trade union activists of being Soviet agents'.[6]

And where security services lead, politicians follow. They provide intelligence officers with the blank cheque they need to criminalise young Muslims via new anti-terrorist measures and provide them with political cover. Thus, when EU politicians and policy-makers, working in tandem with intelligence services, speak of the battle for 'hearts and minds' (a term particularly favoured by the British), what they really mean is that it is time for the colonial strategy of divide and rule to be brought to bear on modern domestic realities. The politicians are seeking to create, through state patronage and clientism, a compliant and loyal Muslim middle-class, middle-aged leadership and a 'moderate Islam' that will cooperate with the state's attempts to bring under the scope of anti-terrorism a series of new offences related to 'undesirable behaviour'. The intelligence services appear to be the driving force behind laws that seriously expand the concept of terrorism-related offences. Today, these involve not just actual material crimes and acts of political violence but also thought crimes – with new laws justified on the grounds of 'preventive justice'. For preventive policing presumes guilt; it does not need proof of an actual material crime, just the suspicion that you may consider such a crime in the future. In short, authorities target individuals not for what they do or have done but based on predictions about what they might do. Hence, the need to create specific new offences related to 'thought crimes' as well as introduce new preventive measures, such as control orders, to prevent them from being realised.

It is an EU-wide strategy, that, while most fully realised in the UK, has its genesis in UN Security Council Resolution 1624, which called on all states to repudiate and take measures against 'justification or glorification of terrorist acts'. After its passing, in August 2006, EU interior ministers, meeting in London, announced a six-point programme to counter terror that included a new legal framework to curb radicalisation and recruitment among Europe's Muslim communities, with a particular focus on the internet. This was followed, in November 2007, by a proposal by the European Commission to amend the 2002 EU Framework Decision on combating terrorism to create three new categories of criminal offence: provocation to commit terrorism (an offence that applies to any statement that creates a 'danger' of such acts being committed); recruitment for terrorism; and, finally, training for terrorism. While the charges of 'recruitment' and 'training' need to show a direct link with terrorist groups or activity, the 'provocation' offence is extremely broad, as it does not require a direct encouragement to commit terrorist acts but applies to any statements that create a 'danger' of such acts being committed.[7]

Proposals such as this are part and parcel of a general trend to shift the focus of anti-terrorist powers in the direction of criminalising ideas. The EU was extending its previous approach to combating terrorism, which focused on the threat posed by foreign nationals ('enemy aliens'), to young second- and third-generation Muslims ('enemy citizens'). Particularly after the killing of 52 commuters in the July 2005 London bombings by three British-Pakistani and one British Afro-Caribbean youth,

British-born Muslims were viewed as a high-risk group whose freedoms must be curtailed. Already, the European Commission, in its 2005 communication concerning 'Terrorist recruitment: addressing the factors contributing to violent radicalisation', had warned of the 'ease' by which 'people come into contact with violent radical groups', through university, media and the internet (in chat rooms and by reading inflammatory articles) and that the media 'can play a role in facilitating recruitment into terrorist groups, by giving expression to terrorist views and organisations and facilitating the contact between radicalised individuals, particularly via the internet'.

Universities and the Monitoring of Muslim Students

A strong message needed to be sent out to Muslim further and higher education students and their parents regarding the political consequences of young Muslims exploring 'anti-social' and 'undesirable' ideas. The exploration of extremist views in books, media and the internet all now comes under the purview of the anti-terrorist laws. EU governments had already instructed universities to keep an eye on foreign students from Muslim countries and to subject them to extra surveillance – an instruction taken to its extreme by the interior ministry of the German state of North Rhine-Westphalia, which now requires all foreign students and academics from Muslim states (as well as North Korea) who require a visa to complete a questionnaire on their fundamental beliefs.[8] But, following the London bombings, the pressure began to mount on other European universities to take extra measures against 'radicalisation'. When two Lebanese nationals studying in Germany were arrested in July 2006, after Improvised Explosive Devices were found packed in suitcases on board two regional trains in Cologne, reports suggested that the students had undergone a swift radicalisation process following the publication in the German press of the Danish cartoons of the Prophet Mohammed. The then commissioner of the Metropolitan Police in London, Sir Ian Blair, also claimed that eleven suspects arrested in August 2006 in connection with an alleged plot to bomb planes en route from the UK to the US had undergone 'rapid radicalisation', in a matter of 'some weeks and months, not years'.[9]

In the UK, a variant of McCarthyism has been introduced in institutions of further and higher education. The opening salvo in this strategy was a speech at the Universities UK conference on 15 September 2005 by education secretary Ruth Kelly in which vice-chancellors and principals of universities and colleges were told that they had a duty to inform the police of 'possible criminal acts', adding that freedom of speech on campus did not extend to tolerance of 'unacceptable behaviour'. Her speech coincided with the release of 'When Students Turn to Terror: Terrorism and Extremist Activity on British Campuses', a report by the Social Affairs Unit, a right-wing think-tank on social and economic issues. Authors Anthony Glees (director of Brunel University's Centre for Intelligence and Security Studies) and Chris Pope (an associate fellow at the Royal United Services Institute for Defence and Security) identified 23 educational institutions (one secondary school and 22 universities) as breeding grounds for terrorism. On the basis of this, the Glees Report (as it is commonly known) recommended that the security services' fight against terrorism needed to be extended to 'subversion', the precursor of terrorism. And, in order to identify potentially dangerous students, Glees recommended close cooperation with MI5 and plainclothes police officers who should be allowed on to campuses to spy on students. Furthermore, university authorities were instructed to undo the 'highly liberal campus environment' that allows extremism to flourish under the banner of free speech as well as limit the 'ethnic composition of any single university' so that it reflects, broadly, the ethnic mix of the UK as a whole.

The Glees report was widely cited in the media, under alarmist and scare-mongering headlines. Naturally, the populist tabloids did not question the methodology of its authors.[10] An analysis by David Renton, a former equalities officer at a union for staff in higher education, showed that this rested on 'searching through acres of newsprint for any single record of Islamist activity'.

Whether the incident had 'occurred in the past month or the past decade', the academic institution where the 'Islamist' had studied was 'named and shamed as an organisation' where extremists were present.[11] Nevertheless, on the basis of Glees' questionable data, academics were encouraged to name names, to report suspicious behaviour to the authorities, and to act against extremists. And in November 2006, the higher education minister Bill Rammell issued new guidelines to universities to target 'violent extremism in the name of Islam', with universities asked to share information with security services regarding suspicious students and external speakers. In February 2008, a leaked Association of Chief Police Officers (ACPO) document suggested that guidelines should be issued to parents, detailing how to stop children searching for extremist websites and advising on how to distinguish the 'legal/ potentially illegal divide'. At around the same time, a consultation document issued by the Department for Innovation, Universities and Skills aimed at institutions of further education provided advice to college authorities on how to deal with 'suspected extremist literature on campus'.[12] College authorities and lecturers were invited to monitor the activities and leadership of religious-based student organisations and to distinguish 'moderate' from 'radical' students (while at the same time noting how quickly the 'moderate' can be 'radicalised'); to monitor the content of talks given by outside speakers and to report suspect students to the police.[13]

Such vague pronouncements manipulate academic fears about the threat posed to the reputation of an educational institution (and possible loss of funding) if campuses were seen, through oversight, to foment terrorism and turns every lecturer into a potential spy on every Muslim student. The loyalty of both the 'moderate' and the 'radical' is placed under suspicion. University College Union (UCU) joint secretary Paul Mackney made such a point when he warned that 'members may be sucked into an anti-Muslim McCarthyism which has serious consequences for civil liberties by blurring the boundaries of what is illegal and what is possibly undesirable'.[14]

New Crimes of 'Undesirable Behaviour'

But, the damage had already been done – a whole set of 'undesirable behaviour' has, bit by bit, been placed under the scope of anti-terrorist laws, leading to a 'substantive expansion of the scope of criminal responsibility and new administrative processes of control that conveniently avoid the guarantees associated with the criminal process'.[15] First, the Terrorism Act (2000) created new offences based on the circulation of information useful for terrorism. Section 57, for instance, made it an offence to be in possession of books or items for the purpose of terrorism, while Section 58, which carries a sentence of up to ten years, made it an offence to collect information useful for terrorism. The Prevention of Terrorism Act (2005) gave the secretary of state power to impose control orders (a form of house arrest) in respect of anyone believed to be involved in 'terrorism-related activity'.[16] And Section 1 of the Terrorism Act (2006) created a specific offence of indirectly encouraging terrorism by the 'glorification of terrorism' (distribution or circulation of a 'terrorist' publication was also criminalised).[17] The 2008 counter-terrorism bill further 'widens the net of innocent people who can be incriminated',[18] at the same time as affording greater penalties for those convicted of the vague offences outlined above, including confiscation of property, bans on foreign travel and requirements to report to the police whenever staying away from home.

Lawyer Gareth Peirce, who represents many young Muslims arrested under Section 58 of the Terrorism Act (2000), warns that as most of the prosecutions brought under this 'profoundly disturbing' measure have succeeded, there now lies ahead the

> bleak prospect of imprisonment for thousands of young people, all Muslim, who have accessed the internet prompted by an interest – shared with millions of their contemporaries around the world, Muslim and non-Muslim – in the workings of political or radical Islam.

'Defendant after defendant has discovered that a long-forgotten internet search has left an indelible record sufficient for a conviction under section 58', she states, adding that even possession of the

Channel 4 film *Road to Guantánamo*, or *21st-century Crusaders*, a compilation of documentaries from the BBC and elsewhere, has been held by the courts to demonstrate 'radicalisation'.

> While the record of use remains permanently, no equivalent reconstruction is available or even required of the mindset of the user at the time. The common elements in each conviction have now become familiar; the defendant has not the slightest idea that such possession was inconsistent with the right to freedom of thought; was not remotely involved in any terrorist activity; and was Muslim.[19]

One case, more than any other, that of Nottingham University masters student Rizwaan Sabir, and Nottingham university staff member Hicham Yezza, illustrates dramatically the extreme vulnerability of young Muslims that Peirce so eloquently warns against. Rizwaan Sabir, as part of his ongoing PhD research on radical Islamic groups, downloaded an edited version of the al Qaida handbook from a US government website. (An extended version of the same document figured on the university politics departments' reading list and was also available from Amazon.) As he did not have access to a printer, he sent the 1500-page document to university administrator Hicham Yezza, and asked him to print it out. At this point a university staff member discovered the handbook on Hicham Yezza's computer and reported Hicham Yezza to the university authorities, who immediately called in the police.

Once the procedure was launched it was quickly out of the university's hands. The results were predictably catastrophic. On 14 May 2008, Rizwaan Sabir was arrested, his home searched, family questioned and computer and mobile phone confiscated. He was accused of downloading material for illegal use, and questioned for six days before being released without charge. Hicham Yezza, who is Algerian but had lived and studied in the UK for 13 years, was also arrested. While he too was released without charge, he was immediately rearrested, accused of immigration irregularities and taken to a removal centre pending deportation. During the entire investigation, the anti-terrorist police maintained a high profile at the university, questioning students and lecturers who, furious at the intimidatory atmosphere on campus, mounted a highly effective political campaign (at one point a demonstration was held in which prominent academics gave public readings from the al Qaida manual). The threat to academic freedom posed by the university's 'disproportionate' response to the possession of legitimate research materials was highlighted, with the outcome that the imminent deportation of Hicham Yezza was prevented. On release, Yezza declared,

> This is not the way I should have been treated ... in a country I love, would protect and where I've done everything I can to engage with and be a good citizen ... I would have appreciated had I been given five minutes simply to answer the questions relevant to the document.[20]

Commenting on the parallel situation in the US, the legal expert David Cole wrote that the post-September 11 shift towards preventive law enforcement leads to a new definition of liability, enabling the authorities to sweep up large numbers of people without having to prove that individuals have engaged in specific harmful conduct. This has been achieved 'by targeting people for what they say before they act and for their associations' under the catch-all offence of providing 'material support' to proscribed groups. In France, as described in chapter 2, this works through the *association de malfaiteurs* offence, under which the vast majority of terrorism suspects are detained and prosecuted. In September 2005, according to government statistics, 300 of the 358 individuals in prison for terrorism offences – both convicted and those awaiting trial – had been charged with *association de malfaiteurs* in relation to a terrorist undertaking.[21] In the UK, one Section 57 prosecution that would seem to fall under Cole's categorisation was that of five young Muslims (four of whom were Bradford University students) who were originally convicted in July 2006 for downloading and sharing extremist terrorism-related material (they were freed on appeal in February 2008).[22] The young men were accused of terrorism on the grounds of a suspected plan to go a Pakistani training camp with the aim of fighting in Afghanistan. The evidence against the five young men appears to have been based solely on an examination of material downloaded from various websites, emails and messages and stored on their computers' hard discs. The Court of Appeal, accepting that the evidence against the men was so weak it should have never gone to trial, overturned the initial ruling, stipulating that in future Section 57 'must be interpreted in a way that requires a direct connection between the object possessed and the act of terrorism'.

In fact, it was precisely the Court of Appeal's interpretation of the law that opened the way for the successful appeal of Samina Malik, the 24-year-old so-called 'lyrical terrorist', against her conviction in December 2007. Prosecuted under Section 58 of the Terrorism Act 2000 (possessing information 'likely to be useful to a person committing or preparing an act of terrorism'), she was sentenced to a nine-month suspended prison sentence. Malik, who worked at an airside branch of WH Smith at London's Heathrow, came under suspicion after she entered into internet conversations with Sohail Qureshi, a man she had never met but whom, unknown to her, the intelligence services suspected of plotting to commit terrorist acts abroad.[23] Police raided Malik's home, seizing terrorist manuals that she had downloaded from the internet and poems she had written about 'Jihad' – one entitled 'How to Behead' and another 'The Living Martyrs'. In the absence of any actual proof that Malik had committed or was preparing a terrorist offence, it was these poems, as well as a shop receipt on the back of which she had written 'The desire within me increases every day to go for martyrdom', that were presented as evidence of her state of mind at her original trial. But there was, as the Court of Appeal later acknowledged in declaring her conviction unsafe, no actual evidence that Malik was involved in terrorism, with the prosecution conceding that 21 of the documents they had provided as evidence at her original trial were no longer admissible. At her original conviction, a tearful Malik had told the court that she was not a terrorist, but had called herself the 'lyrical terrorist' because she thought it was 'cool'. Malik's poetry was indeed lurid, but poet Adrian Mitchell and children's writer Michael Rosen were among those who criticised her initial conviction, asking 'should a person's interests, emotions and opinions be used as evidence to convict them in front of a court?'[24] They concluded that the answer 'would seem to be yes if you are young, working-class and Muslim' and no if you are the best-selling white middle-class novelist Martin Amis who, in an interview with *The Times*, ruminated on whether it would be possible to introduce measures, such as strip-searching at airports and other 'discriminatory stuff', aimed at making the Muslim community 'suffer', until they get their 'house in order' and 'start getting tough with their children'.[25] Later, Amis claimed that his comments were a mere 'thought experiment, or mood experiment', leading Rosen and Mitchell to ask whether the right to '"experiment with the limits of permissible thought" [is] only accorded to people who have the correct skin colour, religion and academic background?'

Framing the Enemy: the Media and the 'Preachers of Hate'

Another variant on the 'Islam scare' has emerged out of the close relationship between the intelligence services and the media. The intelligences services target mosques as sites of international jihadist networks and radicalisation, and the media become preoccupied with the connections between Islamic fundamentalism and 'preachers of hate'. This strain fuses neatly with official interpretations of the causes of terrorism, whether international or domestic. For politicians, who cannot acknowledge that there is a relationship between the rise of political Islam and the brutal interventions and resource wars the West pursues, popularise the views of Orientalist Middle East scholars such as Bernard Lewis, that the roots of terror are located in the Muslim world's hostility to the western 'way of life' and the 'values that we represent'.[26] The same politicians and academic terrorism experts go on to link 'Islamic terrorism' and extremism to young Muslims' failure to integrate, as well as the failures of multiculturalism, which they argue give rise to a dangerous 'fifth column' or 'enemy within'. Instead on focusing on the structural reasons for the marginalisation of Europe's Muslim communities, they and the media have become fixated on the individual profiles of a number of young Muslims – sometimes former convicts turned terrorists, like the British shoe-bomber, Richard Reid, or the French 'seventh hijacker', Zacarias Moussaoui. The orthodoxy has grown that such individuals, alienated from western society and values, and lacking strong father figures, drifted into terrorism because of the influence of charismatic 'preachers of hate'. These, argued the Dutch intelligence services, can be veterans of the Afghan war, propagating extremist radical-Islamic ideology (*Dawa*, i.e. 're-Islamisation'). While stipulating that 'Dawa-oriented forms of radical Islam' are not necessarily violent by nature, the intelligence services allege that the propagation of such 'puritanical, intolerant anti-western and anti-integration ideas' constitutes a security risk.[27] Measures to rid us of such preachers, we are led to believe, will go a long way to removing the threat of terror.

Thus, all foreign imams, poorly educated clerics and orthodox preachers whose viewpoints veer towards fundamentalist readings of religious texts are deemed a security risk and invested with enormous powers to indoctrinate young people, spread hate and act as recruiters for terrorism. The belief is that the radicalisation of young Muslims, driven by sexual frustration and political impotence, takes place rapidly, almost violently as they are whipped into a kind of emotional fervour by charismatic clerics preaching in mosques that have become twilight zones of criminality and murderous Islam.[28] Both tabloid journalism, with its search for easily identifiable villains and 24-hour television news channels, with their desire to undermine rivals and capture the market, find in such lazy arguments the suitable peg upon which to hang 'investigations' into terrorism. And how tempting it is to do so when a handful of imams offer themselves up for representation as cartoon-Ayatollahs. First there was one-eyed, hook-handed, firebrand Finsbury Park preacher and petty criminal, Abu Hamza (currently serving a seven-year jail term in the UK for inciting murder and racial hatred, and fighting extradition to the US). Then there was Norway's Najm Faraj Ahmad (popularly known as Mullah Krekar, owing to his Taliban-style leadership of a militia group in Kurdish Iraq). Not to be left off the list, and now serving a life sentence in a Turkish prison following his extradition from Germany to Turkey on treason charges, is Cologne's former fundamentalist preacher Metin Kaplan (nick-named the Caliph of Cologne following an earlier prosecution for incitement to murder). Finally, one cannot forget Abdul Qadir Fadlallah Mamour, a Turin imam who was deported to Senegal (no matter that Senegal claimed he wasn't its citizen) just hours after boasting to the media that he once knew Osama Bin Laden and warning that if Italian troops were not pulled out of Iraq, there could be a bomb attack in Rome.

Journalistic investigations into the embarrassing and, in some cases, criminal, antics of a few dubious religious figures serve to symbolise to the consumers of European newspapers and television reports the dangers posed to western societies by the rise of Islamic fundamentalism. Such scaremongering pre-dated the events of September 11. The independent journalist Thomas Deltombe in his classic study *Imaginary Islam: The Media Construction of Islamophobia in France*[29] studied the French media's growing preoccupation with Islam from the 1970s onwards, against the backcloth of the Iranian revolution and the civil war in Algeria. Basing himself at L'Inathèque de France – the official depository of TV news – Deltombe viewed the evening news broadcasts of the main French channels from 1975 to 2004, in search of items on France's Arab and Muslim populations. Such news stories, he found, moved, in that period, from 'a peripheral subject of secondary and temporary interest' to a subject 'at the heart of French society'. By the beginning of the 1980s, 'loyalty discourses' were entering the media debate. It asked, for instance, whether young 'Beurs', 'torn between two cultures', were 'really French. Where do their loyalties lie? Are Muslims views compatible with the wider French culture? What is the connection between members of this population and violent events abroad?' Whether integration or the violence in Algeria was discussed, it 'was the "loyalty" of belonging, of France's Muslims that, for the media, was most at stake'.

Deltombe also identified a growing media interest in foreign radical clerics, who, via sermons in unregulated mosques, were spreading their ideas in France and gaining influence over young Arab and Muslim men from the suburbs. Recognising that some of the media concerns about foreign clerics could be justified, did not preclude criticism of particular journalists for their manipulation and distortion of speeches made by these clerics, concluded Deltombe. He linked media distortion to the rise in a particular genre of TV investigative journalism – namely, 'undercover reporting' by journalists, armed with hidden cameras, who would infiltrate mosques in order to expose the Islamist militant groups who were 'indoctrinating' young French Muslims. The only trouble, as Deltombe revealed, was that the information contained in many of these 'investigative reports' was either totally inflated or simply false.

Today, the genre of film-making identified as inherently problematic by Deltombe in France has spread across Europe. Journalists are increasingly going into mosques with a view to exposing radical clerics, extremism and terrorism in hastily constructed, low-budget and badly resourced productions that take the place of high-quality investigative journalism, and include a 'sexy sequence where the reporter looks into his own camera and explains how frightened he feels as he prepares to infiltrate the bad boys'.[30] Whether journalists are acting independently is not clear. But these programmes clearly serve the interests of the intelligence services, which view certain imams as a threat but cannot provide a watertight case that they pose a specific terrorist threat. In the light of intelligence failures, the security services may now seek to prove that there is an incontrovertible link between these clerics and terrorism through 'speech crimes'. Thus, another version of the catch-all offence of 'undesirable behaviour' (brought in to deal with young Muslims) is being brought to bear on foreign imams. In this case, making anti-western, anti-Enlightenment, illiberal, provocative or just plain offensive statements can all be included as incontrovertible proof of 'undesirable behaviour', justifying fast-track deportations (see chapter 6).

Wittingly or unwittingly, documentary-makers contribute not to combating terrorism but to fomenting 'scare scenarios'[31] (which can then be used to justify raids on mosques as well as mass identity checks of mosque-goers). And once television channels commit themselves to the undercover reporter genre, the pressure for journalistic results becomes so great that all sorts of distortions and manipulations become justified. If no evidence of support for terrorism is uncovered, the media are known to accuse the imams instead of promoting segregation, with hostility to integration constituting a 'speech crime'. The Prague Multicultural Centre accused the Czech public service TV station CT2 of screening a documentary that used manipulated footage, originally gleaned through the use of hidden cameras. In this documentary it was ordinary mosque-goers whose supposedly extremist views were intercut with images of terrorism.[32] According to Ahmad von Denffer of the German Muslim League, the only proof provided by the ARD news programme, Panorama, for its claim in a 2003 broadcast that an imam from the Fahd Academy mosque in Bonn preached 'jihad against the non-believers' during Friday prayers was a short scene recorded with hidden cameras during which the words of the imam, who was speaking in Arabic, were totally incomprehensible.[33]

In other cases, television documentaries have actually been presented as evidence to justify the deportation of certain clerics.[34] The German intelligence services sought the deportation of Said Khobaib Sadat, an imam from Afghanistan said to be a follower of the warlord Gulbuddin Hekmatyar, preaching at a Frankfurt mosque, citing evidence from the TV programme 'Report Mainz' in which he allegedly said, 'We must defend our faith against the unbelievers even if to do so we have to die as martyrs.' Lawyers claimed that the TV programme-makers had mistranslated the text.[35] The Turin imam Mohamed Kohaila, whose case is discussed in further detail in chapter 6, was deported on the basis of evidence provided by the documentary *AnnoZero*, broadcast on Italian state-run RAITV on 29 March 2006. Once again, hidden cameras were used to expose the imam who, according to the voice-over, was preaching anti-western extremism in his sermons in the neighbourhood of Porta Palazzo.

Such sensationalised documentaries do little to serve the cause of countering terrorism – a cause that calls for genuine and serious investigative research; nor do they provide a meaningful investigation of the problems posed by religious extremism in a secular society. What serious documentary-makers would do, surely, would be to take a much broader and more holistic view. For a programme on the rise of religious extremism, they would investigate the impact of social conservatism and fundamentalism across all religions (including the majority religion, Christianity) on issues such as gender equality and sexual orientation and set this within the wider framework of the need for mutual tolerance, respect for civil rights (including religious rights) in a secular state and a multicultural society. But this is not what these intrepid truth-seeking journalists and their editors set out to do when they infiltrate the mosque, or go scissor-crazy with hours and hours of footage in the editing suite, cutting and pasting shots to fit a predetermined agenda and to justify use of the undercover reporter in the first place. Instead, such documentaries serve up a routine dish of favourite racial and religious stereotypes, pandering to the fears and stereotypes of the non-Muslim majority, who, through ignorance, equate fundamentalism with terrorism. (Investigative programmes could be made on the documentary-makers themselves!) Could it be that journalists here in Europe have become 'embedded' within domestic intelligence services in ways that parallel attempts by the US and its allies to manipulate global perceptions of Iraq and Afghanistan, through embedding journalists in the military?

Citizenship, Loyalty and Allegiance to the State

During the period of McCarthyism, the McCarran–Walter Immigration and Nationality Act (1952) was introduced, allowing for the deportation of immigrants or naturalised citizens engaged in subversive activities. Today's reforms to citizenship and immigration laws provide another echo of the Red scare, resting on discourses about loyalty and patriotism and the search for the 'enemy within'.

There are several elements to the immigration and citizenship reforms, introduced post-September 11, which are aimed at weeding out Islamic 'subversives'. First, as already implied, immigration laws, similar to the McCarran–Walter Act, have been introduced in most European countries that, while aimed principally at the 'preachers of hate', allow for the deportation of any non-citizen who displays symptoms of 'unacceptable behaviour'. Similarly, measures introduced across Europe, and epitomised by the deprivation of the citizenship section of the UK Immigration, Asylum and Nationality Act (2006), allow for the revocation of citizenship of citizens with dual nationality if they display symptoms of 'unacceptable behaviour', including the speech crimes of glorification of terrorism or fostering racial hatred. What these clauses represent is a wide extension of state power over the citizenry – appreciated by a very small circle of immigration lawyers and constitutional experts. They try to draw attention to the fact that powers to deprive citizens of their nationality constitute a 'recalibration of what it means to be a citizen';[36] 'reduce Britishness' to a 'temporary state, removable at will' by the state;[37] establish new membership norms – a 'conditional order of hospitality' – which lower the threshold of European nationality to questions of allegiance, loyalty and 'compulsory moderation'.[38] The UK's Immigration Law Practitioners' Association (ILPA) points out that in a representative government (as opposed to the tyranny of the majority) 'it should remain the fundamental right of the citizenry to change their government, not of the governments to change the composition of the citizenry by banishment of its awkward elements'.[39]

Once again, the intelligence services are afforded virtually unchecked powers over vulnerable individuals. In the frame this time are long-term residents seeking citizenship, as well as officially recognised refugees, whose naturalisation requests are vetted by the intelligence services not only for support for terrorism, but also, it would seem, for signs of 'undesirable behaviour'.[40] There is no corresponding duty imposed on the intelligence services to explain the grounds for rejection of a citizenship request, and the ability of an individual to seek legal redress or appeal against rejection is severely restricted.[41] In such a climate, it is quite possible that the intelligence services are acting in an oppressive way, particularly towards refugees, cajoling them to act as paid informers for the state.[42] It is a kind of patriotism test, for only by declaring 'allegiance' to the state, by spying on their former countrymen, will certain targeted individuals become candidates for naturalisation. Hassan Assad, a Palestinian under threat of deportation from Sweden to Jordan on account of allegedly funding terrorism, claims to be such a victim. Assad applied for Swedish citizenship, but was refused. He believes that this was because he turned down a request by the Swedish Security Services to act as a police informer. Now the same security services, on the basis of confidential information, accuse him of funding terrorism – an accusation that seems to rest on the fact that, as he openly acknowledges, he had given money to charities providing humanitarian relief to Palestinians in the Occupied Territories and sponsored a Palestinian orphan.[43]

But it is not only the intelligence services that are provided with unchecked powers to judge loyalty. Civil servants as well as police officers have authority to judge the loyalties of individual citizenship applicants, and to decide what constitutes 'acceptable behaviour'. No more so than in France, where naturalisation processes have always been shot through with an assimilationlist logic, although what was meant by 'assimilation' was never clearly defined. Today, according to Abdellali Hajjat, 'the vast majority of cases of "assimilation deficiency" concern very devout or simply practising Muslims, as well as Muslims affiliated to Muslim organisations'.[44] However, cultural and religious selection within naturalisation processes is difficult to prove as public records exclude details that could be challenged in court.[45] According to cultural anthropologist John Bowen, 'candidates can be rejected on the grounds of insufficient assimilation, whether in their dress, their language, their travel outside the country, or the positions they have taken on Islam. The police verify whether a candidate for naturalisation has assimilated, and in their inquiry sometimes ask about private habits.'[46] Bowen cites several cases including that of a lawyer from Morocco who was asked how many times a week she ate couscous, how often she travelled to Morocco, the nationality of her friends and which newspapers she read. A Tunisian was asked why he had made the pilgrimage to Mecca twice. Fouad Imarraine of the Coalition of Muslims from France (CFM) describes this as the '"*politique du guichet*" – the politics of arbitrariness, which means that, on the whim of a civil servant or an intelligence officer, you are going to be judged worthy or unworthy of the Republic, of the French culture, of integration'.[47]

This administrative racism has been accompanied, post-September 11, by a rise in 'constitutional patriotism' whereby citizenship applicants, particularly in France and Germany, must declare allegiance to the state. In both countries, membership of an Islamic organisation that has no association with violence but is critical of the government could be considered enough to justify denial of citizenship. In this way, according to Abdellali Hajjat, the 'definition of assimilation has been transformed'. It now 'involves the state's relationship to Muslim organisations and their degree of allegiance'.[48]

The German internal intelligence services' (*Verfassungsschutz*) practise the most wide-ranging form of religious profiling in Europe. Its classification schemes regard the highly religious as just a notch or two under the potentially violent on a continuum of radicalisation. In fact, any Muslim organisation, even those that are avowedly non-violent, are defined by the intelligence services as 'Islamist' and placed under state surveillance. For membership of an 'Islamist organisation', according to *Verfassungsschutz* annual reports, regardless of whether the organisation is violent or non-violent, offends Germany's 'democratic spirit' by promoting 'self-segregation' through the creation of an 'Islamist milieu, where there is a danger of continuing radicalisation'.[49] Such thinking has had major repercussions on members and sympathisers of the Turkish-German organisation Islamische Gemeinschaft Milli Görus (IGMG, which is linked to the Turkish Refah party and offshoots) said to represent as many as 7 per cent of Germany's Muslims. (It has 400–600 prayer spaces, 26,500 paid-up members and as many as 100,000 sympathisers across Germany.[50]) But because of the intelligence services' 'slippery slope' view of 'gradual radicalisation' through membership of any Islamist group, Milli

Görus has been targeted for investigation for anti-constitutional activities at the federal level as well as in nearly every Land where it is active.[51] Milli Görus has counted around 200 cases, mostly in Bavaria, Baden-Württemberg and Hessen, in which its employees have had naturalisation requests turned down. There was even an instance when an administrative court in Hessen stripped four Milli Görus members of their German citizenship, on the grounds that membership of an Islamist (and therefore unconstitutional) organisation potentially nullified the 'declaration of loyalty' they had signed on naturalisation. (The decision was overturned on appeal.) A Christian Democrat politician complained that 'we cannot meet with half of the Muslims in town because the *Verfassungsschutz* says they are a danger to our values'.[52]

Alongside this official hostility towards the naturalisation requests of Milli Görus employees goes regular denunciations of Milli Görus members in the media. Here, is yet another set of 'scare scenarios', fostering 'moral panics', not just about the terror threat, but implying that the 'growing number of naturalisations turning *Ausländer* (foreigners) into citizens, threatens to change the balance of power between the "established" and the "outsiders"'.[53] One could even argue that the fears of 'foreign infiltration' (*Uberfremdung*), manipulated by the Nazis, have, in the modern context, been transferred from Jews to Turks. Such media demonisation involves journalists quoting unchecked intelligence services reports on a group's activities even though they may include basic translation errors, defamatory material or unfair innuendo and accusation. This has profound effects on the individual, who can be subjected to a variant of the loyalty review boards instigated in the US in the McCarthyite period, or the *Berufsverbot* in Germany in the 1970s, to weed out communist sympathisers from any state employment.[54] In one case, Mustafa Yoldas, highly respected for his inter-faith work and cooperation with the Evangelische Akademie, lost his job as a translator for the federal refugee services after the intelligence services denounced him as a member of Milli Görüs.[55] The International Crisis Group has also described measures introduced by local authorities to identify Milli Görus members as a borderline 'official policy of state harassment to deny Milli Görus members and officials legitimacy or comfort'.[56]

Another example of the kind of 'moral panic' generated by discourses on citizenship occurred in the Netherlands, but this time the scare was about the supposed threat posed by dual nationals. Politicians in their droves are now distancing themselves from the extreme-Right Freedom Party (PVV) politician Geert Wilders, principally because his 15-minute internet film, *Fitna*, against the 'criminal' Qur'an, puts Dutch citizens and interests at risk abroad.[57] Yet in the Spring of 2007, around the time of the March provincial elections, Wilders captivated the media and dominated the parliamentary floor, through his introduction of an emotionally charged parliamentary debate about dual nationals, which was fully supported by the Liberal Party (VVD).[58] The debate included highly personalised attacks on newly appointed Labour Party state secretaries Ahmed Aboutaleb (of Moroccan origin) and Nebahat Albayrak (of Turkish origin), whose loyalty to the Dutch state was called into question on account of their dual nationality. Initially, it looked as though the first minority ethnic members of any Dutch cabinet would be hounded out of office. But a number of important professional and trade union bodies spoke out against what was described as a new form of McCarthyism. The National Federation of Christian Trades Unions (CNV) said that the way dual nationality was being linked to questions of loyalty created mistrust in precisely those professions where the need for trust was paramount. Jan Kleian, the chairman of the union representing the military, ACOM, said that 'Soldiers feel that if the loyalty of state secretaries is being questioned today, the integrity of Muslim soldiers could be up for discussion tomorrow.' And Marleen Barth, chair of CNV Education, said that it was totally unacceptable that people with dual nationality were considered unsuitable for all sorts of jobs because of presumed divided loyalties.[59]

Integration Discourse and Accusatory Processes

McCarthyism, according to the Harvard University sociology professor Daniel Bell, was more a 'tendency of the times' than a political movement. It led, on a large scale, to the introduction of 'moral indignation' into public debate.[60] A similar 'moral panic' is aroused today not just through the prejudices that accrue through prosecutions of 'subversives' under the anti-terrorist laws, but also through the accumulation of anti-Muslim stereotypes via the political debate on national identity, core values and integration. It is precisely through the 'integration debate', that the moral indignation of the majority (identified by Daniel Bell) has been popularised. Within it, Muslims stand constantly accused of being the unassimilable 'Other', with the new yardstick being integration into values. Although what the majority really demands is not integration ('a two-way process of mutual adaptation') but assimilation ('a one-way process whereby the minority are absorbed by the majority'). A debate on integration that makes assimilationist demands presupposes, in Sivanandan's words, that 'there is one dominant culture, one unique set of values, one nativist loyalty'.[61]

And what threatens our open, democratic and uniquely European values more than the Islamist (read Muslim) – a member of a dangerous religious minority that (collectively) holds on to 'alien values'? Through the debate on integration (read assimilation), the moral majority points an accusatory finger at the Muslim minority. You are members of a 'backward culture', you hold on to 'pre-Enlightenment values', shout the majority through their parliamentary tribunes and the megaphone provided by the media. Too much religiosity; too many mosques; too many headscarves; too many beards; too many Muslim cemeteries; too many foreign languages; too many satellite dishes linked to too many foreign TV channels. The tongues of the morally indignant click, their heads shake and their fingers wag. If we the majority, confirmed in the superiority of our values, are self-critical at all, it is only of the liberalism that made us blind to the self-segregatory and threatening trends that have gone unchecked within the 'Islamist milieux'. Hence, initiatives designed to check 'self-segregatory' developments are proposed, such as Rotterdam local authority's 'Islam and integration' project (25 public meetings within which so-called 'experts' discussed 'the extent to which Islam hindered integration into Rotterdam society').

Central to this very public discussion of Islam and integration is a kind of conjuring trick. Muslims comprise something like 3.5 per cent of the total population of Europe and are so diverse – Turks, Kurds, Moroccans, Pakistanis, Bangladeshis, Somalis, Afghanis, Iraqis, Iranians, etc. – and so fragmented in ethnic, national, linguistic and sect terms and so economically marginalised – as to defy any attempt at unity, let alone power. But by removing Muslims from the social reality they face in Europe and linking them to the homogenous and repressive force that is said to be global Islam, the discourse vests them with an illusion of unity and power so subversive as to constitute the 'enemy within'. But recognising that this is no more than a little conjuring trick brings with it illumination. Sivanandan reminds us that while once it was racism that wanted immigrant labour, but not the immigrant and kept immigrants from becoming citizens, now 'it is nativism (the other side of the racist coin, often disguised as patriotism) that, in trying to flatten society into a homogenous whole, demands that ethnic minorities be cleansed of their cultures and recast in Europe's image before they can be "integrated" into society'.[62] In this way, stigmatisation on the basis of colour gives way to stigmatisation on the basis of faith. Just as black people were once problematised, Muslims today are the new 'Other'.

Renagades and Évolués

'The way that the West rolls out the good Muslims has become eerily reminiscent of the McCarthyite era when Communist renegades would be wheeled out to give Americans a state-orchestrated glimpse of the enemy's dark heart.'[63] At the time of writing this, journalist Seumas Milne had within his sights Ed Husain, author of the best-selling *The Islamist: Why I Joined Radical Islam in Britain, What I Saw Inside and Why I Left.* According to Husain the fact that he is one of the highest-ranking defectors from the British-branch of Hizb ut-Tahrir makes his exposé essential reading. But Husain's denunciation of this Islamist organisation and the wider Islamic scene also makes him, from the state's point of view, an ideal 'native informant' on 'subversive' Islamic organisations – one who can be regularly wheeled out by government agencies and the liberal intelligentsia as a suitable role model for young Muslims. Thus, in April 2008, the liberal and New Right intelligentsia came out in force when Husain, alongside another former Hizb ut-Tahrir member, Maajid Nawaz, launched the Quilliam Foundation at the British Museum, [64] promising to 'heal the pathology of Islamist extremism' and promote a new form of 'Western Islam'. [65]

This official promotion of 'good' Muslims – those who have integrated into European values and are therefore worthy of equal rights – is not confined to defectors from Islamist parties. The loyalty debates engendered by the Islam-threat scare scenario imply that being Muslim and being British, German, French, and so on, brings with it a conflict of loyalty, a lack of patriotism, that can only really be resolved if Muslims become more like the majority.

In ways that are remarkable in that they are so predictably similar, in country after country, the European media, wittingly or unwittingly, take on the role of gatekeeper, privileging those voices in the Muslim community that are most supportive of assimilationist agendas. Those privileged – often with very individualistic or extremist agendas – become media celebrities, enjoying inordinate press attention, while the voices of other Muslims, who do not support assimilation, are silenced or ridiculed. The cultural anthropologist Marianne Gullestad described this as a 'star system' that results in a 'diversion of public attention and a crippling of critical awareness'. In her pioneering work, *Plausible Prejudice: Everyday Experiences and Social Images of Nation, Culture and Race*, Gullestad showed how the media elevate individual Muslims supportive of the majority view of immigrant culture as backward and European culture as inherently homogenous and morally superior. 'Star systems', in the context Gullestad provides, could even be seen as a continuation of colonial reward systems under which 'natives', alienated from their indigenous societies, were embraced by the new foreign rulers. In the Belgian

Congo, for instance, the colonisers used to employ a system of rewarding colonised people who alienated themselves from indigenous society: they were raised to the officially designated category of *évolués*.[66]

One such '*évolué*' in Germany is Bassam Tibi, the professor of political science in Göttingen, who first coined the term 'European *Leitkultur*' in 1998 in order to summarise the set of norms and values which, for him, characterised the European cultural community.[67] Tibi, regularly cited in the media as an 'integration expert', argued that the recognition, acceptance and internalisation of this culture of modernity and enlightenment form the yardstick for measuring the successful integration of immigrants. But you do not have to be an academic to be an *évolué*. There are other less intellectual ways of showing assimilation into Europe's superior values. In Norway, young, pretty women, like Kadra Noor (known in the press simply as Kadra), are celebrated as new voices in the fight against patriarchal tradition and backward values, and for integration based on progress and Enlightenment values. Kadra first achieved celebrity status after being invited by the private think-tank, the Human Rights Service (see chapter 3), to turn undercover reporter and participate in two TV documentaries, shown in October 2000, about female circumcision. The programmes created a moral panic in Norway, through their apparent revelation of the lack of firm resistance to female circumcision by some Muslim leaders. The notion that young Muslim women need to be sexually liberated from patriarchal tradition features strongly in Norway, and is also epitomised in the celebrity status afforded the Norwegian-Pakistani stand-up comedian, Shabana Rehman. Among other exploits, Rehman, described by the media as one of the most powerful women in Norway, has been photographed nude with a Norwegian flag painted across her body while dramatically throwing away her Pakistani clothes. And, at the opening of a film festival in Haugesund in August 2005, Rehman, after kissing the Norwegian cabinet minister of culture on her mouth, pulled down her pants and mooned to the public.[68] According to social anthropologist Aud Talle, who analysed the 'morally dubious techniques' and poor investigative quality of the TV programmes Kadra Noor appeared in, as well as the subsequent debates, 'Noor was used (or misused) in order to give majority Norwegians the opportunity to express their self-centred moral condemnation of the practice' [of female circumcision] and indulge in their 'feelings of goodness'.[69] And Gullestad, who had analysed Shabana Rehman's newspaper columns and media stunts, concluded that while the comedian had undoubtedly embarked on a 'radical project of individual emancipation against patriarchal and religious oppression' she had done this by following 'tabloid genre conventions by focusing on the sensational and the sexually titillating'. Rehman had also formulated her criticisms in a way that reinforces the stigmatisation of and paternalism towards Muslim minorities in Norway *en bloc*.[70]

But then assimilationist attractive and chic (apparently a very European feminine quality) feminists of immigrant origin rank high in the list of desirable *évolués*. One such is the former Dutch MP Ayaan Hirsi Ali, who dominated the media discussion of integration and women's rights in the Netherlands for a number of years despite the fact that there were plenty of other feminist voices, including Muslims ones, offering other perspectives. A similar media-created figure is the Algerian-French feminist Fadela Amara, who was of the younger generation that rose to prominence in association with the socialist anti-racist movement SOS Racisme. A Socialist councillor, Amara quickly became a media star through her role in the organisation Ni Putes Ni Soumises (Neither whores nor submissives). Today, Fadela Amara is one of Sarkozy's cabinet ministers. As junior minister, with responsibility for urban issues, Amara, alongside Rachida Dati (justice department) and the equally glamorous Rama Yade (human rights secretary) are regularly wheeled out as proof that the 'assimilated' ethnic has a future in France.

Compare the treatment of such figures with that of the Swiss philosophy professor Tariq Ramadan (particularly in France) and Denmark's first elected female Muslim parliamentary representative, Asmaa Abdol-Hamid. Abdol-Hamid withdrew from office even before she had taken up her parliamentary seat, so fed up was she with the controversy over her headscarf. So incensed was parliament by the thought of having a veiled woman among its members that it instructed a five-member presidium of the Danish parliament to draw up new rules on 'appropriate clothing'. But then headscarf-wearing women everywhere have been targeted for a witch-hunt, as bits of cloth become symbols for certain fears and threats. Only Muslim women like Shabana Rehman, who tear off their clothes, can, it seems, be fully integrated.

Scaremongering: the Joe McCarthys of Europe

And it is the state's attempts to rigorously police the public sphere of religion and religious representation – not least through bans on the hijab and rules on appropriate clothing – that has given succour to the extreme-Right's campaigns against mosques and minarets. For governments that promote assimilationist measures also generate the notion that Muslims must become socially invisible, by force if necessary, if they are to be fully integrated. In the streets of European cities, as well as in the more rural areas, the cry goes up 'Against the Islamisation of Europe'. Politicians and Christian leaders are among those supporting public campaigns and petitions against the construction of mosques, which are denounced for destroying Europe's Judaeo-Christian heritage.[71] But the extreme-Right, unlike our slightly more sophisticated government representatives, are incapable of making a distinction between 'good' Muslims and 'bad' Muslims, so that any expression of religious identity by Muslims is seen as evidence of creeping Islamisation. For at every parliamentary street corner lies a Joe McCarthy. The Dutch have the populist Geert Wilders (PVV), the Austrians had Jörg Haider (Alliance for the Future of Austria). For the Swiss, the billionaire industrialist Christoph Blocher (Swiss People's Party, SVP), and for the Italians both the post-fascist Gianfranco Fini (Alleanza Nationale) and the separatist Umberto Bossi (Northern League). The French, for their part, are blessed with both the demagogic Jean-Marie Le Pen (Front National) and the aristocratic Philippe de Villiers (Mouvement pour la France). De Villiers is also author of *Les mosquées de Roissy* in which he warned that Islamists had 'infiltrated' Roissy-Charles de Gaulle airport and were threatening the security of an airport 'under sharia law'.[72]

In several countries, such as Austria, Germany and Switzerland, extreme-Right parliamentary parties are seeking constitutional change (sometimes by means of a referendum) to outlaw the construction of mosques and minarets.[73] In Switzerland, the SVP (the largest party in the Swiss parliament) has gathered enough signatures to force a referendum on the building of minarets, which they want banned on the grounds that they are 'symbols of political-religious imperialism'.[74] (Never mind that there are only three mosques with small minarets in the whole of Switzerland.) In Belgium and France, legal challenges have been made to ensure that the state gives no financial assistance for the construction of mosques, and in certain areas of Germany, citizens' protest committees are sprouting up every time a mosque is proposed. Meanwhile, in Italy, the local authority in Verona solved its 'mosque' problem by simply demolishing it, transforming the site of the bulldozed mosque into a car park, which they want to be named after the late Islamophobe, Oriana Fallaci. Where once the Nazis spoke of the need to preserve the racial purity of the *Volk* from alien stock, today the leitmotif for extremist campaigns is cultural purity, with the Judaeo-Christian heritage that is said to mark western European culture, constantly evoked. Thus, Jörg Haider, governor of Carinthia, where just 2 per cent of the population are Muslim, warned of the threat posed by the erection of 'institutions which are alien to our culture', and the Conservative (OVP) governor of Lower Austria, Erwin Pröll declares that 'Minarets are something *Artfremd* (strange) and things which are *Artfremd* do not do a culture any good in the long run.'[75] Muslims, as a faith group, are minorities in democratic secular states, with protected rights, including the right to practise their religion. But the anti-mosque campaigners get round this inconvenient fact by denying that Islam is a religion and categorising it instead as a political and criminal ideology that, in the name of security, must be cordoned off from the body politic. It is not *Das Kapital* now that needs to be banned, but the Qur'an, says Joe McCarthy (oops, I mean Geert Wilders) on the grounds that the 'sick ideology of Allah and Mohammed' as written down in this 'wretched book' is similar to *Mein Kampf*.

But Wilders – like McCarthy – has gone too far. He threatens to derail Dutch society and damage Dutch interests abroad. He has even criticised the security services. And the intelligence officers – and they run the political show now – do not like this. Only official nativism will be tolerated in democratic Europe; the 'Islam scare' can only be peddled under licence. Those who seek to go 'freelance' should be careful, for they too may fall foul of the new crimes of 'undesirable behaviour' unleashed by the anti-terrorist laws and the new McCarthyism.

Detention and Deportation

5

THE DEPORTATION MACHINE

We live in an age in which the rich industrialised nations pronounce on human rights abuses abroad while failing to live up to their own standards at home, particularly in relation to obligations under international law. But whereas the abrogation of international law that arose from the 'war on terror' has generated much attention, the degree of illegality that flows from the (undeclared) 'war on refugees' is less keenly observed. The war on terror has undermined the 1949 Geneva Convention on the Treatment of Prisoners of War; the war on refugees has undermined the 1951 Geneva Convention relating to the Status of Refugees. Both wars have eroded international conventions outlawing torture, cruel and degrading treatment or other punishment.

Though the 1951 Refugee Convention is under threat from a variety of directions, some of the most serious abuses of its articles and principles result from the introduction of the EU deportation programme, with its target-based system for removals and its reification of failed asylum seekers as commodities to be parcelled and dispatched out of Europe.[1] It is a programme that eats away at a political culture that professes respect for human rights. As such, the effects of Europe's deportation policies[2] today parallel the plight of refugees during the Second World War. In her consideration of the plight of refugees during and after that war, Hannah Arendt observed that 'the moment human beings lacked their own government and had to fall back upon their minimum rights, no authority was left to protect them and no institution was willing to guarantee them'.[3] The body of international human rights law that was created after 1945 was developed to meet this need – but there is a pressing need today for stronger mechanisms to guarantee that these rights are available and effective for non-citizens, to oblige receiving states to treat the right to asylum as sacrosanct, and to apply the law impartially.

Seventy years after the Holocaust, stateless refugees are being left practically unprotected, 'expelled from humanity', reduced to 'bare life' 'unpeopled',[4] as the protections of international law are gradually eroded. This chapter examines the mechanics of the EU deportation programme, which violates not only the basic principles of the Refugee Convention, particularly that of *non-refoulement* (no return to danger), but numerous other instruments of international law; and the way that civil servants, immigration officials and police officers are being turned into automatons.[5] Under the spotlight here are collective deportations carried out through military-style operations and the brutality involved in individual forced deportations. The EU expulsion policy necessitates the maintenance of a vast carceral system, and this chapter describes what takes place at the *zones d'attente* at international airports, detention centres at maritime borders, removal centres on the outskirts of European cities, and even further afield, as member states extend the detention estate into Libya, Tunisia, Morocco, Mauritania and Senegal. In this prison-asylum complex (a mutation of the ordinary prison system) migrants and failed asylum seekers are warehoused. Here, those displaced by globalisation, economic devastation and war are compulsorily confined while the EU member states search for a third country willing to accept the 'migratory flows' surplus to their policy of 'selective immigration'.

Targets: the Motor for Expulsions

Since 2000, the numbers of asylum seekers reaching Europe have steadily declined. Even so, European politicians, nervous of the electoral pull of the migration issue and the parliamentary muscle of the anti-immigrant lobby, have focused their rhetoric on increasing the rate of return of failed asylum seekers. At the EU level, they have created a machine to render large group deportations of specific nationalities possible, via Frontex (the

EU Agency for the Management of Operational Cooperation at the External Borders of the EU member states), for instance. But the motor that sets the brutal deportation machine into motion is 'targets'.

Each country sets a target for removal that is then blazoned through the media. In 2004, the hardline Dutch interior minister Rita Verdonk announced a policy of 50,000 removals from the Netherlands in three years; also in 2004, the British prime minister Tony Blair reached a deportation formula based on the 'monthly rate of removals' exceeding 'the number of unfounded applications'.[6] In 2007, French President Nicolas Sarkozy set one target for deportations (25,000) and another target for apprehensions of foreigners for illegal entry or unauthorised stay (125,000), with local prefects issued with individual quotas.[7] The imposition of such targets necessarily undermines the whole humanitarian principle of refugee policy – 'need not numbers' – and becomes its obverse, 'numbers not need'. And failed asylum seekers are reduced to a statistic for removal, even when they have strong claims to remain on humanitarian grounds.

But how are targets for deportation enforced? Inevitably, the answer is through officially sanctioned state violence. Deportations on routine passenger flights are neither popular nor economic. At least twelve people have died during violent, forced deportation attempts. Heart failure, asphyxiation, and a combination of panic and stress have been the official causes of death.[8] Not surprisingly, passengers are shaken when they see crying children frogmarched on to planes, or have to witness violent control and restraint methods against adult deportees, who may be bound head and foot, gagged (with special adhesive tape) or have had their heads forced into the special deportation helmet (a chin strap prevents the deportee from moving his lower jaw, an additional strap covers the detainee's mouth). Airline pilots and cabin crew also object to such processes, often on procedural grounds, but sometimes on the basis of human solidarity. States, therefore, increasingly favour systems that render deportations invisible. Special flights and military jets are chartered and fitted-out for deportation; these flights are staffed by police and private escorts, with interpreters and doctors (who have been known to sedate difficult passengers), government officials and other motley advisers on board. These secretive flights often start in one EU country and then stop over in another to pick up more passengers, thanks to the coordinating role in organising joint removals played by EU expulsion agencies.

In some ways, the secrecy that surrounds such flights calls to mind the extraordinary rendition flights set up by the CIA to facilitate the clandestine transfer of captured suspects in the war on terror. And just as it is difficult to trace the journeys of 'enemy combatants', it is difficult for independent organisations to monitor the fate of deportees. They are often rounded up from detention centres in the middle of the night and frustrated in their attempts to contact lawyers and friends about their impending fate. Sometimes, the facts emerge after a public outcry in a receiving country. This has happened in Mauritania, Mali and Benin where there have been angry demonstrations over Spanish and French deportation practices. (Mali only agreed to receive three deportation flights from the Spanish Canary Islands in August 2006 on the basis of strict confidentiality.[9]) Sometimes publicity over such deportations is manufactured by EU member states to serve a deterrent purpose. The UK government, for instance, sent a film crew to video the deportation of approximately two dozen Afghans from Gatwick airport so that the film could subsequently be broadcast in Afghanistan as a warning for those considering refugee flight.

What we do know about such deportations is largely through the efforts of campaigners and organisations like Amnesty International (AI). AI reported in the Spring of 2003 that a group of 54 Senegalese and Ivory Coast nationals were deported on a charter flight from France to Dakar and Abidjan and restrained throughout the entire flight with hard rubber cable wound around wrists and ankles. Some victims also had their faces and legs taped and were beaten.[10] In May 2004, the Caravan for the Rights of Refugees and Migrants in Hamburg reported that failed asylum seekers from Togo and the Cameroon were subjected to pepper spray, plastic shackles, dogs and the deportation helmet during a chartered deportation flight organised jointly by Germany, the Netherlands, Belgium, France and the UK.[11] Women and children were on board a deportation flight that took off one night in June 2005 from Düsseldorf airport. The clients of lawyer Neslihan Celik were on board, and she claimed that adult deportees 'had been given psychiatric drugs. They were forced or pressed to take tablets while they were in the vehicles.'[12]

More recently, the public concern about secretive EU-wide deportation flights has been sharpened by Europe's appalling treatment of Iraqi asylum seekers. Since the US invasion of Iraq in May 2003, more than four million Iraqi civilians have been uprooted in one of the largest humanitarian crises of our times. Approximately two million of these refugees live in desperate conditions and legal limbo in Syria and Jordan, whose governments receive barely any support from the international community. In comparison, just 100,000 Iraqis claimed asylum in the EU between 2003 and 2007.[13] (There are no legal routes to Europe for Iraqis fleeing persecution. Coalition troops and embassies within Iraq do not accept asylum claims. Furthermore, Frontex sees its task as preventing further migratory movements of 'illegal immigrants' from Iraq.[14]) The vast majority of successful Iraqi asylum claims were made in Sweden, with European countries that joined the 'Coalition of the Willing' displaying the meanest attitudes towards displaced Iraqis.

In 2007, forced returns of Iraqis were organised from Denmark, Greece, Poland, Sweden and the UK.[15] The UK started using military flights to deport small numbers of Iraqis to northern Iraq in November 2005, with the largest operation taking place in March 2008, when 50 Iraqis were taken from a detention centre in Dover to Stansted airport in Essex, and flown to Irbil in northern Iraq. On arrival, armed guards from the Kurdistan Democratic Party (KDP) allegedly boarded the flight and beat those who refused to leave on the back of the head with their guns until they bled. There were allegations that British security officials also took part in the violence.[16]

Once a flight is chartered, the authorities need to fill up the plane with nationals from the receiving country in order to make the flight financially viable. This can involve trawling for deportees, both within detention centres and through identity checks on the streets, the metro and train stations.[17] In France, when the authorities have chartered a flight to a specific country and seats are empty, the police have been known to hunt out people of the relevant nationality to fill the charter, even stopping people on the Paris subway system to carry out identity checks. Another unwelcome by-product of targets that pressurise state officials and police officers to meet pre-determined quotas is the injury and death of those who believe themselves targeted for removal. Absolutely panic-stricken in the face of a dawn raid or as a consequence of a police identity check, those hunted may attempt to avoid apprehension, sometimes with tragic consequences. Since September 2007, when the French immigration minister Brice Hortefeux summoned some 20 local government heads and demanded that they 'improve their figures' and step up deportations, there have been numerous such tragic incidents in France as police swoops on street corners, metro stations, outside schools and workplaces have escalated. Chulun Liua, a 51-year-old Chinese woman who had left her only son in northern China to seek work in France, died after throwing herself out of a window to avoid a police raid in Paris.[18] Around the same time in Amiens, Ivan Demsky, a popular 12-year-old secondary school student, whose Russian and Chechen parents were failed asylum seekers, suffered serious head injuries after falling four floors from a window while fleeing with his father from a police raid;[19] and in November 2007 in Marseille, an African broke both his legs attempting to jump from a fourth-floor window.[20] On 4 April 2008, a 29-year-old Malian, fleeing a police identity check, died of a heart attack after jumping into the river Marne in a Paris suburb. After his death, thousands of people demonstrated in Paris to draw attention to the inhuman consequences of French immigration policies. Film director Marie Vermillard, who witnessed the pursuit, during which one police officer commandeered a scooter, asked

What would have happened without the police's persistence? ... This mad pursuit after a man who ran and who had done nothing? Not a criminal, not even a petty crime [had been committed]. No, just a man, who ran because he didn't have papers and ended up dying in this river in a Paris suburb.[21]

Denial of Humanitarian Protection

Every day, the roll call of death and injury grows. But there is more, much more. The EU deportation programme is a juggernaut that, if allowed to proceed unchecked, will violate all our basic human values. To this juggernaut, the most vulnerable must be sacrificed, precisely because they are the easiest to remove. Whereas young, healthy single men can disappear into the underground economy, this is not so easy for families with young children, including the sick. For the notion that the removal of families, even where there is overwhelming evidence of hardship, is vital to retain the integrity of asylum and immigration systems has now hardened into an unbending principle that spills over into the treatment of young people and sick children, some of whom may have severe health problems untreatable in their home country. In the UK, an Iranian girl, aged 15, with a severe congenital heart disease that required constant monitoring to avoid fatal complication, was issued with a deportation order, alongside her mother, a failed asylum seeker. An earlier deportation attempt failed, after the girl collapsed and had to be rushed to hospital.[22] In Sweden, some children have developed symptoms of complete depressive breakdown (the official term for the illness is Pervasive Refusal Syndrome). Unable to thrive emotionally and physically owing to traumatic experiences in their home countries, compounded in Europe by their fear of deportation, they have had to be hospitalised and intravenously fed.[23] Unbelievably, they too have been subjected to deportation orders. In one case, involving Rufat, a 17-year-old boy from Azerbaijan, who was hospitalised in a psychiatric ward and was being fed intravenously, having lost the will to live, the Swedish Migration Board told the family that a specially equipped charter plane would be deployed to deport them, if necessary.[24] In another case, 13-year-old Tanja, who was severely depressed, had to be carried onto the deportation flight to Bosnia. The magazine *Artikel 14* tracked Tanja down to Banja Luka where they discovered that the family had no access to health care, and the sick young girl spent all day lying on a plastic-covered mattress on the floor in a temporary office storage room.[25]

Also among the list of the targeted are torture and rape victims, refugees from war, homosexuals fleeing persecution, women and children at risk from traffickers, unaccompanied children (on reaching the age of 18)[26] and the seriously ill (for example, asylum seekers suffering from AIDS, who could not get treatment in their country of origin).[27] Even though many of these failed asylum seekers may not fit into the strict and, some would argue, outdated Convention definition of a refugee (a victim of political persecution emanating from the state), their removal places them at risk of 'serious harm'. As such, they are deserving of subsidiary protection on the humanitarian grounds laid out in the International Covenant on Civil and Political Rights (ICCPR) and the European Convention on Human Rights (ECHR). States are also obliged to consider the International Convention on the Rights of the Child (COROC) in cases involving the deportation of children.

It would seem, though, that the EU deportation machine is armour-plated against corrosion from any sense of compassion or responsibility. One unwelcome by-product of this inhumane approach is the attempted corrosion of medical ethical codes through the creation of a network of medical professionals willing to subsume the health needs of their patients to government obsessions to hit deportation targets. But this attempt to draw doctors and psychiatrists into a programme for removal based on the bullying of the vulnerable has led to a backlash among medical bodies, the task of which is to maintain independence and protect the ethical standards of their profession. Bernd Mesovic, in a seminal article in the *Frankfurter Rundschau*,[28] was one of the first to draw attention to the growing band of 'medical specialists for deportation' – namely, doctors, 'some with dubious professional qualifications' who are willing to overrule expert medical assessments and declare the seriously ill 'fit to travel'. Lawyer Ursula Schlung-Muntan was also shocked at the growing deployment of an 'immense machinery' to ensure 'fitness to fly', by sending the refugee back to their native country accompanied by security personnel and doctors. Treatment with sedatives during the flight is arranged for those such as the psychologically ill or those at risk of suicide.[29]

In Sweden, where the authorities went to extreme lengths to certify apathetic children 'fit to travel', the threat posed to medical ethics extended into the whole area of high-quality independent medical research. In 2005, stung by public criticism, the immigration services and the government took a much more aggressive approach to the families of children with Pervasive Refusal Syndrome. Parents, the Migration Board suggested, were either deliberately manipulating their children to feign illness, or had gone so far as to poison them in order to intensify the apathy. While doctors and psychiatrics looked on in horror as the government heaped opprobrium on the children's families (the police were called in to investigate the poison claims), the government appointed psychiatrist Marie Hessle to launch an official investigation into the real causes of the children's apathy. One year later, the Migration Board's poison allegations had been discredited, the police investigation wound up. Hessle was criticised for producing a report based on unsubstantiated facts and distorted quotes. It seems that the suggestion that the children had been poisoned or were faking illness was based on the suspicions of doctors who had barely any experience of dealing with apathetic children.[30]

In Germany, the terrible impact on children of the denial of humanitarian protection and the refusal to make allowances for the seriously ill or the vulnerable have been documented by the Antirassistische Initiative in Berlin. It drew attention to two cases involving return to Africa, where the mother of the family died in the aftermath of deportation, leaving the future survival of her children uncertain. One case involved Congolese asylum seeker Tshiana Nguya, in the seventh month of pregnancy when she was forcibly returned to Kinshasa on 26 August 2004, together with two of her three children. Without any money to bribe officials in Kinshasa, she was imprisoned upon arrival and maltreated, raped and humiliated. She was not released until the state of her health deteriorated considerably and she died, alongside her stillborn child, on 7 December 2004.[31]

But so calloused are officials to humanitarian concerns, that they justify deportation on the grounds that they will not be blackmailed by falsified or exaggerated accounts of physical violence or mental trauma. Just as the US authorities at Guantánamo Bay have reclassified detainees' suicide attempts as 'manipulative self-injurious behaviour',[32] EU governments ignore the shocking escalation in suicides and incidents of self-harm among the detained and the desperate by denouncing the victims as 'self-mutilators' or 'emotional blackmailers', 'testing the hospitality' of the nation. So that when in July 2003 in Germany, Hüseyin Dikec died after pouring petrol over himself and setting himself on fire in the regional Aliens Office of Gütersloh, an official was quoted in the newspaper as saying, 'It is unbelievable the lengths that these people will go to avoid deportation.'[33] In this way, yet another offensive dimension is added to the xeno-racist discourse against asylum seekers and refugees. In effect, it turns reality on its head: states are the victims of such behaviour and asylum seekers their victimisers.

Return to Torture and Danger

Those fleeing from war or ethnic persecution and its long-term consequences also merit international protection if the principle of *non-refoulement* (no return to danger), which is central to the Refugee Convention and numerous other instruments of international law, is to be observed. Freedom from torture, from cruel or degrading treatment or punishment, furthermore, is an absolute right guaranteed under the International Covenant on Civil and Political Rights. But, as the war on terror meshes with the (undeclared) war on refugees, the vital principle of *non-refoulement* is held hostage to both anti-terrorist and immigration laws. Not only is protection removed from asylum seekers from regions of the world whose governments have allied themselves to the US and Europe in the war on terror,[34] but (as we have already seen in the case of Iraqis) the rights of refugees are seriously eroded when guarantees of lasting protection under the Refugee Convention are superseded by schemes of temporary protection in Europe until conflicts are resolved. The EU Temporary Protection Directive of 2001 was designed to protect people in 'situations of mass influx' without removing their right to claim asylum, but it has never been used. Instead, EU member states make use of strategies such as refusing asylum but not enforcing removal, which leaves hundreds of thousands of people in immigration limbo, with no rights and no livelihood. Governments today are more ready to use the language of return within days of a declared cessation or military action, or to view military action (in the case of Afghanistan and Iraq) as a means of facilitating returns. The EU has also made provision in the Procedures Directive of 2005 for the creation of an EU 'white list' of 'safe countries of origin' but there is no such actual EU-wide list yet. At present, member states rely on their own 'white lists'.

In fact, in relation to the steady removal of protection from asylum seekers deemed a threat to national security, a precedent had already been set, well before the events of September 11 and the subsequent war on terror. Germany, in particular, had long since taken a hostile attitude towards the struggle for Kurdish self-determination in Turkey, and membership of the Kurdish Workers Party (PKK) was outlawed in the early 1990s. Perceived membership of the PKK was grounds for removal, even if that meant removal to torture.[35] German human rights organisations, concerned about the collusion between Turkish and German intelligence services, which put the lives of rejected asylum seekers at risk, had attempted to monitor the fate of deportees. An investigation carried out by Pro Asyl and the Lower Saxony Refugee Council established that at least five deported Kurdish asylum seekers were tortured on arrival in Turkey.[36] One case documented by Amnesty International (AI) involved Mehmet G, who was deported from Germany to Turkey following diplomatic assurances from the Turkish government that he would not be ill-treated. However, once in Turkey, Mehmet G was arrested, interrogated about his

PKK contacts and tortured with electric shocks. His genitals were squashed and his feet beaten with sticks.[37]

Following September 11, the Kurdish precedent has been extended to other asylum seekers who are also labelled terrorist, due, perhaps, to information provided by foreign intelligence services or suspected membership of foreign organisations blacklisted by the EU or US (see chapter 2). In some cases, the mere allegation of terrorism by the US or a coalition partner in the war on terror has been enough to justify expulsion. The most notorious case in this respect involved two Egyptian asylum seekers, Mohammed Alzery and Ahmed Agiza, who were summarily expelled from Sweden to Egypt in December 2003 without due process or any respect for human rights. The expulsion was carried out by US agents on a plane chartered by the US Defense Department. Forcibly dressed in dark overalls, their hands and feet chained to a specially designed harness, they were taken to the plane blindfolded and hooded. Once in Egypt, Ahmed Agiza was subjected to electric shock treatment with electrodes fastened to his genitals, nipples, tongue and ear lobes.[38]

European governments argue that if a formal guarantee can be given by the government in the country of return that a deportee will not be subjected to torture or ill-treatment, then the absolute prohibition in international law against *non-refoulement* will be adhered to. But this is duplicitous, as the same governments are well aware of case after case that proves the complete opposite.[39] As Human Rights Watch has demonstrated, the widespread and systematic use of torture in many of the countries to which people have been returned from North America and Europe indicates the futility of such diplomatic assurances and similar 'safeguards' against torture and ill-treatment.[40] The very fact that a European government seeks a diplomatic assurance indicates that the self-same government is fully aware that torture is systematic and routinely practised upon certain categories of people, including political dissidents, conscientious objectors and those from certain racial, ethnic or religious backgrounds. Nevertheless, European governments press ahead with this cynical strategy of seeking diplomatic assurances to circumvent the *non-refoulement* principle. For instance, the UK government has secured Memoranda of Understanding (MoU) with Jordan, Libya and Lebanon and an agreement with Algeria that deportees will not be tortured.[41] This is part of an attempt to deport around 30 national security detainees, many of whom are asylum seekers or officially recognised refugees, some of whom were detained indefinitely without trial under anti-terrorist legislation and later subjected to virtual house-arrest under control orders.

Legal interventions have thrown the spotlight on such national security deportations. But not so keenly observed are the everyday deportations of failed asylum seekers to some of the most dangerous regions in the world. As member states' assessments of whether a country is safe for return fall in line with a target-driven deportation policy, the EU moves from a system based on voluntary returns to post-conflict situations to a system of forced returns to situations characterised by danger. But as no official body in the EU monitors the effects of its deportation policies, in terms of the safety and security of deportees, the task of documenting the human cost falls on organisations like Pro Asyl and ARI in Germany, the National Coalition of Anti-Deportation Campaigns in the UK and Docu-Congo in the Netherlands. There is evidence from both the UK and the Netherlands that Congolese asylum seekers have been systematically handed over to the security services and subjected to harsh interrogations and torture.[42]

Similar evidence is available for many other countries. But no case demonstrates more clearly the tragic implications of a wrong country assessment than the group deportation of 220 Eritreans from Malta in September and October 2002. On the basis of a complete misinterpretation of UNHCR guidelines on returns to Eritrea issued in 2002, the Maltese assessed that, owing to the end of the 30-year-war with Ethiopia in 1991 and declaration of Eritrean independence in 1993, it would be safe to expel the 220 Eritreans. AI monitored the fate of the deportees.[43] It found that on arrival at Asmara airport, they were immediately detained – with women, girls and children separated from men. The men were taken to Adi Abeto military detention centre where 180 of them were kept in detention, beaten with leather and rubber whips and tortured over a period of two and a half months. Detainees were tied up day and night and given only short breaks for food and the toilet. Some became paralysed as a result of the treatment. It seems that one man died after he was shot attempting to escape. In December 2002, the remaining detainees were transferred to a secret detention centre on the main Dahlak Island in the Red Sea. One man attempted to commit suicide by tying his hands together and jumping into the sea. 'He got caught in the ship's propeller and his face was badly cut. He was taken out to sea, and we didn't hear of him again, maybe he died', said a survivor.[44]

The Central Role of the Detention Camp

The deportation machine demands the creation of a special prison system, where deportees can be warehoused while states make the necessary arrangements to effect their removal. As travel documents have to be secured and a viable return route established, sometimes to war zones, this can take months. Yet, as immigration detention is for administrative rather than punitive purposes, and detainees are not prisoners in the formal sense, immigration detainees end up imprisoned, but with fewer rights than convicted prisoners. There are few laws regulating their treatment and limited independent scrutiny of detention centres.

The Italian philosopher Giorgio Agamben sees in this growth of imprisonment for immigration purposes a reconfiguration of the concentration camp, which first emerged in Spanish camps in Cuba and British camps for Afrikaner prisoners in the Boer War. Just as the early concentration camps invoked a 'state of exception' based on considerations of 'national security' rather than criminal behaviour, the inmates of *zones d'attente* at airports and certain outskirts of our cities are deemed to have no claim on the nation while paradoxically they are brought more firmly under its control by virtue of their exclusion.[45] Writing on the growth of US immigration prisons run by private contractors in sites converted from military use, and located in remote regions, Jonathan Simon made similar observations.[46] Simon believes that US immigration prisons constitute 'an important mutation of the prison system

as a modern technology of power', which, in dispensing with
Enlightenment notions of the prison as a site of reformation, were
'largely unconstrained by the precedents of twentieth-century constitutional law', invoking an 'earlier tradition of monarchical use
of imprisonment as a site for enforcing undemocratic political
orders'. For Australian scholar-activist Suvendrini Perera, this
'mutant form of imprisonment' has arisen today as a response
to the needs of the new strain of racism first identified by A.
Sivanandan – xeno-racism.[47] For the contemporary detention
camp has been legitimised by a popular discourse that presents
asylum seekers and migrants as politically undesirable, racially
and morally dangerous and economically unproductive.

It is this xeno-racism that explains the appalling treatment
of immigration detainees across Europe. Certain privately run
detention camps have become firmly associated with inhumane
conditions and violence – Yarl's Wood and Harmondsworth
(UK), Fuerteventura (Canary Islands), Lampedusa (Italy), Hal-
Safi barracks (Malta), Köpenick-Grünau and Eisenhüttenstadt
(Germany), the centres 127 and 127bis (Belgium), Vincennes
(France), Schiphol (Netherlands). Inmates' health needs are
routinely ignored and severe depression, self-mutilation and suicide
attempts take place on a regular basis. Methods of punishment
or restraint that violate human rights are also well-documented,
as are the hunger-strikes, violent disturbances, protests and fires
(often started by the desperate inmates in utter frustration), which
sometimes lead to serious injury and even death. The worst single
such incident took place in October 2005 at Schiphol, Amsterdam.
Desperate inmates set fire to their blankets in protest at conditions,
and as the fire raged unchecked eleven detainees, locked in their
cells, perished.[48] But disturbances, often brutally suppressed, have
also taken place at Yarl's Wood (a whole wing of the detention
centre was gutted in a fire that caused £38m damage in February
2002) and Harmondsworth (August 2004, November 2006). In
January 2005 at the Hal-Safi barracks 26 people were hospitalised
when Maltese armed forces, in riot gear and waving batons and
shields, broke up a peaceful demonstration. (Malta is the only
country in Europe that practises a policy of mandatory detention

of all asylum seekers, who can be held for up to 18 months. Hunger-strikes, self-mutilation, suicide attempts and violence are relatively common.) Most recently, in February 2008, riot police responded to the escalation of tensions at Vincennes, Paris (which included hunger-strikes, and incidents of self-mutilation and fire) and several people were hospitalised.[49]

Even though the EU is experiencing a substantial decrease in asylum claims, the number of people held in detention centres is rapidly increasing. Deportation targets place a strain on existing facilities, leading to overcrowding (also a product of the long periods in which asylum seekers are held in detention)[50] and unhygienic conditions. Problems associated with overcrowding and poor hygiene are proportionately worse in countries where prison facilities already fail to meet international standards. For instance, in Lampedusa, Italy, the salt water flowing from showers has, when combined with the heat and the burning sun, contributed to the dermatitis suffered by inmates who receive one bottle of water a day between two people.[51] In Maltese detention centres, the level of hygiene is so poor that diseases such as scabies and fungal infections are widespread. The Hal-Safi barracks is like 'a microwave in summer and a fridge in winter', according to the former UN Human Rights Commissioner Alvaro Gil Robles.[52]

New detention centres are constantly being built,[53] with more units being erected that are capable of accommodating whole families. It is unbelievable that young children can be incarcerated, sometimes for months on end, in the authoritarian, austere insecure environment of a detention camp. Some of the side-effects experienced by detained children, as documented by health professionals, include lack of sleep and nightmares, bed wetting, weight loss, skin complaints and persistent respiratory conditions. Long-term consequences include depression, behavioural change and an undermining of a child's ability to learn. In the UK, the campaigning umbrella group 'No place for a child' estimates that around 2000 children are detained each year. (In one case, a child was held for 268 days.[54]) The UK has 'the most open-ended and unsupervised detention system in Europe'.[55]

In some parts of southern Europe there is even less oversight of what is happening to the detained. The most vulnerable of all to discriminatory treatment (including the denial of the right to seek asylum) and undetected state abuse are the 'boat people' who land in Sicily, Malta, Cyprus, the Canary Islands, Crete, Samos, Los and Chios,[56] having set sail from Morocco, Libya, Mauritania, Cape Verde and Senegal. They are becoming the 'disappeared', deemed not to have arrived at all. Not only are some coastguards accused of recklessly turning the migrants' rickety boats back, even though they are in European territorial waters, but many deportations are disguised as refusals of entry at the border – an administrative measure that does not need to be regulated by a judge and does not ban the migrant from entering the territory in the future. In this way, new arrivals are denied access to the asylum process altogether. And states that do not process asylum claims can also conveniently deny that they have breached the *non-refoulement* principle of the Convention – they have not returned a person to danger, because the person never arrived!

The Mediterranean Solution[57]

In a final twist, the EU is attempting to extend its borders to the North African coastline by co-opting African politicians into its deportation policies. Having militarised the southern maritime borders, to create a 'Schengen of the Sea',[58] the EU has set about solidifying the Euro-Mediterranean partnership, by reaching bilateral agreements with the countries through which Africans travel en route to Europe.[59]

The background to these measures is the EU's concern about the increasing movement of sub-Saharan Africans in the Maghreb. A 2002 report from the International Labour Organisation suggested that each year some 80,000 people from various African countries, notably those beset by civil war or dictatorships, find their way to the Maghreb.[60] Some 80 per cent of these remain in Libya. Of around 16,000 who manage to reach Europe annually, some enter from the eastern side via Cyprus and Turkey, some in small boats to Italy from Tunisia and the rest by the Strait of Gibraltar or the Canaries from the coast of Morocco. Many of these desperate Africans travel to Laayoune, the capital of the disputed Western Sahara, where traffickers and smugglers hold them in tented camps in the rolling dunes of the deserts before taking them on the final stage of their journey to Spain. The EU first sought to stem this movement of sub-Saharan Africans through the introduction of electronic coastal surveillance programmes, deploying control technologies tried and tested in recent wars, such as optronic and radar technology.[61] The EU Border Control Programme led to the introduction of the Surveillance System for the Strait (SIVE), with SIVE soon extended from the Strait of Gibraltar to Ceuta and the Canary Islands. (It will eventually cover the whole of the Mediterranean Coast.) An EU coastal police force was also established, with the first maritime border project, Operation Ulysses, introduced in 2003 and involving armed vessels from Spain, Britain, France, Italy and Portugal patrolling sections of the Mediterranean coastline. As part of joint surveillance operations along the Mediterranean coast, Frontex now patrols the waters of West Africa, intercepting boats before they leave African waters.

An estimated one-third of those attempting the dangerous maritime journey die in the graveyard of the Mediterranean Sea.[62] But neither this human suffering and loss of life nor the militarisation of the EU's borders has stopped the movement of sub-Saharan Africans.[63] It has merely pushed traffickers and smugglers into seeking longer and more dangerous routes, from the northern coast of Senegal, for instance, almost 900 miles away, on a voyage that takes around eight or ten days.[64] As the 'boat people' continue to arrive on European shores, the urgency to co-opt African leaders into deportation plans grows.[65] Hence agreements with African countries for the speedy return of the 'boat people' and the co-option of African leaders into the European Pact on Immigration and Asylum.[66] A 2003 accord between Spain and Mauritania, for instance, enables Spain to deport migrants from Senegal and Mali to Mauritania. The 2004 agreement between Libya and Italy (the details of which remain secret, despite solicitations from the European Parliament) allows for the immediate return of boat people who reach Italy via Libya. Under Italy's rapid expulsion policy, boat people arriving in Italy are denied access to the UNHCR, NGOs and lawyers who could advise them on how to make an asylum claim. Instead, they are almost immediately expelled to Libya where it is virtually impossible for international organisations or human rights groups to access them.[67] (UNHCR is not recognised by the Libyan government and therefore cannot operate its protection mandate there.) From here, Libya deports them, ostensibly to their countries of origin, but many are simply dumped at the desert border. Between 1 and 7 October 2004, the Italian authorities deported a total of 1153 handcuffed migrants from various African, Asian and Middle Eastern countries on military and commercial flights to Libya, days (and in some cases as little as 24 hours) after they had arrived on Lampedusa, Italy's southernmost island. The award-winning Italian journalist Fabrizio Gatti travelled with the African deportees on a lorry from Libya to Niger, reporting that many died during the desert journey, owing to overcrowding in lorries or lack of water.[68]

Once again, the detention camp is central to the EU's expanded deportation programme. Camps on the EU's southern periphery are, typically, located near airports, on former military compounds, and are guarded by paramilitary troops. This makes it much easier to expel rapidly new arrivals to North African and other African detention camps. The temporary stay and assistance centre (CPTA) at Lampedusa, for instance, is located next to Lampedusa airport and has direct private access to the runway, forming a 'simple and discreet way of boarding migrants quickly on civil or military flights back to Africa'.[69] Countries like Libya will then be expected to detain the rejected migrants while they organise their 'reinsertion' (the term deportation is avoided in EU double speak) to their countries of origin. Crucially, though, such repatriation programmes come with either the direct or indirect support of the EU or its member states.

When it comes to Libya, the EU is extremely nervous of direct involvement in detention and repatriation programmes. AI has stated that human rights violations, including beatings with sticks and canes of migrants and asylum seekers (particularly sub-Saharan

Africans), in Libyan prisons, police stations and military camps, take place in a 'context of near impunity'.[70] Hence, the Libya-EU Joint Action Plan limits the involvement of the EU in Libyan detention facilities to the provision of health care and services. Nevertheless, it indirectly funds a deportation programme via the International Organisation for Migration (IOM), through its co-financing of the Programme for the Enhancement of Transit and Irregular Migration Management (TRIM) in Libya. Spain has directly financed the construction of several detention centres in Mauritania, at Nouadhibou, a coastal town on the north-western tip of Mauritania, and in the capital Nouakchott, where migrants, having been flown back by Spain from the Canary Islands, are held at a detention centre that is not subject to any judicial controls.[71] The Nouadhibou centre is run by the Mauritanian authorities, but meals are funded and delivered by the Spanish Red Cross and the Mauritanian Red Crescent.[72] And, in Italy, indirect (and highly secretive) support for Libyan and Tunisian detention centres was provided by the previous Berlusconi administration (2001–06). Following the bilateral agreement signed in Tripoli in August 2004, the Berlusconi government financed the construction of a detention camp for migrants in the north of Libya (Gharyan), close to the port capital Tripoli, and allocated funds for two more camps in the south, in Kufra (south-east Libya, near to the border with Egypt and Sudan) and in the city of Sebha (south-west Libya).[73] In Tunisia, Italy is believed to be working closely with the IOM, and there are allegations that migrants deported from Italy to Tunisia have been transported to the Tunisian-Algerian desert and abandoned there.

ങ ഌ

The enormity, breadth and scale of the deportation machine necessitates the formation of new alliances, which move from the local, to the pan-European to the international. There are many signs that campaigners are moving forward, from the formation of the International Coalition on Detention of Refugees, Asylum Seekers and Migrants to the launch, in April 2008, of the Euro-

African Network – a forum for productive dialogue between NGOs working in the field of migration in sub-Saharan Africa, the Maghreb and Europe.[74] At the centre of Euro-African network are grassroots campaigners from the Moroccan human rights campaign, the Beni Znassen Association for Culture, Development and Solidarity (ABCDS). ABCDS is the only organisation in Morocco offering humanitarian relief to destitute sub-Saharan African migrants who travel through Morocco in their bid to reach Europe. It has already brought together a network of Maghrebian and African NGOs, which extends from Morocco and Mauritania to Senegal and Mali. In April 2008, the ABCDS started a tour of Europe, focusing in the first instance on building links with sister organisations in France, the UK and Germany. In the words of ABCDS London Committee activist Fatiha Hajjat, 'It is time to bring humanity back in the debate, to forge solidarity from the bottom up.'[75]

6

'SPEECH CRIME' AND DEPORTATION

Throughout Europe, immigration reforms have been introduced which now tie citizenship and residence rights to constraints on freedom of speech. For those who breach these constraints, the punishment can be deportation. This chapter analyses 20 cases in which attempts have been made to fast-track 'national security' deportations through the use of immigration law in France, Germany, Italy, Poland and the Netherlands.[1] All involve Muslims, none of whom has been formally accused of involvement in any terrorist offence; 16 involve clerics or religious leaders who have been deported, or threatened with deportation, because of statements that they have made that are alleged to be anti-western, unpatriotic and against democratic rights. Most of those deported were long-term European residents, who could have been charged under existing public order laws but were not.[2]

There can be no reasonable objection to the deportation of a foreign national who incites violence and hatred, if a court rules that deportation is a proportionate response to that crime and if the deportation is in accordance with international law (in particular, the provision that no one should be sent back to a real risk of torture, the death penalty or other degrading treatment or punishment). What is of concern, however, is the lack of transparency and the evasion of due process engendered by policies of administrative expulsion. Grafting anti-terrorist measures on to immigration law avoids the usual checks and balances: duties of disclosure are limited; legal aid may not be available and the safeguards normally provided under criminal law are largely absent.

Reforms to Immigration Law

In the summer of 2004, France, Germany and Spain announced significant changes to immigration and aliens' legislation to make it easier to deport foreigners even if they had not been charged with any terrorist offence. Already, in November 2004, following the killing of controversial film-maker Theo van Gogh,[3] the Dutch government had announced that it would introduce new measures to deal with Muslim clerics who preached hate.

The French government amended the 1945 foreigners' law (which allowed for the expulsion 'in absolute emergency' of any foreigner deemed a threat to the security of the state or public safety) to include any foreigner who committed 'acts of explicit and deliberate provocation or discrimination, hatred or violence against a particular person or a group of people'.[4] The wording of the law concerned socialists and communists who opposed it on the grounds that it was so vague that it could be used as a pretext to expel people for a range of conduct unrelated to the original intention of the amendment. The German immigration law (effective from 1 January 2005) simplified the procedure for the expulsion of foreigners, so that they can now be expelled not only for proven wrong-doing, but also on basis of an 'evidence-based threat prognosis' – proof that someone committed a crime is not needed.[5] Again, civil libertarians criticised the vagueness of the law, pointing out that it provided no clear definition of a 'suspect' and that an expulsion order could be based on little more than 'speculation' or 'premonition'. Measures to revoke the citizenship of naturalised citizens linked to 'unconstitutional organisations' have also been introduced. In Spain, a reform of immigration law enables the deportation of foreigners, including long-term residents, on the basis of suspicion that they may, in the future, commit an 'outrage' against the security of the state. There are no judicial controls over who is deported and the state is under no obligation to furnish evidence against the accused.

After the London bombings of July 2005, more immigration reforms were proposed in the UK, France and Italy. First, the UK home secretary announced new guidelines for the deportation of foreign nationals who posed a security threat, which included a list of 'unacceptable behaviour' encompassing 'public speaking including preaching', 'or using a position of responsibility such as teacher, community or youth leader to express views which foment, justify or glorify terrorist violence in furtherance of particular beliefs' or 'foster hatred which might lead to inter-community violence in the UK'. The list was immediately criticised by civil liberty organisations for casting an 'unacceptably broad net' and amounting to a serious interference with the free expression rights of both foreign and UK nationals.[6] Second, the UK government introduced the Immigration and Asylum Act (2006), which (in sections 56–68) allowed for deprivation of citizenship (for dual nationals) and right of abode (for Commonwealth citizens) for those who displayed 'unacceptable behaviour'.[7] De-citizenship was also a measure favoured by the French interior ministry, which announced that following the London bombings it would have 'no problem' deporting Muslims who inflamed anti-western feeling even if they were French citizens.[8] 'I am going to launch proceedings to deprive French imams who preach violence and fundamentalism of their French nationality; systematically expel those who do not respect our values and are not French; and step up monitoring of places of worship where extremist activities have taken root,' announced the then interior minister Nicolas Sarkozy.[9] Italy, too, responded to the London bombings with new measures. A 1998 law that had allowed for administrative expulsion on national security grounds was extended at the end of July 2005 to include 'proselytism or spreading messages of extremist fundamentalism'. The power to deport was extended to regional prefects, on the grounds that they were the Ministry of Interior's chief officials in Italy's provinces.[10]

While the spur to such 'reforms' was different in each country, all the legislation is remarkably similar in that it is aimed not at those accused of any specific terrorist offence or crime, but at those who have expressed opinions that can be interpreted as pro-violence, anti-western, illiberal or even simply offensive. In this way, the definition of terrorism is being extended to include 'speech crimes'. Such a radical departure is backed by the May 2005 Council of

Europe Convention on the Prevention of Terrorism, which requires states to criminalise the direct or indirect public provocation of terrorism and/or recruitment and training for terrorism. Persons accused of such crimes are to be either tried or extradited. The Convention was agreed, despite the concerns of the Parliamentary Assembly and the Commissioner for Human Rights of the Council of Europe, who felt that it could lead to an erosion of the rights to freedom of expression and association.

The 'Preachers of Hate'

Across Europe, amendments to immigration laws have been introduced on the back of intense public attention directed at so-called preachers of hate. In the UK, the citizenship law was reformed after the press focused on the case of Abu Hamza, a notorious preacher at Finsbury Park mosque. In the Netherlands, new measures were introduced after the Dutch security services (AIVD) described the Al Fourqaan mosque in Eindhoven as one of six mosques where anti-western values were preached.[11] In France, the new law was introduced in response to the case of Abdelkader Bouziane, an imam who appealed against deportation to Algeria. Although Norway and Switzerland did not amend their immigration laws at this time, xenophobic and centre-Right parties were pressing for 'reform'. In Switzerland, Jean-René Fournier (PDC-Christian Democrat), president of the Valais cantonal government, stated that he was in favour of expelling Muslims who 'do not respect our values', which, he said, should be set out in a charter. He also called for Swiss citizenship to be withdrawn from 'fundamentalist Muslims'.[12] In Norway, Progress Party leader Carl Hagen, responding to a Norwegian government white paper on security, demanded stronger measures against groups that publicly expressed views 'that frighten the Norwegian people'.[13] More recently, in Denmark, following the 'cartoons affair', calls were made across the political spectrum for the expulsion of radical imams (including, if necessary, through revocation of citizenship). The calls were made after a group of Danish imams went to the Middle East to rally support against the *Jyllands-Posten* for publishing the cartoons. Danish People's Party leader Pia Kjærsgaard wanted the imams to be tried for treason, and demanded they be forced to sign a declaration of loyalty towards Denmark.[14] In the event, the state prosecutor found that while many of the statements the imams had made were incorrect, there was nothing illegal in what they had said and nothing that promoted violence against Denmark.[15]

In Germany, the furore over the government's attempt to deport Metin Kaplan, the leader of the fundamentalist Caliphate State organisation, provided the backdrop to mounting calls for reform. Kaplan, who had already served a prison sentence in Germany for incitement to murder, was initially reprieved by a court ruling, which stated that his extradition to Turkey was unsafe because evidence against him might have been obtained by the Turkish police's torture of his supporters, and because he faced the threat of torture and degrading treatment if handed over. Subsequently, in October 2004, the German authorities succeeded in deporting Kaplan after a higher court ruled that a written agreement obtained from the Turkish authorities was a sufficient safeguard against his being maltreated. But Kaplan's case allowed the centre-Right parties and the media to portray the Social Democrat-led coalition government as soft on terrorism. For example, Günther Beckstein, then Christian Social Union Bavarian interior minister, described the initial failure to deport Kaplan as 'one of the biggest disgraces for the secret services in years'.[16] There was also a rash of media reports on the formation of Muslim enclaves and anti-German preaching conducted in some mosques, with calls for greater integration.[17] Beckstein, campaigning against Turkey's entry into the EU and critical of Bavarian Turks for living in 'parallel societies', had already stated that Germany's 'law on aliens takes too little account of our country's security situation'.[18]

Hence, the new German immigration law that was introduced included powers to deport 'intellectual incendiaries' or leaders who publicly incited hate, violence and terrorist acts. Regional state officials did not have to seek federal approval before issuing such deportation orders. This gave powerful politicians like Beckstein licence to deport foreign nationals with virtually no judicial check on their decisions. The state of Hessen reported that, in the first two weeks of February 2005, it deported ten imams for 'preaching religious hatred'. Officials from North-Rhine Westphalia announced that they planned to deport 50 individuals, and had placed a further 20 under close surveillance.[19] Beckstein confirmed that he proposed to expel 100 'Islamic extremists' under 'Aktion Kehraus' ('Operation Sweep Out').[20] The German authorities were subsequently at the forefront of a campaign to introduce 'risk profiles'of Islamic clerics across Europe.[21] This led the European Commission to embark on an exercise to identify imams in particular mosques who preached radical Islam as, according to the then EU Justice and Home Affairs Commissioner Franco Frattini, Europe had experienced the 'misuse of mosques, which instead of being places for worship are used for other ends'.[22]

Expanding National Security Crimes

Immigration laws have always contained clauses that allowed for the deportation of foreign nationals on national security grounds. In the UK, for example, the 1971 Immigration Act allowed for the administrative deportation of foreign nationals if they were suspected of endangering national security or committing a serious criminal offence. Such administrative laws, common across Europe, tend to bypass the usual checks on state power embodied in the criminal justice system and due process. Today, the definition of what constitutes a threat to national security is being expanded to include 'speech crimes'. Espousing anti-western sentiments, questioning integration, voicing illiberal sentiments and advocating discrimination against specific groups in society may all now come under the definition of a 'national security' threat that warrants deportation.

In France, reform of immigration law was necessary, it was stated, to deal with those who gave sermons or made speeches that espoused anti-western and anti-Enlightenment values. The then interior minister Dominique de Villepin declared that: 'Today, one can no longer separate terrorist acts from the words that feed them.'[23] Thus, Salafist clerics and others have been expelled for 'proselytising in favour of a radical form of Islam'. Abdelkader Yahia Cherif, an imam in Brittany, was expelled to Algeria in April 2004, because he was alleged, among other offences, to have rejoiced at the Madrid bombings. Orhan Arslan, a preacher at the An-Nour mosque in Mulhouse (Haut-Rhin), was expelled in January 2004 for 'making anti-Semitic and anti-western comments'. Similarly, Midhat Güler, the director of a Paris mosque, was accused of delivering sermons that incited hatred of western societies and of Israel, and allowing Islamic newspapers that glorified *jihad* to be circulated in a prayer room. And Abdullah Cam, deported in September 2005, was accused of using words in his sermons that 'vilify the French state, Western governments and Israel, inciting the faithful to [adopt] a communal response and to [carry out] civil disobedience'.[24] In April 2004, the deportation of Abdelkader Bouziane, the 54-year-old imam at the Al-Furqan mosque in Venissieux, a suburb of Lyon, was carried out after the newspaper *Lyon Mag* published an interview with him in which he was quoted as saying that the Qur'an authorised men to beat their wives and that the stoning of women was permissible. The most recent French case involves Ilyes Hacène, the 38-year-old imam of the Créteil mosque who is a French naturalised citizen (in order to deport Hacène to Algeria it would be necessary to strip him of his citizenship). The intelligence services accused him of commitment to Salafism, preaching 'ideology inciting discrimination, hatred and violence against the Western world and Jews', particularly of Israel and the US. He was further accused of calling on Muslims to pray 'for the mujahideens of Palestine, Iraq, Chechnya and Afghanistan'.[25]

Comparable 'speech crimes' have led to the deportation of Muslim clerics from Italy and Germany. In January 2007, Mohammed Kohaila was expelled from Italy to Morocco after it was alleged that he had made anti-western statements while delivering a sermon at a Turin mosque. In Bremen, in February 2005, a 43-year-old Egyptian imam was identified in the media as a 'preacher of hate', and even though the public prosecutor's office confirmed that it had no evidence on which to base a prosecution, he was deported, seemingly because he had called on Muslims to defend their religion against the 'evils of imperialism'.[26] In Berlin, the constitutional court ordered that Yakup Tasci, imam of the Mevlana mosque, Kreuzberg, be deported on the grounds that he represented a serious danger to public safety. It cited a speech in which he was said to have glorified Islamic martyrs in Iraq and Jerusalem and, in the form of a poem, suggested suicide attacks in Germany.[27] Another case involved Salem El R., the imam of the Al-Nur mosque in Berlin, who was alleged to have said: 'May God protect the mujaheddin in Chechnya, Palestine and Iraq. ... May God let a tornado sweep away the enemies of Islam, smash them and destroy them.'[28]

In the Netherlands, in 2005, the interior minister Rita Verdonk also sought to use immigration law to facilitate the speedy deportation of 'undesirable aliens' who posed a threat to public order and national security. She had her eye on three imams at the Al Fourqaan mosque in Eindhoven, accused by the AIVD of 'contributing to the radicalisation of Muslims in the Netherlands', 'recruiting or tolerating the recruiting of Muslims for jihad' and 'using their sermons to urge Muslims to isolate themselves from Dutch society'.[29] In fact, in November 2006, the court ruled that the expulsion of one of the imams, Eisha Bershma to the Sudan, was unlawful. While the AIVD had shown that the Al Fourqaan mosque in Eindhoven was a breeding ground for militants, it could not be shown that Eisha Berhsma had played an active role.[30]

Youcef Mammery of the Marseille Council of Muslims identifies working-class, badly educated Muslim communities as the real target of these measures. As he noted: 'There are very orthodox people in all religions, who live life on the margins of modern society.'[31] Islamic organisations and the Human Rights League all condemn the hot-tempered rhetoric of badly educated Muslim clerics, but they also defend their right to be afforded the same access to justice as those from other communities. Mammery added that 'extreme doesn't necessarily mean dangerous'. Pointing to the case of Bouziane, he observed that the imam 'wasn't very clever but it wouldn't be fair to say he was dangerous'. He argued that litigation, not expulsion, was the answer to any alleged public order offences.[32]

Previously, the response to crimes of incitement had been to bring charges under public order laws. But the use of administrative expulsion instead of public order legislation means that Muslim clerics are being excluded from the ordinary rule of law. They and they alone are being enclosed within a parallel, shadow justice system that is operated through immigration law, has a lower standard of proof and delivers harsher punishments for those deemed guilty. To date, only Muslims have been caught up in this parallel justice system. Thus, clerics deemed a threat to European values are denied access to the full protection of the European Convention of Human Rights (ECHR), which guarantees the right to a fair trial; to be presumed innocent until proven guilty; to be informed promptly and in detail of the nature and basis of an accusation; and to examine or have examined witnesses against them.

The Role of the Media

Because the threat that these individuals are said to pose derives not from deeds but from words – threatening national security through inflammatory speeches and sermons – the issue of 'credible evidence' is crucial. But the evidence presented against those facing 'national security' deportations is rarely based on more than newspaper articles that quote inflammatory (or merely offensive) statements, or simply regurgitate the views of unnamed security sources. There is little opportunity to challenge possible misrepresentations. For example, when Abdelkader Yahia Cherif was accused by the French intelligence services of rejoicing over the Madrid bombings, they cited comments made during a sermon and a newspaper interview. But his lawyers publicly disputed the allegation that he 'rejoiced' at the Madrid bombings, stating that what he actually said was that there was no 'absolute proof that Islamists were involved in either the September 11 or the March 11 attacks'.[33] Similarly, Abdelkader Bouziane's lawyers argued that extracts from a newspaper article did not accurately reflect his views, pointing out that the 90-minute interview on which it was based was quoted selectively, that the imam spoke poor French and that his comments were seriously distorted.[34] The security services also claimed that Bouziane, following military intervention in Iraq, called during a sermon for a *jihad* against American interests in France. (It should be pointed out that when sermons are delivered in Arabic, the evidence cited by the intelligence services is not direct speech but a translation.) In respect of Bouziane's views on political violence, his lawyers argued that the *Lyon Mag* journalist accurately represented his views, quoting him as saying that he did not want 'to raise his voice, strike or attempt to assassinate anyone in order to convert people to Islam' and that 'it is a great sin to plant a bomb because Allah is angered when innocents are killed'.[35]

In four other cases, from Germany and Italy, the media seemed to be actively engaged in seeking deportation orders on the grounds that the imams were 'preachers of hate' who threatened integration. Two cases rested on documentary evidence provided by televisions stations. A German television station sent undercover journalists to the mosque of Berlin cleric Yakup Tasci and filmed the cleric criticising Germans for being unclean: Germans were, he suggested, dirty and sweaty because they did not shave under their armpits. It was only after this television programme was aired that the senator for internal affairs supported Tasci's deportation for 'seriously endangering public safety and order' and placing in danger the 'peaceful coexistence between Germans and non-Germans'. Lawyers for Tasci appealed on the grounds that some of the statements ascribed to him by the Aliens Office were either wrongly interpreted or taken out of context, while others were never made at all.[36] Similar factors seemed to be at play in Italy, where the deportation of Turin cleric Mohammed Kohaila was approved after a RAI TV documentary programme was broadcast in March 2006. But the documentary, which also used hidden cameras to film Kohaila's sermons, was later criticised by the Turin public prosecutor, who found that a voice-over had misled viewers as to the true nature of the sermon, which contained 'no appeal for holy war, no apology for terrorism and no incitement to law-breaking'.[37]

In another Italian case, Abdel Qader Fadlallah Mamour, an imam in Turin, was deported to Senegal hours after giving an interview to a newspaper in which he warned that if Italian troops were not pulled out of Iraq, there could be a bomb attack in Rome (he also claimed to know Osama bin Laden).[38] Abdul Karim al-Tibsi, a teacher of Arabic and Islam at the Islamic Centre in Rome and a member of the Union of Arab Communities in Italy, was expelled in April 2005 after an Italian newspaper ran an article by an Arab journalist claiming he was a member of a terrorist organisation. The newspaper article appeared the day after al-Tibsi had led prayers in memory of Sheikh Ahmad Yassin, the Hamas spiritual leader assassinated by an Israeli missile attack in Palestine.[39]

Evidence Based on Secret Intelligence

Untested evidence presented by the security services does not constitute 'credible evidence'. In the case of Ahmed Ammar, a Yemeni national deported from Poland in June 2005, the decision was made by the Internal Security Agency, which refused to reveal the grounds for its decision.[40] In France, administrative tribunals have not been provided with wiretap evidence, witness testimony or other material evidence to justify the deportation of the accused. Instead, evidence takes the form of confidential notes issued by the intelligence services, commonly known as *notes blanches* because they are not signed or dated and do not cite sources. In the case of Midhat Güler, director of a Paris mosque, the only security service evidence against him was a *note blanche*, which did not implicate him in terrorist acts but accused him of inciting hatred of western societies and of Israel in his sermons. *Notes blanches* also comprised the evidence against imam Abdelkader Bouziane. According to the government commissioner for the case in the Council of State, one of these 'limits itself to making assertions'; another comprises a discussion of Salafism, while a third, though more detailed, still does not provide 'any ... specific act, any date,

any name ... to support the allegations' made.[41] The deportation
to Algeria of Yousef Mahlili, an imam from Bilbao who moved to
Mourenx to preach in a town close to the French-Spanish border,
was based on a security service assessment that his sermons had
become increasingly radical and critical of Spain, following the
Spanish decision to send troops to Iraq.[42] And in Germany, it was
the evidence of an agent from the Office for the Defence of the
Constitution that led to the deportation of the Berlin imam Salem
El R., for making inflammatory speeches.[43]

No Meaningful Right of Appeal

It is normally on the instructions of the interior minister that
expulsion against those accused of threatening national security
through 'speech crimes' is made. A fair system would establish
a meaningful right of appeal against this executive power, with
appeal taking place prior to deportation. But in cases documented
here from France, Italy and the Netherlands, individuals faced with
rapid deportation procedures following a ministerial expulsion
order only had the right to launch an appeal *after* deportation.
And even that is not a guarantee of due process. Although a
regional court in Lazio ruled Abdel Qadar Fadlallah Mamour's
deportation illegal, as he had merely expressed what amounted to
'personal views', he had already been deported to Senegal and the
Italian interior minister ruled out the possibility of any return.[44]
Similarly, when Dutch interior minister Rita Verdonk told three
imams from Rotterdam to leave the country, or be expelled, they
were told that while though they had a month to launch an appeal,
they could not stay in the Netherlands pending its outcome.[45]

Human Rights Watch has mounted a sustained critique of the
French procedure where the lack of an automatic appeal against
expulsion (during which expulsion is suspended) and misuse of the
expedited procedure have created a situation in which individuals
facing deportation do not have access to any effective remedy.[46]
The interior minister can expedite administrative expulsion by
citing 'absolute urgency' and in so doing bypass consultation with
the Expulsion Commission comprised of two judicial magistrates

and one administrative magistrate, in a hearing at which the
person subject to expulsion and his or her lawyer can participate.
Rapid expulsion, on the say so of the interior minister alone, is
also in contradiction with the *non-refoulement* principle, which
states that no one should be returned to a situation where they face
torture or cruel or degrading treatment. The imam Abdelkader
Bouziane was in fact deported to Algeria, where the use of torture
is well-documented, twice.[47] At Algiers airport, following his
initial deportation in April 2004, Bouziane found himself placed
in a van and taken to an unknown location where he was held
for interrogation for seven days. During this time his family had
no idea of his whereabouts and he was prohibited from using
the telephone.[48]

While Germany and the UK do allow a pre-deportation right
of appeal, crucially it can only be exercised via special procedures
and special courts. Germany has set up a special panel within the
Federal Administrative Court in Karlsruhe as the sole court of
appeal in national security expulsion cases that seems to be based
on the UK's Special Immigration Appeals Commission (SIAC). Set
up in 1997, and formally a 'superior court of record',[49] SIAC is
the sole court of appeal for foreigners living in Britain whom the
home secretary wants to deport on national security grounds, but
evidence on whose cases is considered too sensitive for disclosure
in open court. Following the Anti-Terrorism Crime and Security
Act (2001), which greatly extended SIAC's remit,[50] the workings
of SIAC fell into disrepute, and it became seen as little more
than a 'rubber stamp' for decisions already made by the home
secretary. While some of SIAC's proceedings are held in open
sessions where the appellant and his solicitor are present, others
take place in closed sessions where there is no opportunity for
them to test evidence, and the presumption of innocence does not
apply. Indeed, neither the appellant nor his solicitor can attend
these closed sessions; instead, the interests of the accused are
represented by a 'special advocate' drawn from a panel of lawyers
given security clearance at a level allowing them access to the
classified evidence.[51] Once the special advocate has seen or heard
secret evidence denied to the appellant, he is barred from contact

with the appellant or his lawyers. In 2007 in Norway, the Police Special Branch (PST) called for the introduction of a similar kind of special committee within the Aliens Board where foreigners would be represented by lawyers vetted by the state.[52]

Guilt by Association

For the security services, an indicator of 'threat' is that a person has associated with other suspected wrong-doers, terrorist suspects or their associates. This is very much in accord with post-September 11 counter-terrorism measures which extended the definition of terrorism from concrete acts of extreme violence to 'any form of support' for terrorism, 'active or passive'. In an open court of law, the chances of a successful prosecution based on association with a suspected wrong-doer, without any corroborative evidence of 'conspiracy to commit acts preparatory to violence', would be slim. But fast-track deportations of foreigners via immigration powers bypass open courts and due process.

It is true that, where established, administrative tribunals can provide some checks. In the case of Abdelkader Bouziane, for instance, the French administrative tribunal refused to accept in evidence classified documents, submitted by the interior minister, which linked Bouziane to Salafist groups. And in the case of the Eindhoven imam, Eisha Bershma, as already noted, the courts ruled his deportation unlawful on the grounds that no concrete evidence had been put forward to prove his association with known militants.[53] But the deportations of other Muslims have been justified on the vague grounds of association with terrorists. Abdelkader Yahia Cherif, who was seeking political asylum in France at the time of his expulsion to Algeria, was accused of 'active relations with national or international Islamic movements that are in relation with organisations advocating terrorist acts'.[54] Vague accusations made against Ilyes Hacène include association with Salafists and commitment to a 'Salifi ideology'. Hacène has the support of the Union of Muslim Associations in Crèteil and Dalil Boubakeur, rector of the Paris mosque, who described him as an 'open, moderate young man'. Many in the Muslim community believed that the imam, who had no 'Salafist commitment', had fallen victim to a family dispute.[55]

When crimes of association are created, whole communal, friendship or political networks can become stigmatised as 'associated with terrorism'. As Jean-Jacques de Felice, an attorney who had acted in numerous cases, put it, 'You are the cousin of the cousin of the cousin of someone who's done something, so you are in an *association de malfaiteurs.*' Midhat Güler, a sewing supplies salesman and director of a Paris mosque, was accused by the security services of being an associate of the Cologne imam Metin Kaplan (see above) and founder of the Caliphate movement in France. But his lawyers denied the accusations, saying that while Güler knew Metin Kaplan, he was merely a family friend and Güler had no political link with him or with the Caliphate State.[56] Similarly, Abdullah Cam, the Turkish national expelled from France in September 2005, was accused by the French intelligence services of association with Omer Ozturk and Orhan Arslan, two other alleged followers of Metin Kaplan.[57] In Bremen, an imam of Egyptian descent who had condemned the 'evils of imperialism' (see above) was accused by the security services of links with a Turkish national held at Guántanamo Bay and with a German-Lebanese citizen who, at the age of 17, hijacked a bus in Bremen.[58]

In some countries, national security exceptions to the legal protections against forced removal mean that anyone can be removed, even if they have lived in the country for their entire lives. Muslim religious leaders deported under these provisions have not come recently to Europe; nor were they, like Nation of Islam leader Louis Farrakhan, entering Europe from outside for a limited speaking tour. Most of the cases considered here involve Muslims who have lived in Europe for years, decades even, some have married EU citizens and most have children born there. Abdelkader Bouziane, who had 16 children, had lived in France for 25 years on a renewable residence permit, while Abdullah Cam, who had four children, had lived in France for almost 20 years before his expulsion in September 2005. Midhat Güler had lived in France since 1976; Abdul Karim al-Tibsi had been legally resident in Italy for twelve years; and Ahmed Ammar had been resident in Poland for 14 years. As such, they should enjoy civil rights of residents, including freedom of speech and assembly and be entitled to safeguards under the ECHR that protect the right to family and private life. The ECHR holds that expulsion, which separates someone from his or her family and severs links built up in the country of residence, must be proportionate to a legitimate aim, such as protecting national security or the prevention of crime or disorder. In the past, the European Court of Human Rights has ruled against deporting immigrants who have served prison sentences for serious crimes, on the grounds that such deportation would be disproportionate (a form of double punishment) and a violation of the right to family life. But when Muslim clerics are denied due process, this principle of 'proportionality' also falls.

Political Pressure

Sometimes deportation is linked to the need to satisfy the demands of partners in the international coalition against terrorism. Since 2001, the US has been pressing the European Commission to ease the laws on extradition of terrorist suspects and 'explore alternatives to extradition including expulsion and deportation'. Three deportations from Germany appear to have been undertaken after pressure from the US and Israel. Two of these deportations involved Lebanese men who were long-term residents in Germany and linked to Hizbollah. An unnamed representative of Hizbollah, who had lived in Germany for 20 years on a renewable residence permit, was told that he had to leave the country because he was 'a member of an organization that supports international terrorism'.[59] (Only the military wing of Hizbollah, which had seven seats in the Lebanese parliament at that time, was on the EU list of terrorist organisations. Nevertheless, in its annual report Germany's domestic security agency cited 850 members of Hizbollah living in Germany as constituting a threat.[60]) A German court refused to countenance the unnamed man's appeal on the grounds that Hizbollah was 'waging a war with bomb attacks against Israel with inhumane brutality and against citizens'.[61] In the second case, one Fadi Madi was deported for his 'anti-Israel and anti-US stance', after organising a conference in Berlin that the Simon Wiesenthal Center in Israel had lobbied the German government to ban. Subsequently, an investigation was launched by the German authorities into Madi's 'membership of questionable organisations'.[62] The final case that merits a mention involves the deportation of an unnamed Jordanian national living in North-Rhine Westphalia, who was expelled on the grounds that he had formerly been head of the Al-Aksa group. He was also suspected of collecting donations in Germany to support the Palestinian group Hamas and, by doing so, had violated Germany's 'spirit of seeking understanding among peoples'.[63]

In Cyprus, the deportation of ten Pakistani students in July 2005 was likely to have been carried out in order to appease the US, which had just issued a warning that foreign interests on the island could be targets for an attack. There was widespread consternation when the ten young men, described by their college's director as 'excellent students', were arrested and linked to al Qaida by the Cypriot media. But the interior minister refused to comment on the arrests, citing national security concerns.[64] The deportation of Abdul Karim al-Tibsi from Italy may well have involved pressure from Algeria, another key ally in the International Coalition Against Terrorism. As previously noted, Abdul Karim al-Tibsi was deported from Italy after an Arab journalist published an article alleging that he had terrorist links. (It is not unknown for the Algerian security services to spread disinformation about dissidents via a steady trickle of accusations in the press emanating from unnamed security sources.) Similarly, the deportation to Yemen of Ahmed Ammar, who was studying for a doctorate on Islamic law in Poland, may have been ordered for political reasons; the internal security agency refused to give details of his alleged crimes, but Ammar contended that the motive was his opposition to the presence of Polish troops in Iraq.[65]

Domestically, too, fast-track deportations under immigration law are politically expedient. Deporting a terrorist suspect to a country like Egypt, Algeria, Morocco or Turkey is a convenient alternative to either bringing charges under local anti-terrorist laws or embarking on the process of extradition to another country. Extradition in particular is a lengthy process with in-built legal safeguards, which, crucially, give lawyers and human rights activists time and opportunity to challenge the order.[66] Deporting someone via immigration laws, on the other hand, removes these safeguards.

Of course, there is an apparent logic to the argument that, following the Madrid and London bombings, the pronouncements of fundamentalist Muslim clerics were so dangerous that reforms were needed to allow for deportations. But any law that discriminates between one section of citizens and another and refuses basic due process rights and processes to those it wants to remove undermines democracy and can alienate the very community whose support is most vital to the stamping out of terror.

The Fight for Civil Rights

7

THEY ARE CHILDREN TOO

There is no such thing as your children and my children. Children are children are children. They are the measure of our possibilities; how we treat them is the measure of our humanity. The moment we categorise them as foreign is the moment we lose both.

A. Sivanandan[1]

Today, at the start of the twenty-first century, the industrialised nations of Europe are rich enough to ensure that no child should face hunger or destitution, sexual exploitation or brutality and violence in state orphanages and institutions. Yet the benefits of our child protection laws are denied to asylum-seeking children when they are treated as extensions of adults. In the years to come, the new counter-movements that have been formed to protect children from the violence inherent in detention and deportation policies will surely come to be seen as a key moment in the struggle against xeno-racist laws. As European governments violate the 'best interests of the child' principle of international law, by placing immigration control above the needs of children,[2] the children's rights lobby has mobilised to form national and European consortia, and alliances such as the Separated Children in Europe Programme (SERP).[3] At a grassroots level, new national umbrella organisations, such as Réseau Education Sans Frontières in France and Belgium, have emerged, as have spontaneous anti-deportation initiatives carried out by residents' committees, teachers and schoolchildren, the medical profession and cultural activists.

Together they are kick-starting campaigns for refugee, migrant and children's rights. This is a fight-back that, by establishing that a child is a child no matter what part of the world he or she comes from, challenges the racism (inherent in public discourse) that denies asylum seekers and *sans papiers* individuality and human dignity. And by forcing the media to acknowledge the real reasons for migration and flight, the new campaigns reconnect Europeans with their own history of combating poverty, authoritarianism and displacement. Such grassroots initiatives are not ideologically driven (they often start in small, practical ways, and are motivated by the simple human impulse to protect children and young people), yet campaign literature often deploys the language of resistance against Nazi deportation tactics. A political continuum can be established, stretching back from the anti-deportation and civil disobedience movements of today to the resistance movements that emerged in occupied Europe during the Nazi period.

Reclaiming Children's Rights

When it comes to immigration and asylum, there is only one law, which immigration services would like to see applied to children as to adults. The UK Childrens Act (2004), for example, specifically exempts immigration and asylum services from the positive duty placed on all other statutory bodies to protect the welfare of children.[4] In a climate where governments stubbornly refuse to introduce a children's perspective into the law, one of the first moves by the children's rights lobby has been to reclaim foreign children's right to a childhood by challenging the application on children of asylum determination processes and removal processes designed for adults. For the fundamental principles of the Children's Convention, that in all decision-making governments should prioritise the 'best interests of the child', cannot be observed when the purpose of asylum legislation is to deter asylum claims and expel a fixed quota of failed asylum seekers of whatever age.

The UN Convention on the Rights of the Child (COROC) is further undermined when the 'culture of disbelief' that grows up among immigration services towards adult asylum-seeking applicants is applied, unthinkingly, to unaccompanied and separated children.[5] The age of these children is constantly disputed by immigration officials, leading, in some cases, to children being wrongly classified as adults, detained or left destitute as they are deprived of the administrative and judicial safeguards afforded children.[6] And even when the authorities accept that unaccompanied children are indeed minors, because of their immigration status, they are offered a standard of care inferior to that which native-born orphaned or abandoned children are entitled.

But it is detention, whether of unaccompanied/separated children or children in families, that is regarded by the children's rights lobby as the most serious breach of a state's responsibility towards children,[7] even a form of officially sanctioned child abuse.[8] As European governments expand the criteria for detaining families, particularly in pre-deportation detention, more and more children are being detained, sometimes for lengthy periods. In some southern European countries, such as Spain, Italy and Greece, where the authorities do not have adequate reception facilities to deal with unaccompanied children, many lone children survive in primitive conditions, more akin to detention than reception, in clear violation of internationally recognised rights. Successive children's ombudsmen in Greece have accused the government of treating unaccompanied minors like common criminals. Ombudsman George Karminis gave examples of children as young as twelve who had been detained for weeks and even months in concrete cells and other prison-like facilities that were completely bare except for bedding.[9] By the summer of 2008, as desperate Afghan children detained on the island of Leros staged a hunger-strike to draw attention to their miserable existence,[10] the situation had become explosive. Unaccompanied children returned to Greece from other EU states under the Dublin regulations (which hold that the asylum claim of a refugee must be heard in the first country that asylum seekers arrive in) are treated by the Greek authorities as having abandoned their asylum claim, and are not looked after. In 2008, Germany suspended the Dublin regulations as they apply to unaccompanied children travelling from Greece. Similar action has also been taken by Sweden and Norway.

The situation in Spain is little better. Maltreatment and neglect of 931 minors, mostly from Senegal and Morocco, including violence and sexual harassment, was so rife in four poor and overcrowded emergency reception centres in the Spanish Canary Islands that, in July 2007, Human Rights Watch issued a report revealing that the children received just three hours' education a week, barely any health care, and sometimes were fed just bread and water. A special punishment cell was in operation at the La Esperanza centre in Tenerife where locked-up children were not allowed to go to the toilet and forced to urinate and defecate on the floor.[11]

In response to such degradations, a European Coalition Against the Detention and Forced Removal of Minors has been formed.[12] Hundreds of thousands of people across Europe support its principles, signing petitions against the detention of children and lobbying MPs. Utilising slogans like 'No place for a child' and 'Protection, not prison for children', campaigners are demanding an entirely different legislative framework that is child-centred. Such is the momentum of the movement that children's and prisons' ombudsmen are now in open support, with the UK Chief Inspector of Prisons, Anne Owers, declaring in July 2006 that the Yarl's Wood Immigration Removal Centre in Bedfordshire needed 'a complete overhaul of the detention of children, informed by a proper understanding of the vulnerability of children and the safeguards required in domestic and international law'.[13] And there have been significant legal victories too. In Belgium, for instance, when five-year-old Congolese girl Tabitha Mitunga was detained at the airport in transit to rejoin her refugee mother in Canada, separated from her uncle, and held alongside adults for two months before being deported to DRC, campaigners took her case all the way to the European Court of Human Rights. The Court issued a damning indictment of Belgium's detention policies and held the child's treatment was inhuman and degrading both for the child herself and for her mother.[14]

But it is not just detention that breeds inhumanity towards children. The entire target-driven removal process has coarsened the culture within immigration services; ignoring the vulnerability of children inevitably leads to justifying the use of force against children in the name of preserving the integrity of the asylum system. But the use of force can be a step too far, in the eyes of some sections of the public, at least. In April 2004, there was an outcry in Sweden when national television broadcast video footage of 15-year-old Anisa Muric, barefoot and without her glasses, crying and screaming as she was restrained and forced into a police riot van.[15] There was further revulsion in 2005, and calls for the resignation of the head of the immigration services, when it emerged that immigration staff had officially celebrated the deportation of asylum-seeking families with sick children by parties where coffee and cake, and in one case, champagne were served.[16]

Such cases can become national issues if exposed in the media or the arts. One of the consequences of the deportation machine has been the harnessing of television, theatre, children's literature and music to the refugee cause. Sweden's callous treatment of the so-called 'apathetic children' (asylum-seeking children facing deportation who have become apathetic and withdrawn, often refusing to eat, drink, talk, walk and care for themselves) was exposed by a hard-hitting investigative report for Swedish Television (STV) on 18 December 2006.[17] Two of the UK's best-known actresses, Juliet Stevenson and Harriet Walters, performed in the play Motherland after visiting Yarl's Wood detention centre and hearing of the plight of women and children held there.[18] And in the Netherlands, over a thousand film-makers initiated the extraordinary film-documentary experience, 'The 26,000 Faces Project', which involved filming individual asylum seekers' stories, which were then broadcast in a rolling series on prime-time television.[19] In Sweden, the SVT television station devoted a whole evening to programmes about refugees, and some of the most celebrated pop artists brought out an album, the proceeds of which were given to asylum seekers in hiding.

In fact, members of the public often react to individual stories concerning refugee children in positive ways, and sections of the national media normally hostile to asylum seekers often adopt a different framework when it comes to reporting on the stories of individual children. Frequently it is because of the dedication of campaigners that these become human-interest stories, with children evoking sympathy not hatred. And in many of these cases, those campaigners are either the child deportees themselves or their school friends, in whom the seeds of defiance against inhumane government policies have been sown. In the case of higher education student Olukunle Elunkanlo, who came to Ireland aged 14, and was deported back to Nigeria aged 19, even though he had not completed his studies, fellow students at Palmerstown community school launched such a vociferous campaign that within a month the minister of justice had been shamed into issuing a six-month visa allowing the young man to return to Ireland to sit his final school exams. Eighteen-year-old, Taida Pakic, a Serbian Muslim from Kosovo, who came to the Netherlands aged twelve, one day found herself removed from her classroom in handcuffs. A petition against her removal was signed by 70,000 people, with sections of the public openly criticising interior minister Rita Verdonk for showing such intransigence against a young girl who only wanted to stay long enough in the country to sit the exams that could give her a future. And Viennese protesters took to the streets to support 15-year-old Arigona Zogaj, whose Muslim-Kosovan family were separated when her four brothers and father were deported (her mother, who suffered a nervous breakdown at the airport, could not be removed). Having avoided the deportation police, Arigona was given sanctuary by a Catholic priest. In hiding, she issued a video message that was broadcast on national television in which she threatened to commit suicide if her family were not reunited.[20] Even newspapers that traditionally took a hard line on immigration ended up supporting the reunification of the Zogaj family. 'The gripping plea of the teenager has succeeded in doing what years of human rights campaigners failed to achieve, compelling the media and politicians from across the spectrum to take sides with the family and demand a "humane solution" to deportation', commented *The Times* on 11 October 2007.

Establishing Continuities

> Europe is still a stone wilderness and the smoke which has since long lifted from the last war still discloses a shattered continent. Where it is not shattered physically, it is hurt within its mind and its courage for life. The child groping his way out of the ruins must make his way to life now in this Europe.[21]

With these evocative words, UNESCO launched its 1949 photo-study, *The Children of Europe*. Formed in 1945 to connect us with the intellectual and moral solidarity of mankind, UNESCO, just like UNICEF (1946), was set up at a time of massive turmoil, when Europe was a heaving mass of people on the move, facing famine and disease. Hundreds of thousands of Europeans displaced during the Second World War were still squatting in makeshift camps, leading to the formation of the UNHCR in 1950 and the signing of the Refugee Convention in 1951.[22] A generation of children had been severely damaged by war, left illiterate, disabled or emotionally broken.

War had also given rise to an orphaned generation of juvenile delinquents who had survived the war through living in cellars and worse. 'But there is another reaching and another darkness: the delinquent, the lost, the orphaned', UNESCO reminded the public. 'Left alone, they reach out in the ways they know best. And where there is no encouragement, energy and new strength, they go an old way – the road through the juvenile court into the reformatory.'[23] Profoundly affected by UNESCO's *The Children of Europe*, Ian Serraillier, a pacifist and Quaker teacher at Midhurst Grammar School in Sussex, penned the classic children's adventure story *The Silver Sword*. With its unforgettable portrait of the delinquent orphan Jan, Serraillier provided children with a frank account of war and its by-products, juvenile delinquency and forced migration.[24]

The reconstruction of Europe and resettlement of its child victims after the war needed determination and idealism. Today's Europe too, facing the impact of globalisation, neoliberalism and displacement of peoples, needs that kind of humanitarian regeneration. But politicians and immigration officials are proving themselves either ignorant of or calloused to the reasons for the displacement of children. Across much of the world, it is children who suffer most from war, disease, HIV/AIDS as well as the catastrophic economic effects of neoliberal ideology and the enforced imposition of market economies in the name of globalisation.[25] Save the Children estimates that there are as many as 100,000 unaccompanied refugee children living in Europe today. In an analysis of the cases of 218 unaccompanied/ separated children, Save the Children (UK) established that the main motivations for flight included: fear of child torture; the impact of armed conflict in which 300,000 child soldiers are estimated to be involved; sexual exploitation of girls being trafficked into the European sex industry; death, imprisonment or disappearance of parents in the home country.[26] Certainly, in comparison to Europe's wealth and resources, the number of separated/unaccompanied children who need specialist care within the asylum system, or of foreign children, arriving in Europe abandoned and destitute, is small. Yet politicians turn a blind eye when these vulnerable young people join the ranks of the homeless, either because their age is in dispute or, because, on reaching the age of 18, the permission to stay in Europe that they enjoyed as minors is removed, or because, in the case of the Moroccan street children of Spain, they run away from official reception centres.

Mercifully, though, there are some officials now challenging the myopic and narrow-minded thinking of politicians. For example, the Council of Europe wants more to be done to address the problems of a new generation of 'young vagrants'. In France, 'most are young people from North Africa and Eastern Europe', writes Alvaro Gil-Robles, Commissioner for Human Rights. He continues:

> The overwhelming majority of these children are lost, have little sense of identity and lead a completely hand-to-mouth existence on the streets. Not surprisingly, they become delinquents or, worse still, victims of prostitution networks.[27]

Only a minuscule fraction of the world's orphaned, abandoned or separated children make it to Europe; their presence should evoke curiosity and sympathy. Instead, governments want them to disappear. Against expert advice, as well as legal safeguards, European governments are embarking on new special returns programmes for unaccompanied minors that have but a thin veneer of legitimacy. A central plank of these policies is return to institutionalised care abroad. The Spanish government, for instance, announced in 2007 that it would construct two 'reception centres' in Moroccan territory, and the regional governments of Catalunya and the Canary Islands announced similar plans. Around 2000 unaccompanied children arrived on the islands of Sicily and Lampedusa in 2007, prompting Italy also to consider a Spanish-style solution. It was in 2005 that the UK Home Office first issued proposals for the return of unaccompanied children to Vietnam, despite the fact that Vietnam is recognised as a source country for child trafficking.[28] Now the UK Border Agency (the new name for the Home Office's Immigration Directorate) wants to completely overhaul the treatment of unaccompanied children, introducing an Assisted Voluntary Return programme for failed child asylum seekers, and the enforced return of children who refuse voluntary return under the programme.[29] And in the Netherlands, where over 5000 unaccompanied children applied for asylum during the Angolan civil war, Angolan children are now returned to what is considered a Dutch 'safe zone' at the Dutch-financed Mulemba orphanage in Luanda.[30] Academic Joris van Wijk warned that, as of May 2005, only one Angolan child deported from the Netherlands had actually taken shelter at this state orphanage. Nevertheless, unaccompanied children from

Angola applying for asylum in the Netherlands are now being denied protection because of the orphanage's existence.[31]

Once again governments reach for solutions to the problems posed by the presence of foreign children that simply would not be considered for the children of 'natives'. Many children's homes in western Europe were phased out after the pioneering work of child psychologists revealed the damaging effects of large-scale residential institutions on the development of children, as well as substandard health care and frequent abuse (including sexual abuse) of children by staff and older inmates. All those involved in development work, as well as those who have followed the scandals in state orphanages in Central and Eastern Europe, know that return to orphanages abroad is no answer.[32] A child is a child no matter what region of the world s/he comes from, say UNICEF and Save the Children. It is up to governments to seek durable solutions to the problems of the world's displaced children, and solutions that abide by the international principle that no child should be returned to their country unless the conditions of effective family reunion are met.

Solidarity from Below

But opposition to the treatment of children does not just come from the big NGOs and the organised children's lobby. The most significant development to date has been the coming together of local residents to form grassroots solidarity committees, daily patrols to protect families from immigration 'snatch squads' and anti-deportation campaigns. They come together spontaneously over a local case, but then link up with national coordinating movements like the National Coalition of Anti-Deportation Campaigns (NCADC, UK), Réseau Education Sans Frontières (RESF, France and Belgium), the Swedish Network of Asylum and Refugee Groups (FARR), Solidarité sans Frontières (SSF, Switzerland) the Spanish Commission for Refugee Assistance (CEAR) and the Association for Human Rights in Andalucia, as well as the Euro-wide noborder network, with its rallying cry 'No One Is Illegal'.[33]

It is organisations such as these that are reinvigorating Europe's humanitarian tradition and breathing fresh life into degraded concepts such as solidarity. More than any other action, it has been the sudden violence of arrest by a large number of immigration and police officers in the early hours of the morning that has made visible what was previously hidden. Students are deeply affected when they go to school, only to find a schoolmate has disappeared overnight; teachers are angered too by the impact the sudden removal of a child has on the school environment.[34] It is in the educational environment that the injustice and cruelty of the distinction between foreign and native children is made palpable. As Christian Lapp, a student on Frankfurt Municipal Pupil's Council put it, 'They are our friends, we are learning with them and from them – and then from one day to the next, they're torn from the class and flown to a country whose language they often don't even know.'[35] Or as Amal Azzudin, one of the 'Glasgow Girls' (see below) stated, as she reflected on the dawn raid that led to the arrest of her 15-year-old schoolfriend: 'The dawn raid shook a lot of families, a lot of children were scared.' The school 'hall was full of children crying because they were so scared'. Not just asylum-seeking children, 'but also "indigenous" Scottish children, they were crying and scared thinking our friends have just disappeared'.[36]

The result is the mobilisation of schoolchildren against deportation. English pupils at Mayfield school in Portsmouth, angered by the removal of schoolmate Lorin Sulaiman to Yarl's Wood removal centre, immediately mobilised, and with some success. (The Home Office eventually agreed to review the case, granting permission for the family to stay in Britain for two years.) Within a day of the detention of Amin Buratee at Dover Removal Centre, the entire sixth form at Canterbury High School had mobilised to secure the release of an Afghan teenager who had fled to the UK after losing all his family. They held vigils outside the centre, wrote press releases, gave newspaper interviews, appeared on local radio and television and lobbied their MPs, eventually securing permission for Amin to stay in the country to sit his exams.[37] Out of such UK campaigns grew the National

Declaration Against Deportation of School Students. Teachers, students and all those involved in education were invited to sign the declaration that stated that the best interests of a child or young person studying in a school or college in the UK should come first and that these are best served by allowing him or her to remain in the UK.[38]

In these ways, then, the political consciousness of a new generation of young people has been forged. No more so than in Scotland, where the Glasgow Girls group was formed in 2005 after hundreds of pupils at Drumchapel High School in Glasgow signed a petition opposing the detention of the Murselaj family, including their 15-year-old schoolfriend, Agnesa Murselaj. As more and more children at their school were subjected to dawn raids, this amazing group of young people stood their ground. They visited the Scottish Parliament, challenged the First Minister and gained cross-parliamentary support for their campaign, going on to win the Scottish Campaign of the Year Award in 2004 at the annual Scottish politician of the year ceremony.

In Glasgow, residents' committees have also been formed to protect families from dawn raids. Ordinary members of the community have blockaded flats of families under threat of deportation, and set up daily dawn patrols that look out for immigration vans and alert asylum seekers so that they can escape. In one part of Glasgow, an old corner shop, known as 'Unity' has been taken over. As it is opposite the Home Office building where asylum seekers must report regularly, before going in, asylum seekers sign in at Unity. If they don't come back to Unity after reporting, volunteers raise the alarm that they have been detained for deportation.[39]

Residents' initiatives such as these were formed in response to numerous cases, including that of the Vucaj family, who fled ethnic violence and persecution in Kosovo. They had lived in Glasgow for five years, but one morning, in September 2005, they woke to find riot police in body armour kicking down their door. The family, including Saida, 13, Nimet, 16 and Elvis, 18, were removed from their home in pyjamas and handcuffs.[40] The outrage was such that the Home Office was forced into carrying out a review of the way in which families living in Scotland were removed from the UK, and a protocol was issued between the Westminster and Edinburgh governments securing some protection for children facing removal.

Solidarity organisations often deploy the language of anti-fascism and resistance in their leaflets, statements and press releases. 'The night-time deportations remind me of fascist methods', commented Lothar Kuschnik, superintendent of the Arnsberg church district in Germany, in relation to deportation practices in the Hochsauerland in North Rhine-Westphalia.[41] 'It was like watching the Gestapo – men with armour, going in to flats with battering rams. I've never seen people living in fear like that', commented 67-year-old grandmother Jean Donnachie, part of a residents' initiative on the Kingsway estate in Glasgow.[42] The French civil disobedience movement in support of *sans papiers*, which provides a roster of accommodation (on an anonymous basis) to which a family can be switched as the need arises, acknowledges its inspiration in the citizens' networks formed to protect Jews from deportation during the Second World War. Such committees operate under the coordination of RESF, which, in 2007, issued a petition to defend children and their families from deportation at the end of the school year, entitled *Nous les prenons sous notre protection* (We will take them under our protection). Its initiative had the backing of dozens of celebrities, artists, writers, film-makers, trades unionists, and members of associations and political parties.

But such grassroots solidarity initiatives are under threat. 'Europe mouths "values", "Enlightenment", "tolerance"'... As Sartre said in another context, 'the mouths open, but the words die on the tongue.'[43] Hence, in November 2002, the EU adopted a Directive and a Framework Decision on 'Strengthening the Penal Framework to Prevent the Facilitation of Unauthorised Entry, Transit and Residence', which created new offences of illegal entry.[44] Some European states are implementing these laws in such a way that those people motivated by simple humanitarian principles now face prosecution.[45] In France, where legislation allows for a maximum five-year prison sentence for those found

guilty of the crime of solidarity, the RESF is concerned about the
multiplying lawsuits brought against its members. In Austria, the
case of Arigona Zogaj (see above) led the anti-immigrant BZÖ
to call for more prosecutions under para. 115 of the 'foreigners'
police law' (this makes it a crime to aid and abet immigrants
attempting to stay in Austria illegally). One person they wanted
to prosecute was Green Party spokeswoman Madeleine Petrovic,
a prominent supporter of Arigona Zogaj, who they accused of
helping 'illegal immigrants flee the authorities'.[46]

Such laws, however, seem to have had the contrary effect in
steeling the nerve of individuals supporting asylum seekers and
sans papiers. Today, this can include principled politicians such as
Madeleine Petrovic in Austria or Nathalie Perrin-Gilbert, mayor
of the first arrondissement of Lyons. She told the press that she
had sheltered *sans papiers* in her home and though she was not
revolutionary but 'an elected person' with a duty 'to respect
the country's law', she felt that when a conflict arose between
respect for the law and providing assistance to people in danger,
it was 'important for elected people' such as herself 'to set a
good example'.[47] René Datry, a campaigner against deportation
in France, estimates that as many as 40,000 French families have
volunteered to shelter those at risk. They see it as an issue of
child protection. According to one volunteer, Christine Pitiot,'I
prefer talking about *protecting* children rather than *hiding* them
... Nobody leaves their country without a good reason, whether
they have been persecuted or whether it is for economic reasons.
And everyone has a right to improve their condition.'[48]

A Tale of Two Europes

'The laws of this land have created a new underclass. Not
allowed to work, not allowed to claim support, not allowed to
exist', one church group commented in relation to UK asylum
and immigration laws. The picture is the same across Europe.[49]
Shanty-towns and makeshift camps now exist on the margins of
many of Europe's towns and cities, the best known of which was,
until it was shut down in December 2002, the Red Cross camp at

Sangatte, Calais, which was meant to accommodate 500 people but actually took up to 1300. It is over five years since its closure, but the situation today is worse than ever according to the Refugee Emergency Support Collective, C-Sur; exactly the same number of people are living in alternative shanty-towns.

Children, teenagers and young adults are among those forced into destitution and hunger who inhabit a land that is as unknown to middle-class Europe as the working-class districts of Victorian England were to the bourgeoisie a century and a half ago. And just as then, Charles Booth, Henry Mayhew, Joseph Rowntree and Frederick Engels set out to record working-class life, present-day NGOs, researchers and faith organisations are attempting to record the scale of the problem and counter its worst excesses. Refugee Action's first in-depth national survey into asylum destitution in the UK included 125 interviews in Bristol, Derby, Leicester, Liverpool, Manchester, Nottingham, Portsmouth, Plymouth and Southampton.[50] Almost one in three of those interviewed were women, some pregnant, others with children in the UK. A July 2008 survey by the Joseph Rowntree Trust found 331 destitute people in Leeds' community of failed asylum seekers and refugees, compared with 118 in its 2006–7 survey. The number of destitute children had risen from 13 to 51.[51] According to C-Sur in Calais, migrants who used to live at Sangatte now gather on a patch of sandy heathland they call 'the jungle', situated even further from the town centre where they live in 'slum huts'. One-fifth of the 500 migrant juveniles logged in 2006 in Calais came from sub-Saharan Africa or East Africa, and almost half were girls. Between April and September 2006, doctors working with Médecins du Monde in Calais saw 96 destitute women, seven of whom were pregnant, and 80 children.[52]

The picture painted above may seem bleak, but it is not without relief. This is, indeed, a tale of two Europes. The first Europe consists of government-created bureaucratic machines that reduce officials to automatons. The second consists of ordinary people, often acting in defiance of the law. In reminding governments what humanitarianism and social solidarity mean in practice, and drawing their inspiration from citizens' networks formed to protect

Jews from deportation during the Second World War, they often act with great courage. In an echo of the nineteenth- and twentieth-century European movements to extend protection to the children of the outcast poor, they draw attention to the plight of foreign and asylum-seeker children, persuading a world that demonises the groups they come from, that they are children too.

8

ISLAMOPHOBIA, YOUTH RESISTANCE AND THE MEANING OF LIBERTY

Edward Said, commenting on the 'redoubtable durability' of Orientalist discourse, observed how Orientalism transmitted or reproduced itself from one era to another.[1] In today's Europe, the revamped Orientalism that dominates political discourse has not emerged, post-September 11, because of some sudden atavistic tendency within European societies. On the contrary, the greater circulation of Orientalist ideas is directly linked to the war on terror and the emergence of the security state. Taking the form of a virulent Islamophobia, European Orientalism treats the Orient not as a separate geographical region but as a problem located – owing to Europe's growing Muslim minority population – within the boundaries of Europe (the Occident) itself.

As a result, the circulation of Orientalist ideas does not begin and end in the corridors of Middle East study centres. A growing number of European 'scholars' in social sciences, terrorist studies, anthropology and related fields are daily paraded in the media as impartial experts on Europe's Muslim minorities[2] – who are seldom discussed as citizens or people but, more often, as problems. Europe's growing Muslim minorities are homogenised and problematised in the social sciences today in much the same way as Orientalist experts of the nineteenth century once essentialised the peoples of the East. Living under despotic and decadent political systems, Orientals required Enlightened Europeans possessed of a superior culture to teach them the meaning of liberty.

Emergence of the 'Muslim Problem'

Despite the fact that Muslim migration to post-war Europe took off in the late 1960s, it was only relatively recently that nativist opposition to migration has taken a more explicit Islamophobic, anti-Muslim tone. Racism in the post-war period adopted the form of a generalised anti-immigrant discourse and, for racist movements, the colour, or the 'alienness' of the foreigner was much more important than their faith. But after September 11, as states' responses to non-European minority communities began to change, so too did the shape of popular racism. On the one hand, ill-defined anxieties among policy-makers about 'Islamism' and the problems of a Muslim 'underclass' allowed for the diverse problems of communities of different national and ethnic origin to be collapsed into the problem of integrating a homogenised category of migrants characterised solely by their religion (and a supposed common culture). On the other hand, the institutionalisation of anti-Muslim racism within criminal justice systems and citizenship laws made the political Islamophobia of the extreme-Right respectable. In much the same way as the presence of a people with a different colour was once constructed as a social problem, the presence of people of a different culture and religion has, today, become *ipso facto* problematic.

For just as Orientalism – with its Manichean distinction between western superiority and Oriental inferiority – came with a web of racial and cultural stereotypes, Islamophobia reduces Europe's diverse Muslim communities into a monolithic mass. It obliterates national, cultural, regional, political and religious distinctions, thus giving rise to a proliferation of stereotypical generalisations about 'Muslim culture' and the Islamic mind-set. Most importantly, the many problems faced by young Muslims, socialised in Europe, are regarded as stemming from Islamic culture – which was in fact that of their parents or grandparents. And today's 'integration experts' study patterns, attitudes and statistical trends within 'the Muslim community' and, resorting to old-fashioned paradigms of 'social distance' and 'acculturalisation', concern themselves with the 'social distance' between Muslims' and the 'host' community.[3]

Terrorism experts – often advisers to government anti-radicalisation programmes – create psychological profiles of young Muslim men who, having been brainwashed by the preachers of hate and through rote learning of the Qur'an, have developed infantile and robotic tendencies. Some feminists, often with a pro-assimilation agenda, deny the individual agency of Muslim women and girls who wear the headscarf. They portray them as passive victims of Islamic patriarchy quietly acquiescing to religiously constructed gender norms. Because 'the Muslim' is discussed as the outsider against whom the westerner must shore up liberal values, the fact that young Muslims are not outsiders but European citizens, born and socialised in Europe, is obscured.

A young Muslim's existential reality in Europe is further distorted by the presumption in much of the intellectual discourse that the dominant core culture will instruct him or her into higher values and the meaning of human rights. But, in fact, the young Muslim who today engages in the anti-war or civil rights movements not only challenges Islamophobia but also teaches others about liberty. Such crucial developments pass the 'integration expert' by, so immersed is s/he in statistical projections and social mapping. Hobbled by empty data, s/he fails to see that

> the dominant character of Muslim radicalisation ... points not towards terrorism or religious extremism, but in the opposite direction: towards political engagement in new, radical and progressive coalitions that seek to unite Muslim with non-Muslim in parliamentary and extra-parliamentary strategies to effect change.[4]

 CB EO

In years to come, when historians come to chart involvement in Europe's anti-war movements, the significance of the Muslim contribution to campaigns against the war in Iraq and the Israeli occupation of Palestine will be fully recognised. But equally significant is the development, in the face of European Islamophobia, of new civil rights and self-help movements. These, as I discovered when I carried out a one-year research project on Islamophobia and integration in six European countries for the Institute of Race Relations,[5] encompass struggles against a range of forces: police brutality, racial and religious profiling, state edicts, xenophobic electoral populism, social disadvantage, educational under-achievement. Such movements draw on previous moments of civil rights activism, notably of the Irish and black communities in Britain, the Republicans in northern Ireland and of black movements in the United States.

Self-help and Self-organisation

In the 1970s, in the UK, members of the African-Caribbean community were preoccupied with fighting the mis-education of their children. Members of the Turkish community in Germany, and the Moroccan community in the Netherlands were faced with similar experiences. Children were labelled educationally sub-normal and dumped in special educational programmes outside of the mainstream classroom. In the UK, the African-Caribbean community responded to teachers' low expectations of black children by setting up self-help projects and supplementary schools designed to counter under-achievement.[6] Across Europe today, life is being breathed into this idea, as university-educated Muslims and other committed anti-racist educationalists commit themselves to youth projects addressing the myriad problems caused by social disadvantage compounded by Islamophobia. Such voluntary workers believe that if Islamophobia, which marks the child as alien and eternally different, is allowed to penetrate the child's sense of identity and self-worth, it can create serious emotional problems and a lack of self-esteem.

The Netherlands

Moroccans who arrived in the Netherlands in the first period of post-war migration were mostly labourers from rural areas who were not highly educated. Zakaria Hamidi, now in his late thirties, came to the Netherlands as a young boy in order to join his father and complete his education. Now programme director of De Nieuwe Horizon (New Horizon – a platform for debate and dialogue on Islam and Muslims), Hamidi believes that those Muslims who have progressed through the higher education system cannot divorce themselves from the problems of the poor, working-class communities they were brought up in. The Rotterdam group Ettaouhid, which Hamidi helped found in 2000, spreads the principle of 'self-help' by bringing children and adults together in new networks and developing youth associations so that they can play a more active role in society. In the Netherlands, 'A child is never seen as just "Aisha" or "Mustafa", never seen as just a child,' according to Dutch senior education consultant, Dolf Hautvast, 'they are always seen as a member of a group. They don't feel welcome. This is a very unnatural environment for young children to grow up in.' Hautvast specialises in creating new educational projects for youths at risk and juvenile offenders. (Young Dutch-Moroccans and Dutch-Turks are over-represented in youth offenders detention facilities'.)

The UK

In Birmingham, where many schools have serious structural weaknesses and low expectations for pupils, Pioneers Leading the Way works on self-help principles to address the underachievement of Pakistani and Bangladeshi children. This scheme has provided 150 Pakistani and Bangladeshi mentors for children with low self-esteem, problems around attendance and achievement in 30 local schools. Pioneers encourages undergraduates and other professional volunteers to act as 'academic success mentors' for those at serious risk of failure. The undergraduates begin by receiving a small bursary but, once engaged, some become inspired by Pioneers' ethos of 'giving back to their communities' – and break with previous career paths to commit themselves to education. Azkar Mohammed, Director of Pioneers Leading the Way, described the problems that young Muslim children in Birmingham face:

> The children we mentor live in areas of social deprivation with huge levels of unemployment and have multiple problems, including a lack of self-esteem. If you are constantly told that you are from a failing community which is also potentially dangerous of course this will have an effect. If you come from an area of social deprivation, the only thing you have is your pride. You become defensive of the only thing you have ownership of – your religion.

One way in which Pioneers attempts to deal with these feelings of alienation is by teaching children the history of anti-racism in the UK and by explaining that other communities, such as the Irish, have lived through and overcome similar stigmatisation.

France

In France, Islamophobic discourse owes much to views circulated by pro-Israeli think-tanks and popularised by 'experts' such as philosopher and TV presenter Alain Finkielkraut.[7] Young Muslims are often portrayed in the media as the vehicle for an almost innate anti-Semitism that is imbibed with the mother's milk of Arabic culture, which is said to be eternally hostile to Jews.[8] Some French youths of North African origin, on the margins of society and drifting towards crime, have undoubtedly fallen prey to conspiracy theories and contributed to inter-communal tensions and anti-Semitism. But groups are emerging to counter this. The Jewish-Arabic and Citizens' Group for Peace in Strasbourg is, for example, working to develop new pedagogical approaches involving support structures for young people who use Jews as an outlet for fear and social frustration. This inter-ethnic initiative also counters the Islamophobic myth that anti-Semitism is located within Arabic-Muslim culture. According to Willy Beauvallet and Corinne Grassi, young French North Africans fall prey to conspiracy theories about Jews precisely because they have lived all their lives within the confines of the French *banlieue*.[9] For young French Arabs, the idea of a plot 'fulfils an obvious function: to explain and give consistency to an otherwise incomprehensible situation of poverty and discrimination'. Living a marginal existence, and imprisoned within the *banlieue*, they face a situation of almost daily police harassment. If they identify with the Palestinian cause it is because the Palestinian experience most resembles their own. If they see in the Palestinians a people 'totally deprived of any future' who, nevertheless, resist 'the Israeli Occupation', it is because they too desire to 'resist the forces oppressing them'.

Because the Jewish-Arabic and Citizens' Group for Peace comprehends this identification and it works simultaneously against Islamophobia, it is well placed to counter anti-Semitism. Its creative, challenging approach is replicated in the mosaic of anti-racist and civil rights initiatives now emerging in France to replace the larger, discredited anti-racist organisations, such as the Socialist-led SOS Racisme. For, as the Social Forum of the Banlieues – which has regional collectives in Paris, Lyon, Montepellier and Toulouse – epitomises, the need now in France is for an effective platform for the inhabitants of the *banlieues*.

Alongside the principle of 'self-help' in social and welfare organisations has developed a call for self-organisation and political autonomy to create 'effective political actors, producing our own discourses and developing our own autonomous practices'.[10] As thousands of new African and Arab organisations spring up across France, French-Arabs, French-Africans and other young people advance a new agenda for the deprived suburbs. A powerful dynamic for social change is building up with unifying principles similar to those forged in inner-city communities in the UK in the 1960s and 1970s. French journalist Naima Bouteldja observed that

within the suburbs, a significant proportion of the population are white working class, African, Arabs, and they all face the same stigmatisation because they come from poor neighbourhoods. The *banlieue* is, despite everything, mixed. Eighty per cent of these kids go to the local state school where they mix with each other. So, in France, there is *mixité*.

CB BD

For the Islamophobe, not only are all Muslims the same, but their religious identity is the only thing that colours their politics

(Islamist in any event and therefore inclined to violence and extremism). The reality is that the morality based in religious identification, which is clearly important to many young Muslims, has strong similarities with the political morality of international movements of young Left, Green, anti-globalisation, anti-war and peace activists, though their personal ethics and political identifications are derived from the secular faiths of socialism, environmentalism, humanitarianism and peace. But life does not divide neatly into separate categories – Muslim, Green, Left, Peace – nor are the lives of young Muslims, like the lives of young people everywhere, one-dimensional. The sociologist who tries to put young Muslims in a 'box' labelled faith will find that they have escaped. One need only examine the political loyalties of two of Europe's most dynamic young Muslim Left politicians to understand this. To the horror of assimilationist feminists, both Salma Yaqoob (a Birmingham city councillor for Respect) and Asmaa Abdol-Hamid (the Red-Green alliance parliamentary candidate and city councillor in Odense) are religious Muslims who wear the hijab.[11] Yet they both describe themselves as socialists, feminists and civil rights activists; and both combine the language of faith with the language of political liberation, inspiring a whole new generation of young women in the process.

In the Netherlands, the anti-Muslim diatribes of Pim Fortuyn (assassinated by an animal liberation activist), Hirsi Ali (now a fellow at the US neo-conservative American Enterprise Institute), Theo van Gogh (murdered by an Islamic extremist) and, most recently, the extreme-Right Freedom Party MP Geert Wilders (who wants to ban the Qur'an and stop politicians with dual nationality holding cabinet office), may have taken their toll. But they have also given rise to the highest level of anti-racist activism for years, particularly on university campuses where second- and third-generation students of migrant origin have led initiatives like Stop the Witch Hunt (formed to counter the upsurge in racial violence that followed Van Gogh's murder) and Together Against Racism. Miriyam Aouragh, an anthropologist working on Middle East issues at the University of Amsterdam and a founding-member of both initiatives, described them as providing 'an alternative analysis, not from the vantage-point of religion but from the terrain of civil rights'. Amsterdam Groen Links city councillor Fenna Uliche, a former chair of the National Association of Moroccan Women, agrees that things are on the move in the Netherlands:

> After the death of Theo van Gogh, everyone was defending themselves and saying that we must show people that Islam is a tolerant religion. That was important. But even more important now is that the debate is not just about defending the Qur'an and cultural rights. It is about defending the law and defending civil rights.

Indeed, the momentum against racism in the Netherlands is now such that the larger trades unions have joined forces to oppose the impact of Wilders' campaign against dual nationality on its migrant members.[12]

CB BO

In the economic boom of the 1960s, Europe was desperate for labour. Migration from outside Europe was encouraged, particularly of unskilled or semi-skilled men of working age. As industrial decline and economic restructuring decimated the manufacturing sector into which they were initially absorbed, migrant workers (now settlers) with foreign-sounding names and darker skins were often the first to be dismissed and the last to be re-employed. In the years that followed, the declining rate of migrant participation in the labour force and the resulting levels of unemployment came to be blamed on a cultural deficit, and fears began to grow of a Muslim underclass that was unintegratable.[13]

Though a few second- and third-generation Europeans of migrant origin have gone on to university and managed to escape this ghettoisation (despite there being no official government integration policy), the majority of Europe's Muslims live a life of poverty in traditional areas of immigrant settlement where life is characterised by structured unemployment. In such areas, family breakdown, drug abuse, crime and domestic violence are high. And even those young Muslims and other young black people with skills and some qualifications cannot escape as job applicants with Muslim or African-sounding names are regularly passed over by employers.

These, then, are abandoned communities; and there is no place for them in the globalised, consumerist, celebrity-oriented order: no work, in the present, no route to a future, marked out forever by 'race' and 'culture' as surplus to requirements. The leitmotif is criminalisation. The denizens of such communities are abandoned to a security policing complex, face routine confrontations with the police, unexplained deaths in custody[14] and, finally, 'incapacitation' (as opposed to rehabilitation) 'as the major objective of imprisonment'.[15] In the Netherlands, where Muslims make up just 5.5 per cent of the population, a staggering 20 per cent of adult prisoners and 26 per cent of all juvenile offenders are Muslim. In Belgium, Moroccans and Turks make up at least 16 per cent of the prison population compared with 2 per cent of the general population. And in the UK, Muslims are nearly four times more likely to be imprisoned compared with the rest of the population. While the French government does not provide data on race, religion or ethnicity of the prison population, demographers, sociologists and Muslims leaders suggest that a staggering 60–70 per cent of the prison population are Muslim.[16] By 'criminalising poverty and resistance to saturation policing', argues US prison abolitionist Avery Gordon, 'mass imprisonment removes from civil society potentially active, angry and demanding political subjects to a remote and closed place where they are civilly disabled and socially dead'.[17]

The Archetype of the Young Foreign Criminal

As Europe's prisons burst with Muslim prisoners, the Moroccan, Algerian, Turkish, Kurdish, Pakistani or Somali young man emerges as the archetypal criminal – foreign, hostile and dangerous – who 'did not and could never belong'.[18] At this point, the pragmatic politician puts to one side their Islamophobic prejudices in favour of nativist ones. Whereas the faith of the young Muslim makes of him a likely terrorist, where juvenile delinquency and inner-city crime are concerned, nationality is what truly matters. By stressing the young man's foreign national origins, it becomes easier for xenophobes and blinkered politicians to pathologise the young Arab, young African or young Asian. For crime is not something learnt on the margins of Europe's cities; its causes cannot be located within a continent of glittering wealth and obscene inequality. No, the causes of crime are to be found in foreign lands whence their families came – Pakistan, Morocco, Turkey, Somalia – or in the backward values of their alien parents.

The argument that crime is located in a pathology of alien cultures and foreign families was made respectable by the Dutch right-wing journalist Fleur Jurgens in her bestselling book, *The Moroccan Drama*.[19] Jurgens, whose research was financed by the Police Academy, located the causes of crime in the culture of immigrants from Morocco's Rif Valley. Interviewing over 60 experts of her own choosing, and failing to interview a single Moroccan youth, Jurgens set out to investigate 'how far the family background of problem Moroccan youngsters contributed to their tendency to fail in Dutch society'. The Norwegian interior minister accepted the same twisted logic. After a documentary on Pakistani gangs was broadcast on Norwegian television, the state secretary for integration, immigration and diversity, Libe Rieber-Mohn, drew on the director's claim that Pakistanis 'tend to cheat the state, they learn this in Pakistan' to argue that, as Pakistanis were not used to democracy, it was important that they adopted Norwegian values.[20] In fact, most members of urban youth gangs would have learnt their values in Norway.

But emphasising nationality, not faith, has another benefit for populist xenophobes. If the young offender does not belong to the Muslim minority in Europe, but to, say, the Turkish nation, he is no longer a European problem; rather than being punished and rehabilitated in Europe, the juvenile delinquent can be deported back to the cultural setting where he truly belongs. Seizing on such reasoning, the leader of the Christian Democrats (CDU) in Hesse, Roland Koch, sought to make crime perpetrated by young foreigners the central election issue in the January 2008

German regional elections. Koch tried to make political capital out of a brutal attack on a pensioner by a 17-year-old Greek national and a 20-year-old Turkish national which, caught on camera, had been broadcast by TV stations for more than a week. Koch called for the establishment of US-style private correctional boot camps and the deportation of foreign youth sentenced to one or more years' imprisonment. Emphasising that Germany had, until then, shown a 'strange sociological understanding' for violent members of ethnic minority groups because of a 'false multicultural tolerance', Koch launched his anti-crime election campaign with a list of instructions to ethnic minority parents to desist from foreign practices that ran counter to German principles.[21] German must be the 'language of everyday life', he declared, adding that Germany would no longer tolerate 'the slaughtering [of animals] in the kitchen' or 'unusual ideas about waste disposal'. Adding her support to Koch's campaign, Chancellor Angela Merkel claimed that 43 per cent of all violent crimes in Germany were committed by people under 21, almost half of whom were from immigrant backgrounds. Even though her statistics were immediately disputed, the mass circulation *Bild* newspaper ran with the headline 'Young foreigners more violent than young Germans', going on to feature news stories about 'foreign' repeat offenders on a regular basis.

Koch had set out to repeat the success of his 1999 election campaign in which he ousted the ruling Hesse centre-left administration by launching a successful petition campaign against dual citizenship that played on extreme-Right fears of 'foreign infiltration'. But in a rude awakening for the CDU – the membership of which is falling dramatically, with 60 per cent of existing members in the 50+ group – Koch was trounced at the polls in 2008. His xenophobia had succeeded in rallying the entire opposition (save the neo-Nazis) against him. The Forum for Migrants (which represents 100 small immigrant organisations across Germany within the voluntary sector body the Equal Welfare Alliance), wrote an open letter to the press condemning his 'tactical populism'. The Central Council of Jews in Germany announced that Koch's stance could hardly be distinguished from the neo-Nazi National Democratic Party of Germany. And former Social Democrat Chancellor Gerhard Schröder pointed out that 'young German right-wing radicals commit an average of three violent crimes per day – most of them against people of another skin colour. You do not hear anything about that from Mr Koch or Ms Merkel.'

It would of course be too optimistic to see in Koch's election defeat the lesson that mainstream political parties can no longer make electoral headway in Europe by demonising minority ethnic youth. Nevertheless, grounds for optimism can be found in the growing political confidence of Germany's minority ethnic populations. Their voices have long been stifled by a lack of citizenship rights and the vulnerability that comes from living within a national community constructed around the myth that Germany is 'not a country of immigration'. The coming together of immigrant organisations in the Forum for Migrants is, in itself, a sign of change. But Germany is not France or the UK – the urban landscapes of which have been repeatedly punctuated by uprisings of the dispossessed – so that when marginalised youth spontaneously take to the streets to protest against the police and against racism this, too, is significant. In the days that followed Koch's election defeat, Salih, a 17-year-old youth of Moroccan origin died after being stabbed through the heart in Kalk, a deprived district of Cologne. His assailant was a 20-year-old German youth who the police declared, just eight hours after the attack, would not be prosecuted as he had acted in self-defence to prevent a mugging. Candles were laid at the site of Salih's death and for several days there were nightly demonstrations by up to 300 angry young people demanding justice and protesting against the racism that allowed Koch to demonise them as criminals and foreigners. 'We're sitting on a powder keg', commented anxious former police commissioner Winrich Granitzka, who is also head of the Christian Democratic group in Cologne's city council. 'There's the danger we could see a situation like in the suburbs of Paris.'[22]

This, undoubtedly, haunts Europe's political classes. Mindful that Malcolm X's autobiography continues to be the most requested book by prisoners in the West, they may well fear that in prison young Muslims may find a different kind of Islam – one rooted in the western ghetto experience. The problem for politicians and policy-makers is how to integrate a new Muslim underclass. German politicians look anxiously to the UK, where rioting in the English northern towns caused an estimated £25m worth of damage in the summer of 2001, and to France, where in 2005 cities experienced the worst outbreak of 'rioting' in 40 years (repeated on a smaller scale in November 2007 in the Paris suburb of Villiers-le-Bel).[23] The German educational system was slammed by the OECD for coming last of 17 industrialised nations when it came to supporting migrant children.[24] Now German politicians are talking of a master plan to deal with this educational underachievement, particularly among young Turks – an estimated 72 per cent of whom do not have vocational qualifications and are routinely refused traineeship opportunities. France, too, has been forced to address social deprivation within the *banlieue*, although critics have pointed out that Sarkozy's February 2008 Action Plan for the Banlieues does not actually stipulate whether new funds are to be made available to create the 100,000 new jobs promised for young people.[25]

But such promises do not herald a new dawn for Europe's young ethnic minorities. Europe marches blindly on, criminalising teenage misbehaviour,[26] building new prisons, developing the new penology based not on punishment and rehabilitation of the offender but on 'selective incapacitation'[27] and managing segments of the population through aggregate classification schemes designed for the purpose of surveillance, confinement and control.[28]

The UK, where the age of criminal responsibility (in England and Wales) is set at ten (in Scotland, it is eight, the lowest in Europe), has the largest prison population in Europe.[29] In December 2007, the Labour government announced that 10,500 new prison places would be created by 2014, at the cost of £1.2bn. This would include three new Titan 'superprisons', designed to house large numbers of inmates, and sharing services and facilities, which justice secretary, Jack Straw, denies will be 'monolithic prison warehouses'.[30]

In France, Sarkozy's master plan for increasing opportunities for those from the deprived *banlieues* includes the promise of a 'war without mercy' on crime. Already police carrying out routine ID checks are armed with Taser electroshock weapons and Flash-ball rubber bullet guns. But now 4000 more police officers and more military-style territorial police units for the suburbs are promised. Already, in February 2008, a thousand French riot police and special forces accompanied by armoured police trucks had raided ten apartment blocks in Villiers-le-Bel and surrounding areas, ostensibly to find the suspected ringleaders of the November 2007 'riots' whom Sarkozy had earlier promised to track down 'one by one'. At the same time, Sarkozy brought in a parliamentary bill to introduce a scheme of special 'socio-medico'-legal detention. In such special centres, violent offenders, sentenced to more than 15 years' imprisonment, could face further, and perhaps, indefinite detention. On completing his or her sentence, the prisoner would be further detained if a three-judge special commission believed that he or she might commit further crimes on release. But locking people up on speculation that they might commit a crime in the future undermines international conventions on the right to a fair trial, protection against arbitrary detention and the right not to be punished twice for the same crime, concludes Human Rights Watch.[31]

Now Is the Moment of Civil Rights

This is the shape of the future European security state for the young. But it is being challenged, and not just by lawyers and civil libertarians but by the growing number of young campaigners against Islamophobia and racist stereotyping. Not surprisingly, it is the brutality of the police that galvanises them immediately, but opposition to institutionalised racism is yet more widespread. France has witnessed a steady flowering of new grassroots initiatives such as the Movement of Immigration and the Banlieues (MIB) and DiverCités, a collection of associations from the neighbourhoods of Lyon, which provides training and advice on discrimination, particularly in schooling, prison and law enforcement. Most recently, the grassroots organisation Vérité et Justice (Truth and Justice) emerged out of the wreckage caused by military-style police raids in Villiers-le-Bel. Its young leadership pledged to defend those arrested, to counter police mis-information and to ensure that the perspectives of the youth of Villiers-le-Bel inform the media debate.

And in less likely countries, too, the seeds of revolt have been planted within the hearts of the young. In Denmark, for instance, young people who violently clashed with the police in the Norrebro district of Copenhagen in February 2008 challenged media demonisation of the 'rioters' as Islamic fundamentalists angered by leading Danish newspapers who had decided to reprint the Prophet Mohammed cartoons. In an open letter to the press, entitled 'The Truth Behind the Disturbances', the youths stated that the immediate cause of the riots was the police mishandling of an elderly man who was beaten with truncheons. But among long-term grievances cited was the police's stop-and-search policies, including routine humiliation through strip searches on the streets.[32] Just as in Cologne, the protest of these Danish youths is raw, local and as yet undirected.

But in Norway, civil rights activism among young Norwegians from a minority background has a targeted focus. National demonstrations were organised over an incident in August 2007 when paramedics refused to treat Ali Farah, a 37-year-old Somalian-Norwegian, who had been the victim of a random aggravated assault in an Oslo park during which he suffered serious injuries, including a fractured skull and possible permanent brain damage. Care was refused on the grounds that he was incoherent and had wet his trousers. One shocked eye-witness reported that when Ali, who had been unconscious for several minutes, peed, one of the paramedics called him a 'fucking pig' and refused to take him in the ambulance. (It took weeks for the hospital to apologise, as the ambulance crew, one of whom was a former member of the neo-Nazi Boot Boys, maintained that Farah had appeared intoxicated and posed a security risk.[33])

The appalling treatment of Ali Farah sparked off a huge public debate about latent racism in Norway. Crucially, mass demonstrations in four cities against the racist stereotyping that had denied Farah medical treatment made common cause with the struggles of the African community against the anti-black racism that had led to the earlier death in custody of Nigerian Eugene Ejike Obiara. Obiara had choked to death after being brutally restrained by the police who called in to deal with him after he had become distraught after being refused his welfare benefits at a Trondheim social security office.[34] Though African groups had taken the lead in that campaign – seen as a watershed in anti-racist struggles in Norway – minority youth from all ethnic and faith backgrounds had mobilised for justice. This broad front of support continued in the mobilisations for Ali Farah, with young minority ethnic people leading demonstrations in Bergen and Trondheim to highlight the deplorable lack of treatment and also mark the first anniversary of the death of Obiara.

These, then, are the new inter-racial alliances that cut across faith, ethnic and racial divides to suggest a broad-based, liberatory politics. Based on a philosophy of unity in action, these alliances bring young people together against racism in its many avatars – populist, political, state, xenophobic, anti-black, Islamophobic. What these young people challenge is, to quote Sivanandan, a 'Europe that boasts its Enlightened values' but has never extended these values to the *sub-homines*. Those engaged in shaping a new liberatory politics may well share Sivanandan's view that 'The Enlightenment project ... is not over till its remit of liberty, equality and fraternity is extended to include the non-white peoples of the world.'[35]

NOTES

Introduction

1. The cases cited in these introductory remarks have all been documented in the *IRR European Race Bulletin*. See also the IRR News Service edited by Harmit Athwal at <www.irr.org.uk>.
2. See 'The meaning of Rostock', *Searchlight* (October 2002).
3. See A. Sivanandan, 'Racism 1992', *Race & Class*, Vol. 30, No. 3 (January–March 1989), pp. 85–90.
4. Some chapters in this book are based on essays that originally appeared in *Race & Class* from 2001 to 2006.
5. In both Italy and Austria, overtly extreme-Right political parties have been junior partners in coalition governments.
6. For instance, AN leader Gianfranco Fini, at a three-day conference in Verona in 1998, cited the threat to national identity posed by 'indiscriminate multiethnic dust' and 'incoherent pluri-cultural babel'. An AN document stated that the Italian and other European people were the founders of a 'civil, juridical, aesthetic, ethical and philosophical identity' that should not be 'dissolved into an indistinct and pseudocultural miscellany'. See *IRR European Race Bulletin*, No. 27 (May 1998) and *Searchlight* (April 2008).
7. Nonna Mayer of the Centre for the Study of French Political Life suggested that supporters of Le Pen were separated from supporters of the conventional Right by their greater attachment to social issues and to the notion of some degree of state intervention. See *Le Monde*, 29 November 2006.
8. The FN's first significant electoral breakthrough came in the municipal elections of 1995. Three towns in south-east France fell under FN control, all with a strong element of *Pieds Noirs* – French citizens who left Algeria after the former North African colony won its independence in 1962. In a by-election in February 1997, the FN gained control of Vitrolles, an expanding new town and outer suburb of Marseilles.
9. *New York Times*, 31 May 1997.
10. The FPÖ's greatest victory during this period, in the October 1999 general election where it secured 26.9 per cent of the vote, came on the back of the huge inroads it made into the male, urban and

working-class vote. Haider declared that 'we're more socialist than the socialists, with all the benefits we plan to introduce to help the disadvantaged'. *IRR European Race Bulletin*, No. 32 (March 2002).

11. See *Samora Newsletter*, Nos 3 and 4 (1997).

12. Peter Jensen, '*Der Spiegel*: racial nationalism goes mainstream in a German newsweekly', in *FAIR* (July/August 1992).

13. See 'Mobilising against "foreign criminals": the new electoral politics', *IRR European Race Bulletin*, No. 63 (Spring 2008).

14. The release by the police of statistics that seek to purport that foreigners and asylum seekers are disproportionately involved in crime has been a strong feature in the deteriorating debate in every European country that I have monitored since 1992. For instance, in 1992 in the Netherlands, immigrant crime was a dominant news story after the minister of the interior initiated a 'National Debate on Ethnic Minorities' and the police and press interpreted this as a signal to racialise issues of crime statistics.

15. If the asylum seekers were Roma, the invective was particularly bitter. At the end of 1997, in the UK the Telephone Legal Advice Centre submitted a complaint to the Press Council over the press treatment of Czech and Slovak Roma seeking asylum. Newspaper headlines started 'Giro Czechs hit London' and 'Bounce the Giro Czechs'. The *Sun* newspaper carried a phone poll that produced a ratio of 19:1 in favour of 'booting' the Gypsies out.

16. In some cases, newspapers came out in open support of extreme-Right candidates. Jörg Haider, for instance, enjoyed strong editorial support from the opinion-moulding newspaper, the *Neue Kronen Zeitung* in the run-up to the October 1999 general election.

17. See *IRR European Race Bulletin*, No. 26 (February 2008).

18. See A. Sivanandan, 'Refugees from globalism', *Race & Class*, Vol. 42, No. 3 (January–March 2001).

19. A front-page editorial in the *Wexford People* accused asylum seekers of running up streets waving welfare cheques, frightening old women living alone and attempting to get Irish girls pregnant because a baby would bring a passport. See *IRR European Race Bulletin*, No. 29 (March 1999).

20. In May 1998, police advised asylum seekers living in some parts of inner-city Dublin not to go out at night for their own safety. *IRR European Race Bulletin*, No. 29 (March 1999).

21. See Liz Fekete, 'Populist anti-asylum movement born at Kollum', *IRR European Race Bulletin*, No. 32 (March 2000). An important source of information on events at Kollum and other anti-refugee

incidents during this period is De Fabel van de Illegal <www.defabel.
nl> [last accessed 14 August 2008].

22. On 23 May 2002, the *Guardian* reported that according to a
confidential 'action plan' that had been leaked to the newspaper,
Tony Blair had taken control of asylum policy. Blair argued that
elections in France and the Netherlands proved that centre-Left
parties needed to tackle crime and immigration head-on to prevent
fringe parties exploiting people's anxieties.

23. Even if not invited to become coalition partners, extreme-Right
parties often emerge as the power behind the throne. This has
particularly been the case in the Netherlands and Denmark.

24. Prior to the regional and federal elections of September 1998,
the CSU called for the deportation of entire immigrant families
if underage members were found guilty of criminal offences, and
even if the young offenders were born in Germany. This policy
proposal, likened to the Nazi practice of *Sippenhaft* – or kin
liability, whereby relatives of criminals were held responsible for
their crimes and punished equally – has now been taken up by the
SVP in Switzerland.

25. The Association of Chief Police Officers warned of 'significant public
disorder' unless action was taken to prevent racial tension in parts
of the country to which asylum seekers had been dispersed.

26. Chirac claimed that France was sinking under urban violence and a
mounting crime-wave running at the speed of 'one act of lawlessness
every seven seconds'.

27. See Liz Fekete, 'The electoral extreme-Right – who gains?', *IRR
European Race Bulletin*, No. 41 (August 2002).

28. The approach of southern European countries, as well as France,
has been different in that until 2005 and the introduction of the
Reception Directive there was little state provision for asylum
seekers' welfare needs, which were met by charities and NGOs
like the Red Cross.

29. The *IRR European Race Bulletin* has documented repeated waves
of hostility and violence against asylum centres and the dismal
political responses since 1992.

30. The IRR European Race Audit has catalogued unremitting violence
directed at Roma encampments in Italy, mostly on the outskirts of
cities where refugees from the former-Yugoslavia often live alongside
other homeless people in the most deplorable and primitive
conditions.

31. Spain is one of the few countries in Europe that does not have an
extreme-Right anti-immigrant party embedded in the parliamentary
political process, partly owing to the Popular Party's attempts to

distance itself from the Franco period. However, far-Right racist violence is almost epidemic in Spain, with some of the worst attacks meted out to migrant workers living in deplorable conditions, particularly in Almeria, where the worst outbreak of racial violence in modern Spanish history took place in El Ejido on the weekend of 5–6 February 2000.

32. In February 1995, four Roma were killed after a high-explosive booby-trap bomb was placed next to a Roma settlement at Oberwart in the eastern province of Burgenland. This was part of a five-year spate of attacks, described at the time as Austria's worst wave of bombings since 1945.

33. This was the worst disaster to hit a refugee hostel, and the worst racist attack against foreigners in Germany since the Second World War. There was overwhelming evidence that neo-Nazis started the fire but the police investigation and the press demonised the victims. See Geoffrey Bindman, 'Murder in Lübeck', *Race & Class*, Vol. 39, No. 1 (July–September 1997), pp. 95–100; Liz Fekete, 'How the German press stoked the Lübeck fires', *Race & Class*, Vol. 41, No. 4 (April–June 2000), pp. 19–41.

34. The German Law of Obligatory Residence forbids asylum seekers from moving from their designated accommodation.

35. After the killing of Firsat Dag, a Kurdish asylum seeker, the families fled to London.

36. See Tony Bunyan, 'Towards an authoritarian European state', *Race & Class*, Vol. 32, No. 3 (January–March 2001), pp. 19–27.

37. The proposal is one of many put forward by the Council of the European Union's Future Group of interior and justice ministers from six EU member states. See Ian Traynor, 'Secret EU security drive risks uproar with call to pool policing and give US personal data', *Guardian*, 7 August 2007.

38. The ban on the PKK was followed in 1995 by a decision to lift the ban on deportation of rejected Kurdish asylum seekers. Also in 1993, the French government banned the Kurdistan Committee, as well as the Federation of Kurdistan Cultural Associations and Patriotic Workers. While Switzerland did not ban the PKK, it stepped up surveillance of Kurdish groups and launched proceedings against seven members of the Turkish-Kurdish Socialist newspaper, *Mucadele*. See CARF (May–June 1993).

39. *Guardian*, 7 January 1998; *Independent*, 6 March 1998.

40. See Special Newsletter of FIDH, *France: Paving the Way for Arbitrary Justice*, No. 271–2 (March 1999).

41. Around 120 lawyers were appointed to take part in the trial, which was believed to be the largest and most unwieldy to have taken place in France for 50 years.

42. From 13 to 15 May 2008 mobs went on the rampage, burning the nomad camps in the Ponticelli district of Naples. See 'The Italian general election and its aftermath', *IRR European Race Bulletin*, No. 64 (Summer 2008).

43. Statement of European Center for Antiziganism Research, 'Red Cross Collaborates in Ethnic Filing of Roma in Italy', <www.openpr.com/news/48590/Red-Cross-Collaborates-in-Ethnic-Filing-of-Roma-in-Italy.html> [last accessed 14 August 2008].

44. See A. Sivanandan, 'Nativism vs integration', IRR News Online (15 May 2008).

45. The phrase is that of US prison abolitionist Angela Davis who, building on the work of social historian Mike Davies, uses the term 'prison industrial complex' as a way of countering the prevailing belief that increased levels of crime are the root cause of mounting prison populations in the US. See Angela Davis, *Are Prisons Obsolete?* (New York: Seven Stories Press, 2003); Avery F. Gordon, 'Globalism and the prison industrial complex: an interview with Angela Davis', *Race & Class*, Vol. 40, Nos 2/3 (October 1998–March 1999), pp. 145–57; Elliot Currie, *Crime and Punishment in America* (New York: Henry Holt and Company, 1998).

46. See Alessandro De Giorgi, *Re-thinking the Political Economy of Punishment: Perspectives on Post-Fordism and Penal Politics* (Aldershot: Ashgate, 2006).

Chapter 1

1. This is a conservative estimate of the number of refugees and internally displaced persons (IDPs) in the world today, as it only covers those refugees, returnees, stateless and internally displaced people covered by the UNHCR mandate in December 2007. See UNHCR Statistics Online Population Database, UNHCR <www.unhcr.org/statistics/populationdatabase> [last accessed 11 August 2008].

2. The phrases are those used to describe those migrating to the UK, including refugees, by the UK Home Office in its 1998 White Paper, 'Fairer, faster and firmer' (London, Stationery Office, 1998).

3. Quoted in *IRR European Race Bulletin*, No. 37 (June 2001) from a workshop paper for the Institute of Race Relations.

4. The 1999 Macpherson report (into the racist murder of Stephen Lawrence and the police's conduct) found institutional racism within the police force. From the report came a redefinition of a racial incident and the Race Relations (Amendment) Act 2000, which extended the provisions of the previous act on direct and indirect

discrimination to public authorities and placed a statutory duty on such bodies to promote race equality.

5. See UN Population Division, 'Migration Report' (New York, UN, March 2000).

6. Communication from the Commission to the Council and the European Parliament on a Community Immigration Policy (Brussels, 22 November 2000).

7. See A. Sivanandan, 'Refugees from globalisation', *Race & Class*, Vol. 41, No. 3 (2001), pp. 87–91.

8. See Jerry Harris, 'US: the politics of globalisation', *Race & Class*, Vol. 41, No. 3 (2001), pp. 59–72.

9. I draw heavily in this section on the definitive account of both these processes by John Morrison, 'The trafficking and smuggling of refugees: the endgame in European asylum policy' (UNHCR, July 2000).

10. Patrick A. Taran, 'Migration, globalization and human rights: new challenges for Africa', a workshop paper for Migrants' Rights International.

11. See John Morrison, 'The dark side of globalisation: the criminalisation of refugees', *Race & Class*, Vol. 43, No. 1 (2001), pp. 71–4.

12. See Frances Webber, 'Asylum: from deterrence to criminalisation', *IRR European Race Bulletin*, No. 55 (Spring 2006).

13. *Observer*, 4 February 2001.

14. See Liz Fekete and Frances Webber, *Inside Racist Europe* (London: Institute of Race Relations, 1994).

15. Formed in 1999 to establish a common integrated 'cross-pillar' approach targeted at the situation in the most important countries of origin of asylum seekers and migrants, the High Level Working Group is comprised of 'high level officials' from each member state and the European Commission.

16. *Statewatch*, Vol. 10, No. 2 (March–May 2008).

17. The European Council 'Qualification Directive' (2004) was one of the first instruments to effect this change. Whereas the Geneva Convention gave protection to refugees from conflict until a 'fundamental and lasting change has occurred in conditions in their country of origin and *state protection* has been restored', the Qualification Directive states that protection can be provided not just by the state but 'also by parties or oganisations, including international organizations ... which control a region or a larger area within the territory of the State'.

18. White Paper: 'Fairer, faster and firmer'.

19. Ibid.

20. *Hansard* HC (14 June 2000).

21. See 'Lessons from Europe: how the UK government's asylum proposals will create racism and social exclusion', *IRR European Race Bulletin*, No. 30 (July 1999).
22. Deborah Garvie, 'Far from home: the housing of asylum seekers in private rented accommodation' (London, Shelter, 2001).
23. The phrase is that of the (then) head of the Local Government Association, Mike Boyle, as quoted in *Big Issue* (2–8 August 1998).
24. Monica Hingorani, 'A Right to Life: the story of Ramin Khaleghi', *Race & Class*, Vol. 43, No. 2 (October–December 2001).
25. The Audit Commission estimated that local authorities were being defrauded of up to £100m a year by unscrupulous landlords who made false claims for housing asylum seekers and that this was a 'significant new area of fraud'. Audit Commission, 'Protecting the public purse' (London, 2001).
26. See Frances Webber, 'NASS: Chronicle of Failure', IRR News Service Online (24 July 2003) <www.irr.org.uk/2003/july/ak000010.html> [last accessed 12 August 2008].
27. See 'Seeking profits from asylum detention', <www.corporatewatch. org> (17 June 2005).
28. As with the dispersal system, vouchers were not strictly the invention of New Labour for, under the previous Conservative asylum system, some local authorities had resorted to issuing vouchers to meet their financial obligations to destitute asylum seekers.
29. *Hansard*, HC (14 June 2000).
30. All examples given by the TGWU, Oxfam and Refugee Council in their joint publication 'Token gestures – the effects of the voucher scheme on asylum seekers and organisations in the UK' (TGWU et al. 2001).
31. *Big Issue* (4–10 June 2001).
32. David Woodhead, 'The health and well-being of asylum seekers' (London: Kings Fund, 2001).
33. Home secretary David Blunkett said that the section would be used against people who had been in the country for a while and had then claimed asylum just to gain support. But it soon became apparent that NASS was taking the most draconian approach possible. In a number of high-profile cases, the High Court ruled that NASS's refusal to support asylum seekers breached the law of common humanity as well as the claimants' human rights. See Webber, 'NASS: chronicle of failure', IRR News Service Online, 24 July 2003.
34. *Limbuela* v *Secretary of State for the Home Department* [2005], UKHL (3 November 2005).

35. Unless they could afford to pay, or until their situation became critical enough to entitle them to emergency care.

36. 'Doctors rebel over plan to prevent treatment for failed asylum seekers', *Independent*, 16 January 2008.

37. In April 2008, a Palestinian failed asylum seeker with chronic liver disease, who was unable to return to the West Bank because of Israeli restrictions, but was banned from working in the UK to pay for his treatment, won his legal challenge to the regulations. The High Court held that failed asylum seekers could be entitled to free treatment. The Department of Health announced that it was considering an appeal.

38. In December 2000, the Home Office opened the 200-bed Oakington 'Reception Centre', where it held asylum seekers for 'fast-track' processing of their claims. The success of this system – and the rejection of legal challenges to the 'arbitrary detention' of people who had done nothing wrong – led to the massive growth of 'fast-track' detention and processing of claims. See Bail for Immigration Detainees (BID), 'Detained fast tracking of asylum claims' (2006). Another strand of the fast-track system detains people from a list of 'safe countries of origin' who have no right of appeal from within the UK against the refusal of asylum. The 'safe country of origin' concept (also known as the 'white list') originated in Germany and was adopted by the Conservatives in 1996, removed by Labour and then reintroduced in the 2002 Act. It now forms part of the EU Asylum Procedures Directive, although by June 2008 no countries had been put on the EU list.

39. Since January 2001, the immigration detention estate has increased massively. Full list of UK immigration detention centres provided by Barbed Wire Britain <www.barbedwirebritain.org.uk> [last accessed 12 August 2008].

40. See Sir David Ramsbotham 'Report on a short unannounced inspection of HM Prison Rochester, 31 August–3 September 1999' (HM Inspectorate of Prisons, 2000).

41. See Justice, 'The Schengen Information System: a human rights audit' (London: Justice, December 2000).

42. On 29 March 2008, a total of 1640 asylum seekers were in detention (out of a total of 2305 immigration detainees): see 'Home Office Asylum Statistics 1st Quarter 2008.

43. See coverage in *Guardian* (22 October and 17–20 November 1999).

44. See *IRR European Race Bulletin*, Nos 33/34 (August 2000).

45. See Steve Cohen, 'From the Jews to the Tamils: Britain's mistreatment of refugees' (Manchester: Manchester Law Centre, 1998).

Chapter 2

1. From the prime minister's speech, delivered on 5 March 2004 in his Sedgefield constituency, justifying the military action in Iraq and warning of the continued threat of global terrorism, *Guardian*, 5 March 2004.
2. A. Sivanandan, 'Poverty is the new Black', *Race & Class*, Vol. 43, No. 2 (October–December 2001), pp. 1–5.
3. Since there is such a misuse of terms taking place amid this debate, I should emphasise that I am using the term assimilation to mean the enforcing of dominant cultural habits, values, mores etc. on minorities and the requirement that they relinquish any cultural differences. Assimilation is a flattening, homogenising force as opposed to integration policies, which allow for cultural difference.
4. See Liz Fekete, *Racism: The Hidden Cost of September 11* (London: IRR, 2002).
5. See Liz Fekete, 'Anti-terrorism and human rights', *IRR European Race Bulletin*, No. 47 (2004).
6. In December 2004, the House of Lords ruled that detention without trial of foreign nationals only was unlawful and discriminatory. Despite the ruling, those men still detained under the ATCSA were not released until March 2005, by which time new legislation had been passed allowing for their virtual house-arrest under control orders.
7. Janne Flyghed, 'Normalising the exceptional: the case of political violence', *Policing and Society*, Vol. 13, No. 1 (2002), pp. 23–41.
8. John Upton, 'An authoritarian state is in the process of construction', *Guardian*, 23 February 2004.
9. Gareth Peirce, 'Internment: the truth behind the "war on terror"', public lecture organised by Liberty (15 December 2003).
10. Fouzi Slisli, 'The western media and the Algerian crisis', *Race & Class*, Vol. 41, No. 3 (2000), pp. 43–57.
11. John Upton, 'In the streets of Londonistan', *London Review of Books*, Vol. 26, No. 2 (22 January 2004).
12. Magnus Hörnqvist, 'The birth of public order policy', *Race & Class*, Vol. 46, No. 1 (July–September 2004), pp. 30–52.
13. *Copenhagen Post*, 25 September 2003; *Aftenposten*, 30 January 2004.
14. *Junge Welt*, 6 April 2002; *Frankfurter Rundschau*, 12 April 2002.
15. Campaign against Criminalising Communities (CAMPACC), 'Terrorising minority communities: "anti-terrorism" powers: their use and abuse', submission to the Privy Council Review of the Anti-Terrorism Crime and Security Act 2001 (August 2003).

16. Martin Bright, Evidence to the Special Immigration Appeals (SIAC) hearing, 21 July 2002. In my opinion, Martin Bright, now political editor of the *New Statesman*, seems to have fallen sway to precisely the kind of simplifications he once so intelligently warned against.

17. CAMPACC, 'Terrorising minority communities'.

18. Slisli, 'The western media and the Algerian crisis'.

19. See *Guardian*, 13 September 2003; also *La Vanguardia*, 26 January 2003.

20. *Junge Welt*, 4 January 2003.

21. *Statewatch Bulletin*, Vol. 13, No. 6 (November/December 2003). Official government figures covering 2005/06, the first since the 7 July 2005 bombings in London, showed another big increase in the use of stop and search under the Terrorism Act 2000, with a 34 per cent rise on the previous year. An analysis of the statistics suggested that only one in every 400 stop and searches under anti-terrorism laws led to an actual arrest. See Vikram Dodd, 'Only 1 in 400 anti-terror stop and searches leads to arrest', *Guardian*, 31 October 2007.

22. See 'Freedom: a Sinn Fein educational publication, <http://sinnfein. org/documents/freedom.html> [last accessed 12 August 2008].

23. *IRR European Race Bulletin*, Nos 33/4 (2000).

24. Even before the events of September 11 2001, France had in place what was arguably the most developed pre-emptive counter-terrorism machinery in Europe. The 'association de malfaiteurs' offence was established as a separate offence in 1996. See Human Rights Watch, 'Preempting Justice: Counterterrorism Laws and Procedures in France' (July 2008) <www.hrw.org/reports/2008/ france0708> [last accessed 12 August 2008].

25. Ibid.

26. *Guardian*, 13 September 2003.

27. Alouni is considered the most successful television journalist of the Afghan war and the only one who had a live link from Taliban Kabul.

28. *Guardian*, 15 September 2003.

29. Peter Bergen's full critique of the judgment can be found at <www. achr.nu/art63.htm> [last accessed 12 August 2008].

30. Cited in 'Prejudice and contempt: terror trial by media', *CARF*, No. 69 (Winter 2002/03).

31. *Guardian*, 8 and 13 February 2003.

32. See 'Prejudice and contempt', *CARF*.

33. Ibid.

34. Ibid.

35. *Irish Independent*, 18 January 2003.

36. *Guardian*, 12 January 2004.

37. Giles Tremlett, 'Immigrants sue Spanish PM for claiming terror group link', *Guardian*, 13 September 2003 <www.guardian.co.uk/world/2003/sep/13/spain.gilestremlett>.

38. Ibid. The case against some of the men was subsequently resurrected after it was alleged that they manipulated their mobile phones in a way similar to the Bali and Madrid bombers. Five of the men, known as the 'Dixan Commando' (Dixan is the name of the washing detergent found during the raids on their home) were subsequently found guilty, on the basis of their past activities in Algeria, of forming an extremist cell to further the cause of combatants in Algeria, and sentenced to 13 years' imprisonment in February 2007 (reduced on appeal to six years).

39. See BBC News Online, 'The ricin case timeline' </news.bbc.co.uk/1/hi/uk/4433459.stm> [last accessed 12 August 2008].

40. All the Algerian cases, as of September 2008, are awaiting appeal in the Court of Appeal or the House of Lords.

41. The director of public prosecutions had criticised the plans and six state-vetted 'special advocates', who represent the accused at secret hearings, wrote an open letter refusing to take part in any such trials. *Guardian*, 7 February 2004.

42. On 30 September 2005 the *Jyllands-Posten*, a Danish paper, published twelve cartoons depicting the Prophet Mohammed. Muslim organisations in Denmark and then throughout the world protested as the cartoons (one of which portrayed the Prophet as a terrorist) were reproduced in papers in more than 50 countries. The escalating violence, in which police fired on crowds protesting against the western countries that had published the cartoons, resulted in over 100 deaths.

43. *The Times*, 19 February 2004.

44. Quoted in the *Economist*, 25 October 2003.

45. Agence France Presse, 15 December 2003.

46. As cited by Arun Kundnani, 'The death of multiculturalism', *Race & Class*, Vol. 43, No. 4 (2002), pp. 67–72.

47. *Le Monde*, 16 September 2003.

48. *IRR European Race Bulletin*, No. 41 (2002).

49. Ibid.

50. BBC News Online (21 January 2004).

51. See Paul Silverstein, 'Headscarves and the French tricolour', Middle East Report Online (30 January 2004) <www.merip.org/mero/mero013004.html> [last accessed 12 August 2008].

52. Emmanuel Terray, 'Headscarf hysteria', *New Left Review* (March/April 2004).

53. Silverstein, Headscarves and the French tricolour'.
54. Terray, 'Headscarf hysteria'.
55. See the Migration Policy Institute's analysis of the French integration contract <www.migrationinformation.org/feature/print.cfm?ID=165> [last accessed 12 August 2008].
56. Quoted in *Swissinfo*, 19 January 2004.
57. Comments made on 1 October 2002, at the inauguration of a training school for Islamic preachers and imams. Islam Online, 3 December 2002.
58. Quoted in *Migration News Sheet,* February 2004.
59. See *Muslim News*, 24 August 2003.
60. Quoted in *Italy Weekly*, 13 June 2003.
61. *Guardian*, 25 March 2004.
62. *Copenhagen Post*, 20 February 2004.
63. See *Washington Post*, 16 April 2003; Agence France Presse, 15 April 2003; *Italy Weekly*, 13 June 2003.
64. See A. Sivanandan, 'Nativism vs integration', IRR News Service Online (15 May 2008) <www.irr.org.uk/2008/may/ha000019.html> [last acccessed 12 August 2008].
65. *IRR European Race Bulletin*, No. 48 (2004).
66. *Expatica News*, 24 October 2003.
67. *IRR European Race Bulletin*, Nos 45/6 (2004).
68. A. Sivanandan, 'The patriot game', a working paper for the Institute of Race Relations (2004).
69. Unfortunately, the European Court of Human Rights has upheld the headscarf ban in a number of cases.
70. Human Rights Watch press release, 27 February 2004.
71. Agence France Presse, 21 January 2004.

Chapter 3

I am indebted to A. Sivanandan who helped formulate my thinking on the key concepts of this chapter during an interview that I acknowledge below.

1. A. Sivanandan, 'Race, terror and civil society', *Race & Class*, Vol. 47, No. 3 (2006).
2. *Baltic and Nordic Headlines*, <www.unhcr.se/se/News/pdf/November_2005.pdf> [last accessed 12 August 2008].
3. *Baltic and Nordic Headlines*, <www.unhcr.se/se/News/pdf/January_05.pdf> [last accessed 12 August 2008].
4. *Migration News Sheet* (January 2006), p. 4.
5. *Baltic and Nordic Headlines*, <www.unhcr.se/SE/News/pdf/November_2005.pdf> [last accessed 12 August 2008].

6. *Baltic and Nordic Headlines*, <www.unhcr.se/SE/News/pdf/ November_2005.pdf> [last accessed 12 August 2008].
7. *Guardian*, 15 February 2006.
8. Similar laws have since been enacted in other countries, most notably Germany, where the government argues that the marriage patterns of specific minority groups (that is, Turks) are a major barrier to integration.
9. See Human Rights Watch, 'The Netherlands: discrimination in the name of integration: migrants' rights under the Integration Abroad Act', Human Rights Watch (May 2008).
10. *Copenhagen Post*, 15 September 2004, as cited in *IRR European Race Bulletin*, No. 52 (2005).
11. Currently under review, with the results likely to be published in Spring 2009.
12. Rita Verdonk has since left the VVD and founded 'Proud of the Netherlands'.
13. Human Rights Watch, The Netherlands: discrimination in the name of integration'.
14. *Frankfurter Rundschau*, 17 January 2006.
15. Jörg Haider, then leader of the Alliance for the Future of Austria (BZÖ) (he was killed in a car crash in October 2008) introduced a version of the Baden-Württemberg questionnaire in Carinthia where he was state governor.
16. *Deutsche Welle*, 5 January 2006.
17. OSCE press release, 24 January 2006.
18. *Frankfurter Rundschau*, 2 February 2006.
19. See Anja Bredal, 'Tackling forced marriages in the Nordic countries: between women's rights and immigration control', in Lynn Welchman and Sara Hossain (eds), *'Honour': Crimes, Paradigms, and Violence against Women* (London: Zed, 2006), pp. 332–53.
20. As quoted in ibid.
21. 'The vast majority of immigrant marriages are arranged marriages … We are fed up with forced marriages and the systematic use of the right of family reunification to get families to Denmark at the expense of the young. For a Nordic mind this is a huge offence to freedom, human dignity and self-determination and something we Danes simply cannot accept.' See *Migration News*, Vol. 9, No. 8 (2002).
22. *The News from Russia*, 12 January 2006.
23. See Arun Kundnani, 'From Oldham to Bradford: the violence of the violated', *Race & Class*, Vol. 43, No. 2 (2001). See also Hannana Siddiqui, 'There is no "honour" in domestic violence, only shame!

Women's struggles against "honour" crimes in the UK', in Welchman and Hossain (eds), 'Honour', pp. 263–81.

24. Expatica News, 16 March 2006.

25. Olivier Roy, Globalised Islam: The Search for a New Ummah (London: Hurst, 2004), p. 6.

26. Verena Stolcke, 'Talking culture: new boundaries, new rhetorics of exclusion in Europe', Sidney W. Mintz lecture for 1993, Current Anthropology, Vol. 36, No. 1 (February 1995).

27. Sivanandan, 'Race, terror and civil society'.

28. In conversation with A. Sivanandan (28 April 2006).

29. Samuel P. Huntington, 'The clash of civilizations?', Foreign Affairs (Summer 1993).

30. See Liz Fekete, 'Racism: the hidden cost of September 11', IRR European Race Bulletin, No. 40 (2002).

31. Downloaded from <www.demos.dk/website/artikler-•le>.

32. Marianne Gullestad, Plausible Prejudice: Everyday Experiences and Social Images of Nation, Culture and Race (Oslo: Universitesfor-laget, 2006).

33. Stolcke, 'Talking culture', p. 4.

34. Gullestad, Plausible Prejudice. I am indebted to the arguments of the late Marianne Gullestad on which I build in this section.

35. In discussion with Joan Bakewell, 'Shadow of suspicion', Heart of the Matter series, BBC 1 (17 March 1991).

36. When Westenthaler made these comments he was leader of the Austrian Freedom Party's parliamentary group.

37. Associated Press, 28 March 2006.

38. In 2008, with the election of a new Berlusconi-led government, Calderoli has returned to the Cabinet as a minister without portfolio. Violent demonstrations in Libya, during which 15 people were killed as the Italian consulate in Benghazi was attacked, followed the T-shirt incident.

39. Guardian, 30 April 2002, as quoted in IRR European Race Bulletin, No. 41 (2002).

40. A. Sivanandan, 'Britain's shame', Catalyst (July–August 2006).

41. Address given by the home secretary, Roy Jenkins, in 1966 to a meeting of voluntary liaison committees (London: NCCI, 1966).

42. In conversation with A. Sivanandan (28 April 2006).

43. His statement was made in response to calls for the dismissal of the government-appointed chair of the forum for social integration of immigrants who had described multiculturalism as 'a gangrene' afflicting democratic societies. The full debate is covered in El País, 23 March 2002, Heraldo de Aragón and Agence France Presse.

26 April 2002, as cited in *IRR European Race Bulletin*, No. 41 (2002).

44. As cited by Tasneen Brogger <www.bloomberg.com/apps/news?pid =10000087&sid=aYsZDc.NNfM0&refer=top_world_news> [last accessed 12 August 2008].

45. See Hartwig Pautz, 'The politics of identity in Germany: the *Leitkultur* debate', *Race & Class*, Vol. 46, No. 4 (2005), pp. 39–52.

46. Full text of speech available at <www.europa.eu.int> [last accessed 12 November 2005].

47. Originally published in *Boston Review* (October–November 1997), Okin's essay was later reprinted in an anthology of the same name: Joshua Cohen and Matthew Howard (eds), *Is Multiculturalism Bad For Women?* (Princeton: Princeton University Press, 1999).

48. Okin, ibid.

49. Ibid.

50. Cohen and Howard (eds), *Multiculturalism*.

51. Purna Sen, '"Crimes of honour", value and meaning', in Welchman and Hossain (eds), *'Honour'*, p. 61.

52. Hege Storhaug and Human Rights Service, *Human Visas: Report from the Front Lines of Europe's Integration Crisis* (Oslo: HRS, 2003).

53. See Bredal, 'Tackling forced marriages in the Nordic countries'.

54. One only need look at Storhaug's list of acknowledgements to question her claims to impartiality. Her research on other European countries cites prominent individuals and organisations linked to the anti-immigration lobby as experts on non-western communities. For instance, Sir Andrew Green of the UK organisation Migration Watch is not an academic but a former diplomat who campaigns against immigration. Likewise, the Liberal MP and sociologist Eyvind Vesselbo, who is cited as an expert on Denmark, has written about the dangers posed to Europe by the increasing Muslim birthrate and is also linked to the anti-immigration lobby. Storhaug's work is also replete with discredited racial terminology and typology. For instance, she writes about a lack of 'contact between races' (p. 87) and classifies Travellers in Northern Ireland as 'Tinkers' (p. 137).

55. *Human Visas*.

56. Gullestad, *Plausible Prejudice*.

57. In conversation with A. Sivanandan (28 April 2006). See also 'Freedom of speech is not an absolute', A. Sivanandan in interview with Yohan Shanmugaratnam, *Race & Class*, Vol. 48, No.1 (2006), pp. 75–9 .

58. 'Muslim integration: eyes wide shut. An interview with Alice Schwarzer', Der Spiegel Online <www. service.spiegel.de/cache/

international/spiegel/0,1518,329261,00.html> [last accessed 25 November 2004].

59. Ibid.

60. <www.print.signandsight.com/features/352.html> [last accessed 12 August 2008].

61. In 2006, Hirsi Ali resigned her parliamentary seat after a TV documentary claimed that she lied in her 1992 asylum application. Rita Verdonk, still then interior minister, called for her to be stripped of her citizenship. The escalating row led to the collapse of the coalition government and an early general election at which point Hirsi Ali announced that she was leaving the Netherlands to take up work at the American Enterprise Institute.

62. In 2006, the Human Rights Service awarded Ali its annual prize. According to Storhaug, 'I think she is doing a great service to democracy and the future, because Islamism is the biggest threat to democracy and to Europe.' As quoted by Deborah Scoggins, 'The Dutch-Muslim culture war', *Nation*, 27 June 2005.

63. See 'Notes on the killing of Theo van Gogh in the Netherlands', *IRR European Race Bulletin*, No. 50 (2005).

64. The most striking thing about the film, argues Annelies Moors, is its 'unimaginative resonance with the visual imagery of Orientalism'. Annelies Moors, 'Submission', *ISIM Review*, No. 15 (Spring 2005).

65. The comments were made by Mak in a pamphlet about the fall-out from the van Gogh murder. As cited by Christopher Caldwell, 'Daughter of the Enlightenment', *New York Times*, 3 April 2005.

66. In the Netherlands, where there is no official state ban, individual feminists have taken their own action. Cisca Dresselhuys, editor-in-chief of the mainstream feminist monthly magazine *Opzij*, said that, while she might consider hiring a woman wearing a headscarf for an administrative position, she would not hire such a woman as a journalist, for, in her eyes, wearing a headscarf could not but be the expression of women's subordination and hence clashed with the feminist mission of *Opzij*. See Moors, 'Submission'.

67. See <query.nytimes.com/gst/fullpage.html?res=9805EFDA143CF9 31A25751C1A9659C8B63&sec=&spon=&pagewanted=all> [last accessed 12 August 2008].

68. As quoted by Monica Mookherjee, 'Affirmative citizenship: feminism, postcolonialism and the politics of recognition', *Critical Review of International Social and Political Philosophy*, Vol. 8, No. 1 (March 2005), p. 33.

69. The Ministry of National Education has stated that the 2004 law has had the welcome result of ensuring that religious symbols in

schools have practically disappeared. But this positive evaluation does not take into account those pupils who have chosen to be educated abroad, in private schools (mainly Catholic), or through the National Centre for Education at a Distance. See Dominic McGoldrick, *Human Rights and Religion: The Islamic Headscarf Debate in Europe* (Portland, OR: Hart Publishing, 2006).

70. *Guardian*, 23 November 1989. As cited by Gabriele Dietze in 'The political veil – interconnected discourses on burqas and headscarves in the USD and Europe', in *'Holy War' and Gender: Violence in Religious Discourse* (Berlin: Lit Verlag, 2006).

71. Agence France Presse, 6 January 2006.

72. <www.nextgenderation.com> [last accessed 12 August 2008].

73. In response, the sociologist and feminist Halina Bendkowski organised a counter-petition calling for the state to rescind the residence permits of foreigners who do not recognise the rights of women. See Heide Oestereich, *Der Kopftuchhstreit – das Abedland und ein Quadratmeter Islam* (Frankfurt: Brands and Apsel, 2004), pp. 105–11.

74. Schwarzer made the comments in an essay in *Der Spiegel*. As cited by *New York Times*, 30 June 2006.

75 In a separate but related move, 58 scientists signed an open letter by Professor Yasemin Karakaşoğlu and Mark Terkessidis accusing the female authors of non-fiction books on Islam, currently in vogue, of having written inflammatory pamphlets that make unscientific generalisations on the basis of individual cases and personal experiences. The scientists, whose letter was published in *Die Zeit* (2 February 2006) considered it alarming that, in contrast, scientific studies merit hardly any attention.

76. See Southall Black Sisters, *From Homebreakers to Jailbreakers* (London: Zed Books, 2003).

Chapter 4

1. Gareth Peirce, 'Britain's own Guantánamo', *Guardian*, 21 December 2007.

2. 'Violent Jihad in the Netherlands. Current trends in the Islamist terrorist threat', Ministry of the Interior and Kingdom Relations, The Hague (March 2006).

3. Europol states that eleven member states were targeted for 498 terrorist attacks in 2006, the vast majority carried out by separatist terrorist groups in France (principally Corsica) and Spain. Despite the smaller number of Islamist terrorism attacks in the EU in 2006, half of the arrests made that year were related to Islamic terrorism.

The average age of those arrested for any terrorism-related offence was 36, although two-thirds of those arrested were in the 26–46 age group. Europol, 'TE-SAT 2007. EU Terrorist Situation and Trend Report 2007', Europol, The Hague (March 2007).

4. As cited by the *Washington Post*, 12 March 2007.

5. Only five of the 242 suspects examined in Bakker's study, 'Jihadi terrorists in Europe', were women. However, the Dutch intelligence services say that it is only a matter of time before more young women, under the influence of 'Moroccan lover boys', become more actively involved in violence.

6. Magnus Hörnqvist, 'The birth of public order policy', *Race & Class*, Vol. 46, No. 1 (July–September 2004), pp. 30–52.

7. See Ben Hayes, ' "White man's burden": criminalizing free speech', *Statewatch*, Vol. 18, No. 1 (January–March 2008).

8. The University of Münster has stated that it will oppose 'this discriminatory questioning of students and academics'. *Frankfurter Rundschau*, 24 May 2008.

9. Both cases cited in Europol, 'TE-SAT 2007'.

10. In July 2008, the Federation of Student Islamic Societies criticised the flawed methodology in 'Islam on Campus: a survey of UK student opinions', another report in this genre by the Centre for Social Cohesion.

11. David Renton, 'Document on student extremism seriously flawed' <www.irr.org.uk/2008/april/ha000019.html> [last accessed 13 August 2008]. See also Islamic Human Rights Commission, 'You ONLY have the Right to Silence. A Briefing on the Concerns regarding Muslims on Campus in Britain' (London: IHRC, 2006).

12. 'The Role of Further Education Providers in Promoting Community Cohesion, Fostering Shared Values and Preventing Violent Extremism', <www.dius.gov.uk/publications/extremismfe.pdf> [last accessed 13 August 2008].

13. By June 2008, the Home Office was ready to announce that a nationwide 'deradicalisation' programme was being developed to 'bring back' those who had 'already crossed the line' in terms of ideology and outlook but had not yet committed any criminal offence. An extra £12.5m (on top of the £40m already spent) would be provided to local authorities to fund partner community organisations in order to 'facilitate debate and amplify mainstream voices' against Islamist extremists. *Guardian*, 3 June 2008.

14. As cited by BBC News Online (16 October 2006). <www. news. bbc.co.uk/1/hi/education/6055184.stm> [last accessed 13 August 2008].

15. See David Cole, 'The new McCarthyism: repeating history in the War on Terrorism', *Harvard Civil Rights-Civil Liberties Law Review*, Vol. 38 (2003).

16. Control orders under the Prevention of Terrorism Act 2005 are used against terrorist suspects who are British or who cannot be deported. The terms of orders are draconian, and most people on control orders for any length of time begin to exhibit signs of psychiatric distress. But the most notorious feature is the secret evidence on which a control order is generally based.

17. The 2006 Terrorism Act also allowed the state to ban non-violent organisations if they were deemed to 'glorify' terrorism. Elsewhere in Europe, legislation also allows for the surveillance of Islamic groups *per se*.

18. By, for instance, creating the new offence of seeking or communicating information about any current or former member of the armed forces that could be useful to terrorism – a provision that could be used against the peace movement. See 'This is about more than 42 days', a letter to the *Guardian* (3 June 2008) from Lord Rea, Sir Geoffrey Bindman, Bruce Kent and 17 others.

19. Peirce, 'Britain's own Guantánamo'.

20. See Nottingham University Students and Staff, press release, 21 May 2008; *Times Higher Education Supplement*, 22 May 2008; *Education Guardian*, 31 May 2008; Hicham Yezza, 'Britain's terror laws have left me and my family shattered', *Guardian*, 18 August 2008.

21. As cited in Human Rights Watch, 'Preempting Justice: Counter-terrorism Laws and Procedures in France' (July 2005).

22. *Guardian*, 14 February 2008.

23. Sohail Qureshi was convicted in January 2008 under Section 5 of the Terrorism Act 2006 of preparing to commit terrorist offences overseas. At the trial, it was alleged that Qureshi wanted to use Malik as a source of information on the security situation at Heathrow airport.

24. 'Race, class and freedom of speech', letter to the *Guardian*, 7 December 2007.

25. Martin Amis made the comments in an interview with Ginny Dougary of *The Times*, 9 September 2006. See <www.ginnydougary. co.uk/2006/09/17/the-voice-of-experience> [last accessed 13 August 2008]. See also Ronan Bennett, 'Shame on Us', *Guardian*, 19 November 2007.

26. For an overview of the ways in which Orientalist Middle East scholars set the framework for the discussion of Islamic terrorism, see Richard Jackson, 'Religion, Politics and Terrorism: A Critical

Analysis of Narratives of "Islamic Terrorism"', Centre for International Politics Working Paper Series No. 21 (October 2006); Arun Kundnani, 'Islamisim and the roots of liberal rage', *Race & Class*, Vol. 50, No. 2 (October–December 2008), pp. 40–68.

27. See Ministry of the Interior and Kingdom Relations, 'Violent Jihad in the Netherlands'.

28. The EU Commission initiated a mapping project to identity imams in particular mosques preaching radical Islam. EU Justice and Home Affairs Commissioner Franco Frattini stated that Europe has experienced the 'misuse of mosques, which instead of being places for worship are used for other ends'. See *Expatica News*, 23 May 2007.

29. Thomas Deltombe, *L'Islam imaginaire, la construction médiatique de l'islamophobie en France* (Paris: La Découverte, 2005). See David Tresilian, 'Television versions of French Islam', Al Ahram Weekly Online, Issue 765 (20–26 October 2005).

30. The phrase is that of *Guardian* journalist Nick Davies, and although not related to the rise of Islamophobia in TV reporting, his critique of the rise of the 'undercover reporter genre' is illuminating. Davies argues that there has been a collapse of factual international programming, together with a collapse of investigative journalism in favour of low-cost I-teams (favouring the investigation of consumer products, for instance). And the I-teams approach even penetrates current affairs programming, which favours low-cost, low-risk human interest output. See Nick Davies, *Flat Earth News* (London: Chatto & Windus, 2008).

31. For a more general critique of media scare-scenarios, see Sabine Schiffer, 'Muslims, Islam and the Media: Taking the Initiative Against Scare Scenarios', <www.qantara.de/webcom/show_article.php/_c-478/_nr-308/i.html> [last accessed 13 August 2008].

32. *Prague Post*, 1 March 2006.

33. Ahmad von Denffer, 'Muslime unter Generalverdacht?' Deutsche Muslim Liga, Bonn (2004).

34. Iskender Pasa mosque in Rotterdam threatened to sue *De Telegraaf* after the newspaper reported that the imam of the mosque had been deported for preaching hate. But the person expelled was not the imam (he led Friday prayers the day after his reported expulsion), but a volunteer at the mosque who had been arrested for not having a valid residence permit. See *Migration News Sheet*, March 2005; *Expatica News*, 25 February 2005.

35. *Frankfurter Rundschau*, 27 January 2006.

36. Matthew J. Gibney, 'The deportation of citizens', paper delivered at Conference on Terrorism and Migration, University of Southampton (17–18 November 2007).

37. Liberty, 'Immigration, Asylum and Nationality Bill 2005: Liberty's Amendments' (December 2005).

38. See Derek McGhee, *The End of Multiculturalism? Terrorism, Integration and Human Rights* (Oxford: Oxford University Press, 2008).

39. Immigration Law Practitioners' Association, 'Immigration, Asylum and Nationality Bill – HL Bill 43 House of Lords report. Briefing on clauses 7, 42 and 51 to 55 – "Terrorism" Provisions', February 2006 <www.ilpa.org.uk/briefings.html> [last accessed 13 August 2008].

40. This, in turn, is linked to the EU December 2001 Common Positions on Combating Terrorism, which instructs all member states to vet all asylum seekers to determine whether they have any connection to terrorism, including 'any form of support, active or passive'.

41. In the UK, it is possible to apply to an administrative or constitutional court for a judicial review of a decision to refuse citizenship, and in those proceedings to seek reasons for the decision. Seven unsuccessful applicants for British citizenship are currently challenging the refusal of the Home Office to give detailed reasons for the refusal, instead of just being told that they are suspected of terrorist associations. The cases are likely to be heard in late 2008.

42. Whether intelligence services are attempting to recruit vulnerable refugees as spies is, understandably, a very difficult area to research. One civil liberties lawyer told me that many of those subjected to control orders in the UK, or facing deportation from there on national security grounds, have said that the order was preceded by a request by the security services to inform on members of their communities, which they had refused.

43. *Svenska Dagbladet*, 27 February, 23 March 2007. See also <Ramiswall.blogspot.com> [last accessed 13 August 2008].

44. As quoted by Liz Fekete, *Integration, Islamophobia and Civil Rights in Europe* (London: IRR, 2008).

45. One case that did receive wide publicity was that of Faiza Silmi, a woman from Morocco, who had lived in France for eight years with her French husband, and has three French children, but was refused citizenship on grounds of insufficient assimilation. See Naima Bouteldja's interview with Faiza Silmi for Press TV, <www.presstv.com/Programs/player/?id=65353> [last accessed 12 August 2008].

46. John R. Bowen, *Why the French Don't Like Headscarves: Islam, the State, and Public Space* (Princeton: Princeton University Press, 2007).
47. As quoted in Fekete, *Integration, Islamophobia and Civil Rights in Europe*.
48. Ibid.
49. See the critique provided by International Crisis Group, 'Islam and Identity in Germany', International Crisis Group Europe Report No. 181 (Brussels, 14 March 2007).
50. Ibid.
51. See Nina Mühe, 'Muslims in the EU – Cities Report, Germany', Open Society Institute, EU Monitoring and Advocacy Programme (2007).
52. Quoted in Jytte Klausen, *The Islamic Challenge: Politics and Religion in Western Europe* (Oxford: Oxford University Press, 2005), p.29.
53. See Mühe, 'Muslims in the EU – Cities Report, Germany'.
54. At the end of the Second World War, the Constitution of the new Federal Republic of Germany included clauses forbidding denial of the Holocaust or attempts to reinstate the Third Reich. But gradually the definition of what threatened the constitution was broadened to include those professing communism. In 1950, a decree made loyalty to the constitution a condition for public service employment; by 1978, the *Berufsverbot* decree had banned communists from employment in government service.
55. Mühe, 'Muslims in the EU – Cities Report, Germany'.
56. International Crisis Group, 'Islam and Identity in Germany'.
57. Wilders' film features footage of the September 11 attacks and the Madrid train bombings, preceded by verses from the Qur'an, with the implication that the Qur'an instructs Muslims to commit acts of terrorism. All mainstream Dutch TV companies refused to broadcast *Fitna*, and eventually on 27 March 2008 it was broadcast on LiveLeak.com. The Dutch government repeatedly condemned the film. Some Dutch multinational companies have stated that they will sue Wilders if his film leads to a commercial boycott of Dutch products in the Muslim world.
58. A fuller account can be found in *IRR European Race Bulletin*, No. 60 (Summer 2007).
59. All trades union leaders cited in *Expatica News*, 13 March 2007.
60. Daniel Bell, 'The status theory', in Thomas C. Reeves, *McCarthyism* (Malabar, FL: Robert E. Krieger, 1973).
61. A. Sivanandan, 'Attacks on multicultural Britain pave the way for enforced assimilation', *Guardian*, 13 September 2006.

62. A. Sivanandan, preface to Fekete, *Integration, Islamophobia and Civil Rights in Europe*.

63. Seumas Milne, 'Denial of the link with Iraq is delusional and dangerous', *Guardian*, 5 July 2007.

64. Speaking at the meeting was Paddy Ashdown, a former Bosnian proconsul and one-time head of the Liberal Democratic Party, Jemima Khan and *Guardian* columnist Timothy Garton Ash. The Conservative frontbencher Michael Gove (author of *Celsius 7/7 – How the West's Policy of Appeasement Provokes Fundamentalist Terror and What Has to be Done Now*) and David Green director of the Conservative think-tank Civitas, are among the Quilliam Foundation's advisors.

65. For critiques of the strategy of the Quilliam Foundation, see Ziauddin Sardar, 'To lionise former extremists feeds anti-Muslim prejudice', *Guardian*, 24 April 2008, and Seumas Milne, 'All Mod cons' <commentisfree.guardian.co.uk/seumas_milne/2008/04/all_mod_cons.html> [last accessed 13 August 2008].

66. This important insight was made by Ronan Bennett, *Guardian*, 19 November 2007.

67. See Hartwig Pautz, 'The politics of identity in Germany: the *Leitkultur* debate', *Race & Class*, Vol. 46, No. 4 (2005).

68. Details of Rehman's media stunts are provided by Marianne Gullestad in *Plausible Prejudice*.

69. As quoted in ibid.

70. Ibid.

71. A snapshot of anti-mosque campaigns in Europe from late 2006 to January 2008 can be found in Liz Fekete, 'Cultural Cleansing?', *IRR European Race Bulletin*, No. 62 (Winter 2008).

72. In 2006, 72 baggage handlers, nearly all Muslims, were stripped of their security badges at Charles De Gaulle airport because of alleged links to groups with 'potentially terrorist aims'.

73. Fekete, 'Cultural Cleansing?'

74. SVP MP Dominique Baettig, as cited in *The China View*, 9 July 2008.

75. Ibid.

Chapter 5

1. What follows draws on two previous IRR studies, 'The Deportation Machine: Europe, Asylum and Human Rights' (2005) and 'They are Children Too: A Study of Europe's Deportation Policies' (2007).

2. The correct legal term is 'removal', since deportation is reserved for those who have committed criminal offences or otherwise

threatened the public good, but I prefer to use the term 'deportation' in its popular meaning.

3. Hannah Arendt, *The Origins of Totalitarianism* (San Diego: Harcourt, 1985).

4. Arendt warned that refugees were 'expelled from humanity'; Italian philosopher Giorgio Agamben writes of the *Homo sacer*, reduced to 'bare life' and thus deprived of rights; Australian indigenous critic, Tony Birch, speaks of the 'unpeopled', the 'non-people' whose human suffering may not be seen or recognised. See Suvendrini Perera, 'What is a Camp...?', *Borderlands ejournal*, Vol. 1, No. 1 (2002).

5. Arendt wrote of the relationship between the ability to think and the capacity for evil. The banality of evil referred to those who follow orders and convention and lose the ability to think. See Dana Villa, ed., *The Cambridge Companion to Hannah Arendt* (Cambridge: Cambridge University Press, 2000).

6. Press Release, Home Office, 16 September 2004. Removals from the UK increased from 8400 in 2000 to over 60,000 in 2007. See Home Office, Control of Immigration Statistics 2000; Asylum Statistics 2007.

7. In June 2008, immigration minister Brice Hortefeux announced that France was well on track to meet the target for 2008. See Agence France Presse, 19 June 2008.

8. Eleven of these deaths are cited in 'The Deportation Machine'. A further case occurred in July 2007 when the Nigerian Osamuyiu Aikpitanhi died during a Spanish deportation attempt.

9. See *Migration News Sheet*, September 2006.

10. 'Concerns in Europe and Central Asia January–June 2003', Amnesty International Index: EUR 01/016.2003.

11. *Junge Welt*, 28 May 2004; Statement from the Caravan for the Rights of Refugees and Migrants, Hamburg, 15 June 2004.

12. Interview with Neslihan Celik, 30 June 2005.

13. See 'Five years on Europe is still ignoring its responsibilities towards Iraqi refugees', a statement by the European Council on Refugees and Exiles, ECRE, (March 2008); Press Release, International Rescue Committee, 18 March 2008.

14. Frontex Public Bulletin (September 2007), cited in ECRE, ibid. The acceptance rate in Greece in 2006 for Iraqi asylum seekers was 0 per cent. See Markus Sperl, 'Fortress Europe and the Iraqi "intruders": Iraqi asylum-seekers and the EU, 2003–2007', UNHCR Research Paper No. 144 (October 2007).

15. Germany took the unique step of systematically revoking the refugee status of thousands of Iraqis who were granted protection before

2003, placing them in a situation of uncertainty and precariousness. See Sperl, ibid.

16. *Guardian*, 29 March 2008.

17. In June 2008, the British home secretary Jacqui Smith announced the creation of around 80 immigration squads to track down failed asylum seekers or those who have overstayed their visas. Press Release, Home Office UK Border Agency, 19 June 2008 <www.bia. homeoffice.gov.uk/sitecontent/newsarticles/localimmigrationteam-stobe> [last accessed 13 August 2008].

18. See Angelique Chrisafis, 'The crackdown', *Guardian*, 3 October 2007.

19. Associated Press, 22 September 2007.

20. Associated Press, 6 November 2007.

21. *Le Monde*, 7 April 2008.

22. The girl lodged an asylum claim, which eventually succeeded on appeal, and she and her mother were finally allowed to stay.

23. The appalling treatment of these children was exposed largely thanks to the work of the magazine *Artikel 14* and the TV investigative journalist Gellert Tamas who is currently writing a book on the subject. For further information on Swedish asylum policy, see Sanna Vestin, *Flyktingfällan* (Stockholm: Ordfront, 2006).

24. Rufut's mixed-race background singled him out for racial assault in Azerbaijan, after which he became seriously depressed, but the family had hoped for an improvement in his condition in Sweden, and appealed against the decision to deport him. *See Artikel 14*, No. 4 (2004).

25. Ibid.

26. In March 2007, the Home Office changed its policy on the granting of Discretionary Leave (DL) to failed unaccompanied asylum seeking minors, from a grant to the 18th birthday to DL to the age of 17.5 years, which applies to decisions made after 31 March 2007. Home Office APU 3/2007 (March 2007).

27. In May 2008, the European Court of Human Rights upheld the British government's decision to deport an AIDS sufferer to Uganda, where she would die prematurely because of the lack of available treatment there. *N v UK* (26565/05) 27.5.08. In January 2008, the leading medical journal the *Lancet* described as 'atrocious barbarism' the removal of kidney patient Ama Sumani from her hospital bed for deportation to Ghana, where she died two months later. *Guardian*, 20 March 2008.

28. *Frankfurter Rundschau*, 18 February 2004.

29. As quoted in *Frankfurter Rundschau*, 4 January 2001. In the UK, deportation of the mentally ill and suicidal is endorsed by the higher

courts provided safeguards to prevent actual suicide are in place before, during and after deportation flights. See *J* v *Home Secretary* [2005], EWCA Civ 629

30. See the TV documentary, *Uppdrag granskning* produced by Sveriges Television (SVT) on 18 September 2006. Terese Jonsson provided me with a summary of the programme in English.

31. *Migration News Sheet*, June 2006.

32. David Rose, *Guantánamo: America's War on Human Rights* (London: Faber & Faber, 2006).

33. Anti-Racist Initiative, 'Federal German refugee policy and its lethal consequences 1993 to 2004' (Berlin: ARI, 2005).

34. Through, for instance, the 2004 Qualification Directive, which excludes from refugee status and from subsidiary protection people who commit 'acts of terrorism', although no one who is at risk of torture may legally actually be deported.

35. Germany, as a member of the Council of Europe, could not legally send anyone back to a real risk of torture, and Article 53 of the German Foreigners Law protected all, including suspected terrorists, from expulsion to torture. The risk of torture was simply not acknowledged.

36. *IRR European Race Bulletin*, No. 38 (2001).

37. *IRR European Race Bulletin* No. 30 (July 1999).

38. Foundation for Human Rights and Swedish Helsinki Committee for Human Rights, 'Alternative report to "Comments by the Government of Sweden on the Concluding Observations of the Human Rights Committee", 2003', Press Release, Human Rights Watch, 4 May 2004. See *Agiza* v *Sweden*, Communication No. 233/2003, CAT.

39. In the case of Mehmet G, the Turkish authorities did not even reply to a letter from their German counterparts demanding an explanation for the torture. In the case of Mohammed Alzery and Ahmed Agiza, the guarantees the Swedish government received were totally deficient, and the procedures that the Swedish government installed to monitor those assurances fell short of international prison-monitoring standards, including those of the UN Special Rapporteur on Torture and the International Committee of the Red Cross.

40. Human Rights Watch, '"Empty Promises:" Diplomatic assurances no safeguard against torture', *Human Rights Watch*, Vol. 16, No. 4 (April 2004).

41. See AI, 'United Kingdom. Deportations to Algeria at all cost', AI Index: EUR 45/001/2007, 26 February 2007. Unusually, SIAC and the Court of Appeal refused to rely on the MoU with Libya, and

accepted that terrorist suspects could not be deported there. See *DD and AS* v *Home Secretary*.

42. See Arun Kundnani, 'The grim fate that awaits those deported to Congo', IRR News Service Online, 2 December 2004.

43. Amnesty International, 'Eritrea: you have no right to ask', 19 May 2004.

44. Ibid.

45. An excellent discussion of the work of Giorgio Agamben and Jonathan Simon on the relationship between immigration imprisonment and wider questions of incarceration is provided by Suvendrini Perera, 'What is a Camp...?'

46. See Jonathan Simon, 'Refugees in a carceral age: the rebirth of immigration prisons in the United States', *Public Culture*, Vol. 10, No. 3 (1998), as cited by Perera.

47. Perera, 'What is a Camp...?'

48. See Helen Hintjens, 'Two very Dutch Fires', IRR News Service, 9 February 2006 <www.irr.org.uk/2006/february/ha000012.html> [last accessed 13 August 2008].

49. The League of Human Rights, the Syndicat de la Magistrature and the Union of Lawyers are conducting an independent investigation. See *Le Monde*, 26 February 2008.

50. Until June 2008, there was no EU-wide agreement on the length of time failed asylum seekers and migrants could be held pending removal. The EU Return Directive has established that non-EU migrants can be detained for up to 18 months.

51. See Rutvica Andrijasevic, 'How to balance rights and responsibilities on asylum at the EU's southern border of Italy and Libya' (Central for Policy Studies, Central European University & Open Society Institute, 2005/2006); Lorenzo Trucco, 'Lampedusa – a test case for the subcontracting of EU border controls', in *European Civil Liberties Network Essays*, No. 13 (2005) <www.ecln.org/essays/essay-13.pdf> [last accessed 13 August 2008].

52. Evidence of the serious health risk faced by detainees at Hal-Safi barracks was given by Greta Apap, a doctor employed by Medicare Services to work in Maltese detention centres, at the hearing of an Eritrean who alleged he had been subjected to serious violence in detention. See *Malta Today*, 7 November 2007; *Migration News Sheet*, December 2007.

53. For example, the Dutch government's extensive prison-building programme includes a detention centre at Alphen aan de Rijn (total capacity 1300), which has its own court and hosts offices of the International Organisation for Migration (IOM). See *Statewatch*, Vol. 18, No. 2 (April–June 2008).

54. See *Society Guardian*, 12 July 2006.
55. A. Baldaccini, *Providing Protection in the 21st Century* (London: Asylum Rights Campaign, 2004), as cited by Christine Bacon, *The Evolution of Immigration Detention in the UK: The Involvement of Private Prison Companies* (University of Oxford, Refugee Studies Centre Working Paper No. 27, 2005).
56. Greece has one of the lowest refugee recognitions rates in the EU. Of 1687 refugee applications examined between January and March 2006, only six were accepted. See '"The truth may be bitter, but it must be told": The situation of Refugees in the Aegean and the Practices of the Greek Coast Guard', Pro Asyl & Group of Lawyers for the Rights of Refugees and Migrants, Athens (October 2007); Amnesty International, *World Report* (2006).
57. For a discussion of how the Mediterranean solution mirrors the Australian Pacific solution, see Penny Green, 'State crime beyond borders: Europe and the outsourcing of irregular migration control', in S. Pickering and L. Weber (eds), *Borders, Mobility and Technologies of Control* (New York: Springer, 2006).
58. An alternative expression for the network of agreements with Mediterranean and North African states to control Europe's southern borders, which mirrors the original 1985 Schengen agreement designed to protect Europe's opening borders from non-EU migrants.
59. See Liz Fekete, 'The "Mediterranean Solution": rescinding the rights of boat people', *IRR European Race Bulletin*, No. 56 (2006); Amnesty International, 'The southern border – the State turns its back on the human rights of refugees and immigrants' (AI Index: EUR 41/005/2005).
60. Cited in *Atlantico Canarios*, 24 November 2002.
61. The architects of military defence systems designed to repel invasion did not give much thought to upgrading emergency search and rescue coastal patrols, leading to countless unnecessary accidents and a senseless loss of human life. See Liz Fekete, 'Death at Europe's borders', *Race & Class*, Vol. 45, No. 4 (April–June 2004), pp. 75–83.
62. Michael Pugh, 'Drowing not Waving', *Journal of Refugee Studies*, Vol. 17, No. 1 (2004), pp. 50–69.
63. The APHDA 2006 annual report states that in 2006 the number of arrests for attempted illegal entry rose fourfold, from 11,781 to 47,102.
64. APHDA's statistics suggest that Senegalese nationals are the second largest category of deportees from Spain.

65. The cost of expulsions for the Spanish state from April 2004 to October 2006 amounted to over €45m, according to APHDA.

66. The European Pact on Immigration and Asylum, adopted by the European Council in October 2008, has been critiqued by the African Assembly for the Defence of Human Rights (RADDHO).

67. See Sara Hamood, *African Transit Migration through Libya to Europe: The Human Cost*, American University in Cairo (January 2006); Andrijasevic, 'How to balance rights and responsibilities on asylum at the EU's southern border of Italy and Libya'.

68. *L'Espresso*, 24 March 2005; 'Sahara: last journey of the damned', *IRR News Service Online* (10 August 2005) <www.irr.org.uk/2005/august/ak000011.html> [last accessed 13 August 2008].

69. Helmut Dietrich, 'The desert front – EU refugee camps in North Africa', <www.statewatch.org/news/2005/mar/12eu-refugee-camps.htm> [last accessed 13 August 2008].

70. Libya has in the past held migrant workers in military camps – and there are fears that it is these military camps that will be integrated into the EU's deportation programme.

71. *El País*, 21 March 2006. Amnesty International claims that pressure from Spain is leading to serious human rights violations in Mauritania, both of migrants deported from the Canary Islands and people arrested in new measures that mean that foreign nationals are arrested arbitrarily by the Mauritanian police and returned to Senegal and Mali 'with no judicial oversight or right of appeal'. See AI, 'Mauritania: "Nobody wants to have anything to do with us": Arrests and collective expulsions of migrants denied entry into Europe', AI Index AFR 38/001/2008, July 2008.

72. AI has criticised Spain for its treatment of 23 men who were held for three months in a hangar in Nouadhibou following the interception by the Spanish sea rescue service of a boat near the coast of Mauritania and following their refusal to be repatriated. See 'Mauritania: "Nobody wants to have anything to do with us"'.

73. The fullest account is provided by Andrijasevic, 'How to balance rights and responsibilities on asylum'.

74. See Liz Fekete, 'Conference on Sub-Saharan African migrants stranded in Morocco', IRR News Service Online, 3 April 2008. Up-to-date information on the Euro-Africa Network can be found on the website of the Migrants Rights Network, <www.migrantsrights.org.uk> [last accessed 13 August 2008].

75. Fatiha Hajjat was speaking at the London Conference in support of ABCDS on 1 April 2008.

Chapter 6

1. The 20 cases included here are: France: Abdelkader Yahia Cherif, Abdelkader Bouziane, Midhat Güler, Yousef Mahlili, Orhan Arslan, Abdullah Cam, Ilyes Hacène; Germany: an unnamed Egyptian imam, Yakup Tasci, Fadi Madi, an unnamed Lebanese national linked to Hizbollah, Salem El R., an unnamed Jordanian linked to Hamas; Italy: Abdel Qader Fadlallah Mamour, Abdul Karim al-Tibsi and Mohammed Kohaila; Netherlands: Eisha Bershma, Mohammed Mahmoud and one unnamed imam; Poland: Ahmed Ammar.

2. The fact that those accused of speech crimes are pursued via immigration law makes it an extremely difficult area to monitor, and the cases documented here do not represent all the cases of deportation for speech crimes, only those where information was available. For more information on France, see Human Rights Watch, 'In the name of prevention: insufficient safeguards in national security removals', *Human Rights Watch*, Vol. 19, No. 3(D) <www.hrw.org/reports/2007/france0607/> [last accessed 13 August 2008].

3. Van Gogh was murdered by a Muslim fundamentalist after he produced the film *Submission*.

4. *Migration News Sheet*, July 2004.

5. Amnesty International, 'Counter-terrorism and criminal law in the EU' (AI Index: IOR 61/013/2005).

6. 'Exclusion or Deportation from the UK on Non-Conducive Grounds: a Justice Response' (London: Justice, 2005). See also Human Rights News, 'U.K.: Proposed Anti-Terrorism Measures Threaten Fundamental Rights' <hrw.org/English/docs/2005/08/10/uk11620.htm> [last accessed 13 August 2008].

7. In addition to these immigration reforms, Section 1 of the Terrorism Act (2006) created a specific offence of indirectly encouraging terrorism by the 'glorification of 'terrorism'.

8. Agence France Presse, 7 July 2005.

9. See Agence France Presse, 19 July 2005.

10. Richard Bernstein, 'What is Free Speech and What is Terrorism?', *New York Times*, 14 August 2005.

11. *Expatica News*, 23 February 2005.

12. *Migration News Sheet*, December 2004.

13. *Aftenposten*, 17 November 2004.

14. Islam Online, 24 March 2006.

15. *Migration News Sheet*, February 2007.

16. As cited in Amnesty International, 'Counter-terrorism and criminal law in the EU'.
17. *Deutsche Welle*, 24 November 2004.
18. As quoted in *Expatica News*, 16 June 2003.
19. Islam Online, 16 February 2005.
20. Reuters, 23 January 2005.
21. The *Times*, 24 December 2004.
22. As quoted in *Expatica News*, 23 May 2007.
23. *Wall Street Journal*, 9 August 2004.
24. Human Rights Watch, 'In the name of prevention'. An intelligence report, dated 1 July 2006, which summarised the case against Cam, stated that 'His physical appearance (beard and head gear) leaves no room for doubt as to his fundamentalist convictions.'
25. The case is reported in *Le Monde*, 2 December 2007; Altermedia. info, 4 December 2007; *Le Parisien*, 14 June 2008.
26. *Migration News Sheet*, March 2005.
27. *Berliner Morgenpost*, 23 March 2005.
28. *Berliner Morgenpost*, 10 May 2005.
29. *Migration News Sheet*, March 2005; *Expatica News*, 25 February 2005.
30. Reuters, 2 November 2006.
31. BBC News, 31 May 2004.
32. Ibid.
33. *Le Monde*, 20 August 2004; *Guardian*, 23 March 2004.
34. Agence France Presse, 23 April 2004; *Migration News Sheet*, July 2004.
35. Human Rights Watch, 'In the name of prevention'.
36. *Berliner Morgenpost*, 23 March, 15 April 2005; *Berliner Zeitung*, 16 April 2005.
37. *Il manifesto*, 10 January 2008; *Migration News Sheet*, February 2008; *Andkronis International*, 15 August 2007.
38. See *IRR European Race Bulletin*, No. 47 (2003).
39. Harnid Ghemrasa, 'Italy expels Algerian over "Yassin Prayers"', Islam Online, 25 April 2005.
40. Amnesty International Report 2005: the state of the world's human rights <www.web.amnesty.org/report2005/index-eng>.
41. As cited by Human Rights Watch, 'In the name of prevention'.
42. *Migration News Sheet*, July 2004.
43. *Berliner Morgenpost*, 10 May 2005.
44. *Migration News Sheet*, January 2005.
45. Mohammed Mahmoud, one of the imams from the Eindhoven mosque who received an expulsion order, had the right to appeal from within the country as he was married to a Swedish citizen

resident in the Netherlands. *Migration News Sheet*, September 2007; *Expatica News*, 26 June 2005.

46. Human Rights Watch, 'In the name of prevention'.
47. After the first expulsion on 21 April 2004 (the day after he was detained), Bouziane successfully appealed from outside France and returned to the country, only to be expelled again on 6 October 2004, when the Supreme Administrative Court overturned the lower court's ruling. See ibid.
48. Ibid.
49. The formation of SIAC in 1997, to replace an advisory panel of 'three wise men', sitting in secret and giving unenforceable advice to the home secretary, was originally seen as a progressive measure. The European Court of Human Rights had judged the advisory panel in breach of the Convention on Human Rights, and SIAC was seen as institutionalising a measure of fair procedure previously missing.
50. The Anti-Terrorism, Crime and Security Act (2001) extended the role of SIAC to cover appeals by aliens indefinitely imprisoned without charge because they are suspected of involvement in terrorism, but cannot be deported owing to a risk of torture or ill-treatment. In 2004, Brian Barder, a retired diplomat who was one of the original lay members of SIAC, resigned in protest at the role the special court was playing in the extension of emergency powers and the fact that it could no longer act 'as an effective champion against error or abuse by the executive'. See Brian Barder, 'On SIAC', *London Review of Books*, 18 March 2004. In March 2005, indefinite detention of undeportable alien suspected terrorists was ended following the House of Lords ruling that it was unlawful in December 2004 (*A and others* v *Secretary of State for the Home Department* [2004], UKHL 56) and replaced by control orders.
51. Ian Macdonald QC, a leading immigration and human rights lawyer and one of the first senior barristers to be appointed a special advocate, resigned in November 2004. See 'Ian Macdonald resigns from SIAC' <www.gardencourtchambers.co.uk/news/news_detail.cfm?iNewsID=268> [last accessed 13 August 2008].
52. *NRK*, 2 February 2007.
53. Bershma had already been deported to Sudan, and it is not clear whether he intended to return to the Netherlands.
54. *Migration News Sheet*, May 2004.
55. *Le Parisien*, 14 June 2008 <www.leparisien.fr/home/maville/valdemarne/articles/L-IMAM-DECHU-DE-SA-NATIONALITE-FRANCAISE_298564807> [last accessed 13 August 2008].
56. *Migration News Sheet*, June 2004.

57. Human Rights Watch, 'In the name of prevention'.
58. *Migration News Sheet*, March 2005.
59. *Migration News Sheet*, February 2005.
60. Deutsche Presse Agentur, 17 May 2005.
61. *Migration News Sheet*, February 2005.
62. *Deutsche Welle*, 19 September 2004.
63. Deutsche Presse Agentur, 20 May 2005.
64. Agence France Presse, 9 July 2004.
65. See 'Amnesty International Report 2005: the state of the world's human rights'.
66. It could also be argued that such deportations merely displace the problem of terrorism.

Chapter 7

1. A. Sivanandan, Foreword, in Liz Fekete, *They Are Children Too: A Study of Europe's Deportation Policies* (London: IRR, 2007).
2. Belgium, Germany and the UK have issued reservations to the UN Convention on the Rights of the Child (COROC), placing the welfare of children second to the interests of immigration control. In practice, children's rights are frequently ignored by European governments, whether or not they have issued reservations to the COROC. The parliamentary Joint Committee on Human Rights has repeatedly recommended the withdrawal of the UK's reservation. In February 2008 the government announced a consultation on lifting the UK's reservation.
3. See <www.separated-children-europe-programme.org/index.html> [last accessed 13 August 2008}.
4. This has been widely criticised and reforms are forthcoming.
5. Unaccompanied children are defined by the UNHCR as children under 18 who have been separated from both parents and are not being cared for by an adult who, by law or custom, is responsible to do so. Separated children are children under 18 who are separated from both parents or from their previous legal or customary primary caregiver, but may be cared for by extended family members. Child experts have also pointed out that some children arrive in Europe with adults (hence they are not strictly unaccompanied) who are not their parents or legal or customary primary caregivers as the result of being trafficked or smuggled. See Jacqueline Bhabha and Nadine Finch, *Seeking Asylum Alone: Unaccompanied and Separated Children and Refugee Protection in the UK* (Human Rights at Harvard, 2006).

6. For a description of the safeguards for unaccompanied and separated children in the UK, see UK Borders Agency website, Asylum Policy Instructions (API) on children, <www.bia.homeoffice.gov.uk> [last accessed 13 August 2008].

7. International standards as stipulated by the UNHCR and in the UNCRC, the UN Rules on Juveniles Deprived of their Liberty stipulate that children should only be detained as an exceptional measure of 'last resort'. To detain children for the administrative convenience of immigration authorities does not constitute last resort and is therefore in violation of international law.

8. A Ugandan asylum seeker, detained when he first arrived in Britain, told the English Children's Commissioner that detention was a form of 'child abuse'. See Medical Foundation for the Care of Victims of Torture News Service, <www.torturecare.org.uk> [last accessed 13 August 2008].

9. See *PICUM Newsletter*, December 2005.

10. *Guardian*, 3 June 2008.

11. Human Rights Watch, *Unwelcome Response: Spain's Failure to Protect the Rights of Unauthorised Migrant Children in the Canary Islands* (HRW, July 2007).

12. Sign its appeal at <www.nominorsindetention.org> [last accessed 13 August 2008].

13. Refugee Council online news, 26 July 2006, <www.refugeecouncil.org.uk> [last accessed 13 August 2008].

14. European Court of Human Rights press release issued by the Registrar. Chamber judgment *Mubilanzila Mayeka and Kaniki Mutunga* v *Belgium*. Directorate of Communication, Press Release – 582 (2006).

15. *Artikel 14*, No. 2 (2003); *Expressen*, 19, 20 October 2003.

16. *Frankfurter Rundschau*, 21 December 2005.

17. Sveriges Television, 'Uppdrag granskning'.

18. See <www.asylumaid.org.uk/data/files/publications/76/Issue_No._73_March_final_pdf.pdf> [last accessed 13 August 2008].

19. See <www.26000gezichten.nl/news.php?id=27> [last accessed 13 August 2008].

20. *Migration News Sheet*, January 2008; Associated Press, 5, 6, 7, 9, 12 October 2007.

21. *UNESCO Courier*, February 1949, </unesdoc.unesco.org/images/0007/000739/073912eo.pdf> [last accessed 13 August 2008].

22. See 'The Wall Behind Which Refugees Can Shelter', *Refugees Magazine*, Issue 123 (July 2001). <www.unhcr.org/home/PUBL/3b5e90ea0.pdf> [last accessed 13 August 2008].

23. *UNESCO Courier*, February 1949.

24. See Afterword by Jane Serraillier Grossfield in Ian Serraillier, *The Silver Sword* (London: Red Fox, 2003).

25. Annual Report, *The State of the World's Children 2005 – Childhood Under Threat* (UNICEF, 2004).

26. *Separated Children Coming to Western Europe* (London: Save the Children, 2000).

27. *Report by Mr Alvaro Gil-Robles, Commissioner for Human Rights, on the Effective Respect for Human Rights in France following his visit from 5 to 21 September 2005* (Strasbourg: Council of Europe Office of the Commissioner for Human Rights, February 2006).

28. Many of the Vietnamese children considered for forced removal under the Home Office proposals are likely to be girls, in their early teens, smuggled into Britain by human traffickers to work in nail bars, brothels and cannabis factories. See *Guardian*, 18 August 2006.

29. UK Border Agency, 'Better Outcomes: The Way Forward: Improving the Care of Unaccompanied Asylum Seeking Children' (January 2008).

30. The Dutch have also used the fact that they gave money to Congolese orphanages to justify attempts to repatriate a six-year-old Congolese boy who lived in the Netherlands since 2002. *Migration News Sheet*, July 2007.

31. Joris van Wijk, 'Dutch "safe zone" in Angola', *Forced Migration Review*, No. 23 (2005).

32. See 'Family Matters: A Study of Institutional Childcare in Central and Eastern Europe and the Former Soviet Union' (Everychild, 2005).

33. More information on these organisations can be found at NCADC (UK) <www.ncadc.org.uk>; RESF (France) <www.educationsans-frontieres.org>; RESF (Belgium) <resf.be/wordpress/?page_id=86>; FARR (Sweden) <www.farr.se/content/blogcategory/13/30>; CEAR (Spain) <www.cear.es>; APHDA (Spain) <www.aphda.org>; and the noborder network <www.noborder.org>.

34. A national investigation by RESF (France) has resulted in the publication of *La Chasse aux Enfants* ('The hunting of infants'). See <www.educationsansfrontieres.org/spip.php?article 12800> [last accessed 13 August 2008].

35. *Frankfurter Rundschau*, 25 August 2005.

36. From an interview with Amal Azzudin in *Shared Futures: Supporting the Integration of Refugee Children and Young People in School and the Wider Community* (London: Salusbury World, 2008).

37. Arun Kundnani, 'National declaration against deportations of school students launched', IRR News Service Online, 21 April 2005.

38. Ibid.
39. See Rachel Stevenson and Harriet Grant, 'Land of no return', *Guardian*, 13 June 2008.
40. Indymedia Scotland website (29 September 2006) <www.imcscotland.org>.
41. *Jungle World*, 13 July 2006.
42. Stevenson and Grant, 'Land of no return'.
43. Sivanandan, Foreword to *They Are Children Too*.
44. See Frances Webber, 'Asylum: from deterrence to criminalisation', *IRR European Race Bulletin*, No. 55 (Spring 2006).
45. The EU directive permits (but does not require) states to refrain from prosecuting those helping people enter or remain in breach of immigration laws, if they do so for humanitarian reasons.
46. *Der Standard*, 18 October 2007.
47. See *Libelyon*, 10 October 2007.
48. See Diane Taylor, 'How far would you go?', *Guardian*, 4 November 2006.
49. An important umbrella organisation is the Platform for International Cooperation on Undocumented Migrants (PICUM), <www.picum.org>.
50. Refugee Action, *The Destitution Trap: Research into Destitution among Refused Asylum Seekers in the UK* (London: Refugee Action, 2006).
51. David Brown, 'More destitution in Leeds' (Sheffield: Joseph Rowntree Charitable Trust, 2008).
52. *Observer*, 24 December 2006.

Chapter 8

1. Edward Said, *Orientalism* (New York: Pantheon, 1978).
2. See Liz Fekete, *Integration, Islamophobia and Civil Rights in Europe* (London: IRR, 2008); Matt Carr, 'You are now entering Eurabia', *Race & Class*, Vol. 48, No. 1 (July–September 2006), pp. 1–22.
3. There is a growing recourse among academics and policy-makers to very old-fashioned 'race relations' paradigms of social distance, much of which draws on US political scientist Robert Putnam's theory of social capital.
4. Salma Yaqoob, 'British Islamic political radicalism', in Tahir Abbas (ed.), *Islamic Political Radicalism: A European Perspective* (Edinburgh: Edinburgh University Press, 2007).
5. Fekete, *Integration, Islamophobia and Civil Rights in Europe*. In the course of conducting this research, I interviewed over 50 activists

and scholars in Europe, some of whose remarks I draw on in this chapter.

6. To counter the relegation of African-Caribbean children into ESN schools (schools for the educationally subnormal) in the early 1970s a host of supplementary schools were created in communities run by volunteers. See *Race Today* (April 1973).

7. French political commentator Alain Finkielkraut is not only a lecturer in social sciences but a media celebrity, having presented 'Républiques', a weekly discussion-based radio programme on France Culture, for 20 years.

8. The importance of Finkielkraut in constructing a cultural–religious framework for considering issues of anti-Semitism and violence cannot be overemphasised. For a critique of his stance on cultural issues, see Nathalie Rachlin, 'Alain Finkielkraut and the Politics of Cultural Identity', *SuBstance*, Vol. 24, No. 1/2 (1995).

9. Willy Beauvallet and Corinne Grassi, 'Blaming the "other": Judeophobia and Islamophobia in France', *News from Within* (December 2003).

10. Call for the National Social Forum of the Banlieues, 22–24 June 2007, Paris.

11. The hostility that Abdol-Hamid encountered during the 2007 general election and her disappointment at the Red-Green alliance's failure to stand up to Islamophobia has led her to temporarily withdraw from politics.

12. Trades unionists of migrant origin believe that because of their dual nationality they are now considered unsuitable for all sorts of jobs because of presumed divided loyalties.

13. See Carl-Ulrik Schierup, Peo Hansen and Stephen Castles, *Migration, Citizenship, and the European Welfare State: A European Dilemma* (Oxford: Oxford University Press, 2006).

14. In France, in particular, a large number of unarmed teenagers and young men of North African, Arab, African and Roma origin have died in police custody, mostly shot dead by police officers.

15. See Angela Y. Davis, *Are Prisons Obsolete?* (New York: Seven Stories Press, 2003), p. 73.

16. Statistics on Muslims in Dutch prisons cited in 'Muslims in the EU: Cities Report', Open Society Institute EU Monitoring and Advocacy Programme (2007). The UK statistics were cited by the justice secretary, Jack Straw, using 2006 data from the Offender Management Caseload Statistics. Statistics on Muslim prisoners in other countries were cited in the *Washington Post*, 29 April 2008, citing the Open Society Institute and French researchers.

17. Avery F. Gordon, 'Abu Ghraib: imprisonment and the war on terror', *Race & Class*, Vol. 48, No. 1 (2006).
18. Orlando Patterson, as cited by Gordon, ibid.
19. See the critique (in Dutch) by Pieter van Os, *De Groene Amsterdammer*, 20 April 2007.
20. *Aftenposten*, 4 March 2007.
21. See *IRR European Race Bulletin*, No. 63 (2008).
22. Spiegel Online, 1 February 2008.
23. For the causes of the UK 'riots', see Arun Kundnani, 'From Oldham to Bradford: the violence of the violated', *Race & Class*, Vol. 43, No. 2 (October–December 2001).
24. OECD, 'Where immigrant students succeed: a comparative review of performance and engagement in PISA 2003' (OECD, 2006).
25 'Plan Banlieues: La Pagaille des Idées', *Libération*, 9 February 2008.
26. Research by the UK charity NACRO suggests that the explanation for a rise in youth crime figures can be found in the criminalisation of minor teenage misdemeanours that would have previously been dealt with by an informal ticking-off.
27. The idea underlying 'selective incapacitation' involves achieving a reduction in aggregate crime levels by locking up a large number of criminals for a large proportion of their criminally active careers.
28. Malcolm M. Feeley and Jonathan Simon, 'The new penology: notes on the emerging strategy of corrections and its implications', *Criminology*, Vol. 30, No. 4 (1992).
29. The prison population in England and Wales has risen 38 per cent since Labour came to power in 1997. See George Monbiot, 'Crime is falling – but our obsession with locking people up keeps growing', *Guardian*, 24 June 2008.
30. *Guardian*, 6 June 2008.
31. Press release, Human Rights Watch, 'France: internment for former violent offenders violates human rights', 28 January 2008.
32. *Migration News Sheet*, March 2008.
33. *Aftenposten* English Web Desk (8, 14, 16, 30 August 2007).
34. See Liz Fekete, 'Landmark fight against police racism in Norway', IRR News Service Online (12 July 2007).
35. A. Sivanandan, 'Race, terror and civil society', *Race & Class*, Vol. 47, No. 3 (2006).

INDEX